REVOLUTIONIZE YOUR CUSTOMER EXPERIENCE

Revolutionize Your Customer Experience

Colin Shaw
Founding Partner of Beyond Philosophy

First published 2005 by
PALGRAVE MACMILLAN
Houndmills, Basingstoke, Hampshire RG21 6XS and
175 Fifth Avenue, New York, N.Y. 10010
Companies and representatives throughout the world

PALGRAVE MACMILLAN is the global academic imprint of the Palgrave
Macmillan division of St. Martin's Press, LLC and of Palgrave Macmillan Ltd.
Macmillan® is a registered trademark in the United States, United Kingdom
and other countries. Palgrave is a registered trademark in the European
Union and other countries.

ISBN 1–4039–3603–X

This book is printed on paper suitable for recycling and made from fully
managed and sustained forest sources.

A catalogue record for this book is available from the British Library.

A catalog record for this book is available from the Library of Congress.

10   9   8   7   6   5   4   3   2   1
14   13   12   11   10   09   08   07   06   05

Printed and bound in Great Britain by
Creative Print & Design (Wales) Ebbw Vale

Contents

List of figures and tables   vi
About the author   viii
Endorsements   x
Acknowledgments   xiii
Foreword   xv
Preface   xviii

1 Are you missing the gorge?   1
2 Please hold, your call is important to us   25
3 The guiding principles   48
4 The enablers   70
5 Sensory experiences   81
6 Naïve orientation   91
7 Transactional orientation   109
8 Enlightened orientation   127
9 Natural orientation   148
   Naïve to Natural™ self-assessment summary sheet   165
10 Understanding, action, and embedding   166
11 Case study: from the most ridiculed to the most respected   181
12 Case study: Build-A-Bear Workshop   198
13 Conclusion: dare to be different   209

Notes   214
Index   216

Figures and tables

Figures

1.1 The Naïve to Natural Model™: holistic understanding
to detailed implementation 17
1.2 The Naïve to Natural Model™ 21
2.1 Evolution of Naïve to Natural™ orientations 32
2.2 Economic development of orientations 34
2.3 The Naïve to Natural™ orientation areas 37
2.4 A Transactional financial services organization 38
2.5 The Naïve to Natural™ orientation area: people 39
2.6 The Naïve to Natural™ orientation area: strategy 40
2.7 The Naïve to Natural™ orientation area: systems 41
2.8 The Naïve to Natural™ orientation area: measurement 41
2.9 The Naïve to Natural™ orientation area: channel approach 42
2.10 The Naïve to Natural™ orientation area: customer expectations 43
2.11 The Naïve to Natural™ orientation area: marketing and brand 44
2.12 The Naïve to Natural™ orientation area: processes 45
2.13 The Naïve to Natural™ orientation area: culture and leadership 46
3.1 The Naïve to Natural™ orientation areas 51
3.2 The Customer Experience Hierarchy of Needs™ 64
3.3 Share of Mind™ 65
6.1 The Naïve to Natural™ orientation areas 92
6.2 A Naïve manufacturing company 93
6.3 The Naïve to Natural™ crossover points 104
7.1 A Transactional financial services organization 111
8.1 An Enlightened high tech company 129
8.2 Key factors at the crossover point between Transactional
and Enlightened orientations 132
8.3 The Customer Experience Hierarchy of Needs™ 133
8.4 The Naïve to Natural™ crossover points 142
9.1 A Natural airline company 150
9.2 Customer Experience: transport 158
9.3 Moment Mapping®: retail banking 161

10.1	The Charles Handy "S" curve	168
10.2	The conscious competence learning model	169
10.3	Competence levels across the Naïve to Natural Model™	170
10.4	"Knowing me, knowing you" Customer Experience framework	172
10.5	The steps to changing orientation	174
11.1	Yorkshire Water's Customer Experience triangle	185

Tables

2.1	A story displaying all of the orientation areas affecting the Customer Experience	36
3.1	A Customer Experience with an ISP technical support agent	58
6.1	Conversation between manager and employee at a mail order company	101
7.1	A Customer Experience with a PC sales agent	116
7.2	Typical complaints process: "guilty until proven innocent"	122
9.1	Moment Mapping®: *It's A Bug's Life*	156

About the author

Colin Shaw
Founding Partner, Beyond Philosophy

Colin Shaw is the Founding Partner of Beyond Philosophy, the world's leading experts in the Customer Experience. From their offices in the United Kingdom and United States, Colin and his team help organizations think through the ramifications of commoditizing global markets and advise them on how to create competitive advantage through a differentiated Customer Experience.

They typically work at board level in blue chip organizations. The Beyond Philosophy™ client list reads like a "who's who" of all the big blue chips from both sides of the Atlantic. They have undertaken many highly successful implementations and can demonstrate case studies of clients who have improved their Customer Experience and made a significant impact on the bottom line. Colin has visited Senior Government Officials at No. 10 Downing Street on a number of occasions to advise them on how to improve the public service's Customer Experience.

There is one fundamental principle for Beyond Philosophy™ that is encapsulated in its company name. Colin and his team believe that it is OK to have a great thought or idea, but it means nothing unless you go beyond the philosophy and do something. Hence the name Beyond Philosophy™. The organization's strengths lie in developing strategy but then, critically, operationalizing that strategy.

Owing to his expertise, Colin has appeared on CNN, BBC TV, and BBC Radio. He has conducted many radio interviews and "phone-ins" and is quoted in publications such as *The Times*, the *Independent, Marketing, Marketing Week, Customer Management, Utility Week*, and many other business publications. As a result of his activities, Colin is kindly being called by others the...

"Guru of the Customer Experience."

Colin has enjoyed over 20 years of experience working in blue chip companies, including Mars Ltd, Rank Xerox, and BT. He has worked at a senior level in a number of different functional areas including sales, marketing, customer service and training, culminating in his appointment as Global VP,

Customer Experience at one of the world's largest global companies, leading over 3000 people. This experience gives him a very rounded approach to business – he knows what makes businesses tick and understands the trials and tribulations of running operational units, including the pleasures, the pitfalls, the politics and the policies.

One of Colin's passions is public speaking. His style is very interactive, thought provoking, and amusing. He is an accomplished speaker who has delivered many key-note speeches and is a member of the Professional Speakers Association and the National Speakers Association.

Colin now indulges in his real passions; creating and managing organizational change, strategic thinking, developing original concepts, inventing innovative but realistic solutions, and critically working out how these can be practically implemented.

Whilst his intellectual rigor is without question, he still manages to keep both feet firmly on the ground. He is most importantly a father of three and husband to Lorraine, his lifelong partner. Colin is a loyal supporter of Luton Town Football Club (soccer) and collects 1966 World Cup Soccer Memorabilia.

Beyond Philosophy™ can be contacted through its offices:

UK Office
212 Piccadilly
London
W1J 9HG
+44 (0)207 917 1717

US Office
Suite 310
5401 South Kirkman Road
Orlando, FL 32919
(+1)-407-876-6707

www.beyondphilosophy.com
contact@beyondphilosophy.com

Endorsements

"We have worked with Colin and the Beyond Philosophy™ team for several years as we have set about the task of revolutionizing our Customer Experience. This second book by Colin Shaw justifies his reputation as the 'guru of the Customer Experience'. A revelation. Read it."
Peter Scott, *Customer Service Director, T-Mobile*

"Not often do you see an approach that you can both intuitively and rationally buy into. However, the Naïve to Natural Model™ is an exception. The index will enable forward thinking organizations to secure competitive advantage. Beyond Philosophy's expertise in the Customer Experience marketplace shines through in every aspect of the approach."
Gary Price, *Customer Services Director, EGG plc*

"There have been many books written about demographics and psychographics, but rarely do books cover those critically important subjects, and weave them together with the elusive topic of true Customer Experience. Consumers are changing while, at the same time, brand and product choices are exploding. It is critical that we all stop and do not 'miss the gorge' to ensure we understand our customer needs, in order to succeed profitably into the next decade."
Karl Schlicht, *Director, Lexus (GB)*

"The Naïve to Natural Model™, for the first time, provides a numerical measure of the Customer Experience that an organization delivers. This is invaluable information. Read it, understand it, and prepare to Revolutionize Your Customer Experience™."
John McGregor, *Director of Banking, Sainsbury's Bank*

"At Hamleys, the Customer Experience has always been an integral part of our organization's DNA. As an organization we are committed to taking the action necessary to deliver a captivating Customer Experience. If you read one book this year, for the sake of your business, make it *Revolutionize Your Customer Experience*. This book will inform, excite and inspire you to take action."
Delia Bourne, *Marketing Manager, Hamleys*

"Reading this book, with its informal and anecdotal style is like enjoying a discussion with an old, trusted, friend. Take a seat, sit back, enjoy, and learn."
Simon Fox, *Managing Director, Comet Group plc*

"There are few people I have met who have such an in-depth understanding of the Customer Experience as Colin Shaw. I met Colin several years ago, when he was still working as VP of Customer Experience in one of the UK's largest companies. At that time he was successfully grappling with how to revolutionize the Customer Experience of that organization. Thank goodness that he decided to establish Beyond Philosophy™ so that we can all now benefit from his many years' experience and expertise in this area. Thank goodness for this second book – a must read for anyone serious about improving their Customer Experience."
Alan Gordon, *Route Director, Stena Line*

"Colin Shaw's second book is a great piece of work, which for the first time provides evidence of how organizations are oriented around the Customer Experience. Organizations will critically learn how to align towards the customer and the steps they need to take to improve this."
Gary Fox, *Director, Customer Experience, Dell Computers, EMEA*

"Colin Shaw's second book on managing Customer Experiences takes the emerging discipline one major step further. Colin brings concrete tools, applied frameworks, and global examples of what it means to win on experience, to take the outside in view and to turn it into a superior Customer Experience."
Stéphane Marceau, *Vice President, Consumer Strategy, Bell Canada*

"Colin's second book consolidates and enhances the blueprint laid out in his first book about how to build a great Customer Experience. This new book unveils Beyond Philosophy's Naïve to Natural Model™, which builds on the groundbreaking thinking from their first book. This thought-leading model, which we fully endorse, provides a logical path for how organizations can Revolutionize Their Customer Experience™."
Waynn Pearson, *City Librarian, Cerritos Library, California*

"Beyond Philosophy's Naïve to Natural Model™ is one that holds great promise. The guiding principles feel intuitively correct and through the use of their scientific approach, organizations will ultimately be able to understand how to Revolutionize Their Customer Experience™."
Klaus Buellesbach, *Director of Customer Services, Scholastic Book Fairs*

"Every company is offering an experience – whether they know it or not. What kind of experience are you offering? Read Colin's book and learn how to improve that experience."
Robert Stephens, *Founder and Chief Inspector, The Geek Squad*

"A breath of fresh air in an otherwise stuffy, stifling world of business books. Colin Shaw is at his best in this fresh, dynamic book that is an absolute must for all business people today."
John Clayton, *Operations Director, Richer Sounds*

Acknowledgments

Writing a book is always a challenge. Writing a book with a fast growing business is even more of a challenge. I would like to acknowledge a number of people's help.

Firstly, John Ivens. Due to personal circumstances John has bravely decided to take a back seat at Beyond Philosophy™. Having said that John has been instrumental in getting this book to market. His commitment to this project has been without question. Undoubtedly he has been supported by his partner Catherine Walsh. I thank them both.

I would like to thank the growing team at Beyond Philosophy™. They have had to put up with me not being around as much. Specifically thanks to David Ive and his wife Sue. Dave and Sue had been friends for some time before we decided to join forces. Dave is proving to be an invaluable Partner at Beyond Philosophy™. Next, Joanna Kelly, my long suffering PA who has had the unenviable task of being my memory. She runs my life and does a far better job than I could. Thanks to Andrew Mullen and Jackie Cooper, from our marketing team. Also to Mark Grieves, Director of Consulting, and Eamonn Murray, Principal, as well as the rest of the growing consultancy team. All the team has been instrumental in contributing to the book and the continued expansion of Beyond Philosophy™.

I would like to express my gratitude to all of our clients, fortunately too numerous to mention! You are the pioneers, the people with the belief, and the vanguards of a new age. Thank you for your custom and your words of encouragement. Thanks to all the people who completed our Naïve to Natural Model™ and all those companies who kindly gave up their time to be interviewed and appear in this book.

Thanks to my brother Neil for his ongoing encouragement and being our guinea pig, also to Christine, Paul, Sarah, and Mark. Maureen and the Champion family are much appreciated for their continued presence and for being there when needed.

My Dad deserves a special mention. He has been someone I have looked up to all my life. He has set the standard for others to follow. Dad has always been a strong influence in my life. He is someone that you can always rely on and will help you out no matter what the problem. I have inherited Dad's work ethic and drive to succeed. During my youth, I was probably a bit of a disappointment to him as one teacher described me as the "clown of the class." I hope he feels I am doing a little better now, as, like most kids, having your parents' approval is important even when you are 46!

Thanks to all our friends particularly Brian and Sue, Garrett and Danni, Graham, Hazel, David, Bernadette, Iain, Fenella, Paul, Anne, Martin, Laraine, Stuart, and Pauline, and a special mention to Derek, Mandy, and Amy Morgan. Derek was unfortunately diagnosed with cancer a while ago. I am pleased to say he has now beaten it. The way he did this was a source of inspiration to me and others. He remains positive and played it by the numbers, a very brave man. Well done Derek.

Thanks to my wife, Lorraine. In my first book I explained what she means to me, that hasn't changed. She is my life and my reason for being. I love you.

I would like to dedicate this book to our three children Coralie, Ben, and Abbie. They are the best children a father could have. They are the thing I am most proud of in my life. They are Lorraine's and my legacy when everything else is gone.

Coralie, our eldest. My "bestest big girl in the whole wide world." She has Lorraine's affection and my common sense. She is a natural mother and knows just what to say and when to say it. She always takes care of everyone and is totally reliable and responsible, unusual for a girl of her age. Thank you for being you.

Ben, or Benny Bot! Ben is blessed with a good brain, which unfortunately, like his Dad, doesn't contain a memory! Ben has an incredible self-belief and a great sense of humor both of which will aid him well through life. At the same time he manages to mix it with a softer gentle side, remarkable for a boy of 18.

Finally Abbie, "my little princess." Abbie has a remarkable zest for life and is always laughing. She has a wonderful sense of humor and makes everyone happy around her. This is her greatest asset. Again she has her sensitive side. Her love and care for animals is something I am very proud of.

Finally, I am proud to say we all have a strong family ethos, which is vital to Lorraine and me. As I say it to you every night when I kiss you good night as you sleep, "I love you more than words can ever say." I am very proud of each of you.

Foreword

by Stephen Brewer,
CEO, Caribbean Mobile, Cable & Wireless

Never before, in the history of business, has it been so difficult to find true sustainable differentiators. The majority of businesses have, over the last 30 years, been obsessed with driving quality, reliability, and reducing prices as a means of differentiating themselves. These activities have actually been self-defeating for most organizations, as they have simply served to drive faster and faster commoditization of their own marketplace. Coupled with the advent of the Internet, this means there are few markets and industries today that are not now suffering from the onset of commoditization, with the dramatic and painful effect this is having on profit margins. Even the vast sums spent on branding are failing to provide the means of delivering true differentiation.

Those organizations that are succeeding are those that have been quietly obsessed with building a great Customer Experience – those who recognized the importance of providing an emotionally engaging, captivating Customer Experience that creates genuine customer loyalty, by which I mean the emotional desire of customers to come back and consume that experience again and again. Colin's last best selling book, *Building Great Customer Experiences*, provided an insight into how organizations could unleash the power of emotions to achieve this.

His new book affirms his unrivalled status as the "guru of the Customer Experience" as he explains how those organizations who have, and are now, focused on using customer senses as an integral part of their Customer Experience are laying the foundations of true long term sustainable differentiation and competitive advantage.

Colin introduces his revolutionary "Naïve to Natural Model™" which he and his team at Beyond Philosophy™ have developed, drawing on their combined years of experience and expertise in looking at and working in the whole area of Customer Experience.

This powerful tool enables organizations to plot where they are in terms of the development of their Customer Experience and the degree to which they are oriented around delivering a "Natural" Customer Experience – an experience that is underpinned by stimulating customer senses throughout the experience and one that leaves customers and clients with a positive, emotionally captivating experience.

Beware those organizations in the "Naïve" and "Transactional" orientations – those who have either failed to recognize, or failed to act upon their recognition, that the deliberate and systematic evoking of emotions in customers is the basis of building long-term loyalty. If you are not to become one of the casualties of commoditization, you need to start preparing now to Revolutionize Your Customer Experience™. Gain first mover advantage in your market place by Revolutionizing Your Customer Experience™ into the "Enlightened" or "Natural" orientations – and genuinely enjoy the benefits of sustainable differentiation.

At Cable & Wireless, we have recognized that in order to survive we have to embrace the philosophy of Revolutionizing Your Customer Experience™. We are committed to embedding a Customer Experience culture within the organization and understand that if we are to truly leverage the long-term sustainable benefits, we have to adopt this as a long-term approach – as a strategy that cannot be compromised by short-term considerations. "Natural" organizations adopt an unswerving loyalty to the Customer Experience – they have the Customer Experience in their psyche, in their corporate DNA, at the very heart of their being. That is what we are committed to at Cable & Wireless.

It is often only with hindsight that we understand and see where a trend started to emerge. The Customer Experience has long been a competitive battleground for companies. However, generally our thinking has been constrained to believe this meant the product, delivery times, opening hours, pricing and reliability of the product. It is clear that the dynamics of the battleground are changing fast. It is only those "Enlightened" and "Natural" companies who have recognized the power of unleashing emotions and using sensory stimuli as part of the Customer Experience, and have then acted to embed this within their organization, who will ultimately create the ability to deliver a sensory experience that is emotionally engaging that can be long terms winners.

Revolutionizing Your Customer Experience™ is critical if you are not to be one of the long-term losers. I have undertaken work with Colin, as he, like this new book, provides practical steps to help organizations understand what they should be deliberately doing in the area of emotions and senses.

I believe that at some point marketing theory will have to be rewritten to include the dynamics of the Customer Experience. Colin's books, *Building Great Customer Experiences* and *Revolutionize Your Customer Experience™*, will form the backbone of this new marketing philosophy, as organizations are forced to change their paradigm and their Customer Experience orientation if they are not to be swept away by the tide of change.

Foreword

I am delighted to recommend this book to you. I fully endorse the Naïve to Natural Model™ as it provides the framework by which organizations, including Cable & Wireless, can approach the task of Revolutionizing Your Customer Experience™.

Stephen Brewer, CEO, Caribbean Mobile, Cable & Wireless
Former MD, Vodafone
Former CEO, Vodafone Ireland

Preface

What is happening to business today? Everything is becoming a commodity, everything. Many organizations are struggling to find a sustainable differentiator as commoditization reaches epidemic proportions. This commoditization drives prices lower and lower, which then has a subsequent effect on profitability. The natural knee-jerk reaction from management is to cut costs, but this can only take you so far. Surely a new differentiator must be found?

Two years ago 71 percent of senior business leaders believed the Customer Experience was the next competitive battleground.[1] Today that figure has risen by a whopping 24 percent to 95 percent.[2] Why? What is a Customer Experience anyway? Why is it deemed so important?

In our last best-selling book *Building Great Customer Experiences* we looked at the early development of the Customer Experience market. We outlined our Seven Philosophies for Building a Great Customer Experience. In this book we reveal our latest thinking gained from over seven years of focusing exclusively in this arena and being involved in many practical implementations with many organizations across the globe. We have also conducted research with customers and organizations alike, from both sides of the Atlantic. All this has led us to discover a trend, previously unidentified, of how an organization is oriented around the customer to enable it to deliver a great Customer Experience.

We have debated these concepts with business commentators, academics, and senior business leaders, and are proud to reveal them in this book. To represent this discovery we have devised a ground-breaking model that enables organizations to understand where they are, and what they need to do to deliver a great Customer Experience. By organizations recognizing their current position they can clearly understand what they need to do to Revolutionize Their Customer Experience™.

Our new research,[2] which we share for the first time in this book, unequivocally shows organizations are on a distinct four-stage journey to become more customer focused and to enable them to deliver a great Customer Experience. We call this:

The Journey from Naïve to Natural™

The four stages are:

Naïve – Transactional – Enlightened – Natural

As consumers in everyday life, we can all recognize the types of organizations depicted in Beyond Philosophy's Naïve to Natural Model™. As business leaders, we should not ignore the power of this revolutionary model, which makes it easy for organizations to understand where they are in terms of the development of their Customer Experience, but more importantly, outlines the practical steps that should be taken to secure the competitive advantage of becoming a "Naturally" oriented company.

Kathryn M. Haley, Vice President, Client Experience,
RBC Royal Bank of Canada

The Naïve to Natural Model™ reveals how an organization is internally equipped to deliver a great Customer Experience across nine orientation areas, all of which have a massive effect on the Customer Experience. The orientation areas are:

1. People.
2. Culture and leadership.
3. Strategy.
4. Systems.
5. Measurement.
6. Channel approach.
7. Customer expectations.
8. Marketing and brand.
9. Processes.

In explaining the journey from Naïve to Natural™ we shall address the factors that make an organization move from evolution into revolution. We shall address what forces organizational change. We look at where you are today and where you need to be tomorrow. We look at how you can use this to identify a market opportunity or to exploit a weakness in the competition. Finally, but most importantly, we explain how can you drive your organization to Revolutionize Your Customer Experience™!

We have discovered organizations are invariably forced to change from one orientation to another by market conditions or some other shift in their environment. It is at these moments of change, between the four stages – Naïve, Transactional, Enlightened, and Natural – that an organization is forced into Revolutionizing Its Customer Experience™, thus making a step change in its approach. In this book you will hear from many senior business leaders who have already traveled the path from Naïve to Natural™. They will give you advice on what you should be doing and how you should be doing it.

To help you ascertain where your organization is on the Naïve to Natural Model™ and what you need to do to improve, we provide a self-assessment tool. Whilst this will provide a limited evaluation, a more comprehensive version is available free of charge on our web site: www.beyondphilosophy.com.

Finally, in this book you will discover:

- the benefits of progressing from Naïve to Natural™
- why Naïve and Transactional organizations struggle to maintain competitive advantage in the longer term
- how Transactional organizations are actually driving the commoditization of their own market places – and the impact this is having on their profitability!
- why Enlightened organizations have embraced customer emotions as a means of differentiating themselves and increasing customer loyalty
- how Natural organizations use theatrical techniques as a key part of their customer strategy
- why customers' senses are critical to Natural organizations
- why Natural oriented organizations find it easy to build Customer Experiences that improve the bottom line
- how your organization can build captivating Customer Experiences.

1   Are you missing the gorge?

The world is going mad!

- An airline gives away two million free seats...
- Need a new car? No problem, you get one free when you arrange a new mortgage.[3]
- Going into hospital? How about choosing your own room decoration, including the artwork to hang in your room? Didn't you know improving the Customer Experience makes patients heal faster?[4]
- How can a public library with a city population of 52,000 people be attracting 3500 people a day?[5]
- Would you like a Chilly Willie (an ice cream)? The natural place to get one is a hi-fi specialist![6]
- Would you like to fly a MiG jet? What about being a zookeeper? Or how about driving a rally car? These can be bought in a box at your local store: it's one of the highest growth retail sectors.[7]
- Would you like to drink water from a 23,000-year-old glacier? Buy it in a bottle: it's more convenient that way![8]
- How about getting married somewhere unusual? What about honeymooning at an Ice Hotel[9] that is constructed each year entirely from ice?

What is happening? The world is going mad!

Would your organization like to dramatically improve its Customer Experience from 51–91 percent and save approximately £8.5 million ($15.5 million) as a direct result? We will reveal how a utility company we have worked with has done exactly that.[10]

Organizations across the globe are improving their Customer Experience and saving money. This is why:

95 percent of senior business leaders say the Customer Experience is the next competitive battleground[2]

... an increase of 24 percent in two years!

The big question is what are *you* doing about it? Nothing? Then watch out! You are going to be left behind as more and more businesses become enlightened and are transforming their organizations.

But before we go into this, let's stop for a moment and take a step back. What is this Customer Experience anyway? Why are so many people talking about it? Why is it so important? To explain, I invite you to imagine this: it's four weeks before Christmas and your partner asks that fateful question: "What would you like for Christmas, darling?" "Oh goodness," you think, "What do I want for Christmas?" Nothing comes to mind. "I must think of something for them to buy me." You remember seeing a small camcorder you liked and you think, "I shall probably never use it, but let's put it down on the list anyway, at least it's a start." You look at the shopping catalogues: "Maybe that will jog my memory" ... but it doesn't. You remember the CD that you half want so that goes down on the list too...

Why do we have this difficulty? A hundred years ago, it was easy. People wanted so many things, some just to survive, so why is this question so difficult today?

The reality is for many people in the developed world we already have what we want. If you want a CD or a DVD player you simply go and buy one. After all they are now only a few dollars. In fact, people have more than they want. Have you looked in your garage or loft recently? Look at the junk that has accumulated.

How many TVs, VCRs, or DVD players do you have? I guess more than one. Why? Relatively speaking we are more affluent than we have ever been. The combination of more competition, improved manufacturing methods, and many other things have resulted in a plentiful supply of goods and services. There is now so much choice across many markets that everything is becoming a commodity. In the ground-breaking research we conducted for this book[2] we found that:

84 percent of organizations believe their market is commoditizing.

The time from "innovation to imitation" is now a matter of weeks. Many businesses are struggling with the effects of commoditization, reducing prices and reducing profit; all of which is leading to cost cutting. In fact:

76 percent of organizations believe commoditization is now affecting their profitability.[2]

Some of our clients even question the merits of investing vast sums of money in research and development as, in today's business environment, it often fails to give them sufficient edge over their competition for long enough to pay back their investment. For example, can you remember which organization was first to the market with picture messaging for cell (mobile) phones?

Do you remember, or even care? One thing is for certain, the advantage only lasted a matter of weeks before everyone else was offering the same functionality.

Enlightened organizations know that customers do not always buy the cheapest products. This was summarized for me in a very clear and unambiguous way by Michael Porter, when I was speaking with him at the European Customer Management Conference.[11] Michael said:

When everything is equal, people buy on price.

This is such a simple statement, but one that articulates a number of things to me. It means that if everything is equal people will buy on price. When this happens, unless you can increase volumes dramatically, your profitability will erode. It means that if you don't want this to happen, then you should be striving to make things "unequal." Let's invert Michael's statement:

When everything is unequal, people do not buy on price.

Is this what you want for your organization? Do you want to have something that is different from your competition that your customers value? Of course you do.

Customer relationship management (CRM) was to be the business differentiator, until all organizations starting doing it. The cry goes up: "If everyone is doing it we need to do it otherwise we will be left behind." So everyone jumps on the bandwagon, but they don't know why! Little surprise then that something like 60 percent of CRM implementations fail to meet their objectives. Yet, we are all really busy as we strive to be customer-focused! Rubbish! Our research[2] reveals that after years of "customer-focused" rhetoric:

47 percent of organizations still categorize themselves as "product-led."

You see, we are constantly busy doing "stuff." Stuff, stuff, and more stuff. The more organizations downsize, the more stuff we all have to do. We are doing stuff just to keep up with other organizations that are doing stuff. The game appears to be: who can out stuff the other? However, stuff is not good enough! Stuff is not the answer and will not solve the problem. Because:

Stuff is just stuff.

Organizations are facing a huge chasm between where they are today and where they need to be tomorrow just to survive. Unfortunately:

You can't jump a chasm in two jumps.

3

A number of organizations are rushing headlong into oblivion. "But we are really busy!" is the cry! But busy doing what? People are so busy they do not see what is happening all around them. When we calmly sit down with clients to help them understand what is happening, you can see the light bulbs being turned on. They become enlightened and can clearly see the path ahead.

To explain this further I would like to tell you a story that a really nice guy called Declan Coyle[12] told me. Declan is Director at Andec Communications. I believe this encapsulates the issue.

Declan's story:

A few years ago, when I was in Taiwan, we were staying in a wonderful part of the world near the Taroko Gorge. We were visiting there for a number of reasons, but one reason was to explore the whole subject of Buddhism and enlightenment. On this particular day we had decided to take the day off and three of us had decided to walk the Taroko Gorge. We learnt from the locals that it normally takes about five and a half hours to complete the walk, but we decided to set ourselves a target and walk it in five hours. We were going to beat the average!

We set off at a great pace, stomping loudly across the terrain. After an hour or so the sweat was pouring from us and I remember looking at my watch and thinking we were making good time. As we came up to a small hill I looked over to my left and saw about eight Chinese Buddhist nuns with their heads clean shaven, sitting by a stream. I remember thinking, "What are they doing, they are very still?" Coincidently, our path led us right past them.

As we were passing, one of them said, "Just a moment!" I was shaken and somewhat amazed so I stopped immediately, as I thought they might be in some sort of trouble.

"Yes, can I help you?" I asked.

The smallest nun turned to me and looked at me with bewilderment on her face. "Excuse me," she said, "but you're missing the gorge."

"What?" I said, somewhat surprised. "Missing the gorge? What do you mean, I'm missing the gorge?"

"From the moment I saw you coming along in the distance, I knew you had to be from the West, as you were walking at such a fast pace. You are missing the gorge!"

I was shocked and somewhat puzzled that she had stopped me to tell me something so ridiculous. I was going to miss my target if I wasn't careful.

"Missing the gorge, missing the gorge, how can I be? I'm in the gorge, I have cuts on my leg from the gorge, how can I be missing the gorge?" I said, rather annoyed.

"You are missing the gorge," she reiterated. "Please spend a moment and sit down with me and I will explain."

I looked up at Tommy and Larry as they were disappearing into the distance and I remember thinking, "I will have to jog to catch them up," but I decided to sit down as she intrigued me.

"Please sit down, and close your eyes and listen," she said.

"Listen to what?" I asked. "This is silly." I sat down anyway and did as she asked.

"I want you to hear the gorge, I want you to listen to it," she said calmly.

My mind was telling me that there was nothing to hear. How can you hear a gorge? But then it happened and I started to hear things. The water running by the side of the stream, the birds chirping in the distance, the rustling of leaves on the bushes and trees, the wind blowing past my ears, my heart beating, my breathing. Suddenly I started to feel serene. Then I realized ... I was listening to the gorge! I could hear all the sounds that I hadn't heard before. I could feel the sun on my face, the wind gently caressing my skin, the beads of sweat dripping down my face.

"Now open your eyes, look and see, really see!"

I opened my eyes. I saw the blue water of the stream, the white foam as it raced across the rocks, the wonderful colors of the rocks, the plants and trees coming out of the crevices, violets and pinks. Then I looked up and saw the blue sky like a dome above.

"Now breathe in deep ... breathe the gorge!"

I filled my lungs with air, fresh air. I realized she was right: I had been missing the gorge; this was wonderful. Only now did I realize what she meant. She spoke very softy. "Do you see what I mean? You were missing the gorge." "Yes," I replied. I didn't want to move. Then she said something that was to hit me like a sledgehammer in my solar plexus.

"I hope your action today is not a symbol of your life? Are you missing the gorge in your life, rushing from one thing to another without thinking?"

It was one of those moments when everything comes together and I thought, "My goodness, she's right... I am missing the gorge in my life!" A sense of enlightenment came over me. I am not spending the time to see all the joy that is happening around me. I am so busy rushing from one thing to the next that I have missed the gorge.

Ever since that day I now spend time thinking about what I am doing, trying not to miss the gorge. So let me pass on the favor the nun gave to me. "Are you missing the gorge?"

What a great question: "Are *you* missing the gorge?" A great question about your life, a great question to apply to your organization's Customer Experience. Are you missing the gorge with your Customer Experience? In other words do you ever actually stop and see what you are doing, *really* see? Do you ever stop and look at the detail of what is happening with your Customer Experience? Can you put your hand on your heart and say what your customers really think and feel about their experience with your organization? Do you consider why this is happening? Do you ever stop and think about what is happening across the market, the world and the subsequent effect this will have on your organization's Customer Experience? Unfortunately the majority of people would not give a positive answer.

We are so busy doing "stuff" that we are missing the gorge, not seeing what is happening all around us. We have become blind to the signs that are all around us, if only we took time to stop, look and listen. In our experience people are not taking the time to get off the merry-go-round and do one of the key things we, as leaders and managers, are paid to do – *think!*

The Customer Experience gorge is full of dangers and opportunities. The danger is that you carry on stomping through the undergrowth, oblivious to the world around you. You can continue to rush headlong like lemmings to the commoditization precipice that awaits blind and unaware organizations. These organizations say they are customer-focused whilst their Customer Experience is, at best, bland or boring. The gorge is strewn with organizations that do not know where they are going with their Customer Experience or what they are doing; they are blind to the world around them. Therefore you have a choice. If you wish to continue on the lemming rush to commoditization and the inevitable cannibalization of your profits, just carry on doing what you are doing. Put this book down now, don't waste your time reading any further. We wish you good luck. *You'll need it!*

On the other hand, you may wish to use us as your guide; every day more and more organizations are putting on their walking boots, loading their backpack with customer information, getting the maps out to plot their direction, and setting off on their journey. This path is well covered but takes you safely past the commoditization precipice. However, only the people who are enlightened can see the path. This path has been forged by some daring pioneering organizations that are led by enlightened dynamic leaders, some of whom have kindly contributed to this book, several of whom we have had the pleasure to work with.

Kathryn M. Haley, VP, Client Experience, RBC Royal Bank of Canada told us the following:

> *I hear a lot of people saying that it is difficult to transform the experience in financial services but I personally think the work that is underway to improve our client experience will radically change the way we go to market. Ten years from now, I think it may ultimately change marketing textbooks. When you look at the client experience it is more holistic than people typically understand.*

Peter Scott, Customer Service Director, T-Mobile:

> *The whole market is changing as people become more affluent and more demanding in the products and services that they are buying. As a service organization we need to step beyond just providing a transaction to meet*

people's requirements, it's now about staging experiences, even entertaining people, taking them through an experience that engages their emotions and by engaging them we can build relationships, which in turn develops loyalty. Where we have been able to do this, we have seen an improvement in customer satisfaction, better first call resolution, higher sales results, and reduced churn; all of which have a positive impact on bottom line profitability.

Throughout this book we will share with you examples of the path such organizations have trodden. We will share the reasons they started the journey in the first place, and having trodden the path, the lessons they have learnt. Duane Francis is CEO of Mid-Columbia Medical Center, Oregon. It provides a great Customer Experience to its community. Duane shared with us some of his thoughts:

We were a normal hospital 20 years ago. We were deep in the trenches of what we call the medical arms race. We were marketing to gain market share, saying we were better than the other guys. But then we took a step back and looked at what was happening and what we could do. We felt that medicine was cold and unfeeling, and while it was very effective in many cases, it didn't make people feel good. Typically, the patients are objectified as a problem or a trauma. They are diagnosed, patched up, drugged up, and sent home. Effectively they were being treated as a transaction. We thought that there was a better way. We chose to focus on improving our Customer Experience.

We ran the financial analysis of what it was going to take for us to build the cancer center. We didn't think that it was going to cash flow for five years or make any money until year seven. We like to call it a healing cathedral, it is just incredibly patient focused and oriented and it is a true healing environment. This didn't make financial sense at the beginning, but the reality is we have been making money since the first day that we opened the cancer center. People travel thousands of miles for treatment here.

The results are amazing. Overall length of stay has steadily gone down even though the level of average illness that we see with our patients has gone steadily up; we are able to get them in and through the hospital in a shorter amount of time. In essence they are healing faster.

So many organizations from many different markets are focusing on the Customer Experience. One person who recognized he could take a boring business, computer repairs, and turn it into a special Customer Experience is Robert Stephens whose title is Founder and Chief Inspector (CEO) of The Geek Squad. The Geek Squad is now part of Best Buy,[13] one of the United States' largest specialty retailer of consumer electronics. The Geek Squad fixes and installs computers. A very commoditized market, and not a particularly glamorous business, that is until Robert came along:

> *I now realize there are two kinds of businesses. There are the glamorous ones and the unglamorous ones and computer repair is not a glamorous field.*
>
> *There is a lot more room for creativity in the boring businesses. We decided that we could differentiate ourselves by providing a unique Customer Experience, so we dressed our people up like secret agents, with black trousers, pencil ties, white shirts, and sunglasses. We gave them Geek Mobiles to drive around in; it's a bit like the Ghostbusters, but more sophisticated. It's more like a James Bond movie. You see we are the essence of heroism. We are on call 24 hours a day to fix your computer problems, we have to think on our feet; we are a secretive organization as sometimes people don't want other people to know that we were there! When they have caused a problem they want us in and to get us out the back door before anyone notices! But the best part I can tell you is that I still harbor visions of working for her Majesty's Secret Service, because it is not boring, that's why it's exciting. The best part about Geek Squad is that we are real. If your customers are happy, and the employees are happy, you can get away with anything and all this is great because it's profitable.*

This was taken from the web site:[14]

> **The Geek Squad was established to protect society from the assault of computerized technology:**
>
> *That and the fact that we can't land dates. You can now rest assured that every portable and stationary computer system, corporate, and civilian, will be protected from this point forward. If you feel threatened, contact a Geek Squad Agent immediately.*

In this case, the basic commodity is the service, fixing the PC, and The Geek Squad does this very well. But this is not a differentiator. If you cannot do the basics then you shouldn't be in business today. Critically what The Geek Squad does is take it one stage further and provide an experience. It provides a bit of fun, a bit of entertainment, a bit of theater. It is providing a great Customer Experience.

Robert Stephens again:

> *You have to listen to those two voices in your head. You know when you are on the verge of "compromise and mediocrity." There is always the other path of being different. I don't like being different just for difference's sake, but I think there is a way to do both, to accomplish substance with style. From the way our cars look, to the music on hold, all these are important.*

8

It is important to recognize from the beginning:

This is a journey not a destination.

So now is your opportunity to stop, sit down and get off the merry-go-round of life!

Pretend I am Declan's nun sitting with you by the stream as we explore, together, the world around us. Close our eyes, listen, and think as we explore what a Customer Experience involves. As we travel through the chapters, we will provide the answers to five key questions:

1. What is happening out there?
2. What are you doing?
3. Where are you now?
4. Where should you be?
5. How are you going to get there?

OK, let's start:

Let's take a step back and consider how we find ourselves here. Just after the Second World War, in Europe, there was a massive shortage of goods and services. Some goods even needed to be rationed. Due to these shortages, people accepted that products they were buying were potentially of a poor quality and unreliable, and accepted the fact that, in the main, organizations were not focused on the customer.

Contrast this with today's business environment. We have seen globalization, the birth of massive multinational organizations operating across international boundaries, drives on total quality management (TQM), business process re-engineering, ISA 9001. We have experienced the massive impact of technology; PCs, Moore's law; communications, mobile technology. We have seen value chain integration, the emergence of brands, the birth of the Internet, manufacturing jobs moving around the globe, and now service jobs following them with call centers moving to India. We have seen outsourcing, downsizing, right sizing. The list is endless. The outcome is a vast improvement in choice, reliability, availability, and a reduction in price of products and services. This has fuelled competition, which results in many organizations providing similar products at similar prices. This is why:

85 percent[1] of senior business leaders say that just differentiating on the physical side of the Customer Experience (price, product, and quality) is no longer sustainable ...

Ironically just focusing on price, product and quality further drives commoditization and reductions in profitability. It is a vicious spiral.

9

A depressing read. So where does it all go from here? The bad news is it gets worse, *a lot worse*. Following the Second World War a unique phenomenon occurred, which has had a dramatic effect on the world economies ever since: the birth of the "baby boomers" (people born between 1946–64). As this group represents significant proportions of the population in the United States and in the UK, they have had a dramatic effect on everything they touch, from the introduction of pop culture to the hippy movement. They have also had an enormous impact on the economy as they have moved through their various life stages. The boomers are now reaching another life stage change: "empty nesters." This change affects what they buy, which in turn, affects the organizations that serve them.

Elliott Ettenberg[15] is the author of a great book called *The Next Economy*. In a recent debate on the subject Elliot made the following observations about the market dynamics we are just about to enter.

The next economy is all part of this baby boomer change in life priorities as they move towards and into retirement. Most boomers, by this stage in life, have the majority of goods they need. They are therefore no longer buying "needs." They are buying "wants." They are looking for things that they haven't experienced before. But more importantly they reduce buying the majority of goods and services one finds dominating most retail shopping today.

Baby boomers in North America account for about 28 percent of the population and represent about 52 percent of all consumption. The effect of these people changing their buying habits, for no other reason than they are reorganizing their lives, will be dramatic. Business, as usual, will be caught napping once again. Boomers will be buying fewer need items. Those they will buy will be on the basis of cost. There will be no margin on these basics. Wants on the other hand will be quite profitable. People always seem to pay more for what they want.

If you go through the average shopping center in North America today about 80 percent of the goods and services are need based and will no longer be on the shopping list of the baby boomers. The impact of that represents about a 30 percent reduction on demand. That is enough to get all of North America worried.

But the longer-term issue is even more disturbing. The generation behind the boomers, Generation X (born 1965–76), is a lot smaller in terms of size and buying power. They count for only 16.4 percent of US population compared with the 28.2 percent of the baby boomers, so they can't make up for this slacking demand created by the change in lifestyle of the boomers.

The savior will be Generation Y (born 1977–94) who account for 25.8 percent of the US population. They are already very brand loyal, they are very market savvy. With the high divorce rates and then remarriage, they are already a multi billion dollar business because many of them have four parents and eight grandparents all buying stuff for them. They are about as big as the boomers' population and they are even more brand loyal. So we have a 20-year gap between the decline of the baby boomers and the market impact of Generation Y. Businesses should be planning for this. They are not.

Demand will be driven by luxury goods and services catering to those who have the means and the desire to consume. Businesses that do not adjust to this evolving reality will perish. Those that do will flourish.

People want experience. People will pay for experience. So if you think competition is tough now, imagine what it is going to be like over the coming years. Kathryn M. Haley, VP, Client Experience, RBC Royal Bank of Canada can also see the trends building up:

Consumer behavior over the next ten years will not be as predictable as the last ten. Competing for tomorrow's customers will require companies to build capabilities that respond to a diverse and unpredictable marketplace. This implies the Customer Experience is going to be that much more important and businesses are starting to understand that.

This means that Charles Darwin's observations are going to be even more relevant than before:

It is not the strongest of the species that survives nor the most intelligent, but the ones most responsive to change.

The issue is people will be buying experiences not products or services. Products and services in today's society are a given. If you cannot deliver your product on time, or the food that a restaurant serves is not the right quality, then you will not be in business for very long. The Customer Experience is the wrap around your product or service, and is what provides the differentiation.

Hamleys is a giant toy store in the heart of London's West End. Hamleys opened its doors in 1760. Now let's get this into context. It started business before the Revolutionary War of Independence between America and Britain, before Captain Cook set foot in Australia. So some time ago! I guess if you have been in business since 1760 you would know one or two things about retailing. Steven Hamilton has the interesting job title of "Theatre Director" at Hamleys, which I guess will give you an indication of its thinking.

We are all about retail theatre, that is really important for what we do. Whether it is Crazy Chris jumping up and down blowing the bubble gun outside the store to take our theatre onto the streets or the magicians inside the store, it's all about retail theatre. A couple of weeks ago we organized a

11

nationwide competition to find a Elvis lookalike. Another example is we get our people to dress in authentic costume to celebrate over 270 years of Hamleys. It is all about retail theatre. Of course ultimately you want to drive sales, increase footfall, and all those things but we consider we are all about "memories and nostalgia."

We are seeing a growth of people wanting to spend money on experiences. Lots of people sell toys, but we go one step further and provide a total store experience. For instance we have also started to do corporate parties. The fifth floor is closed to the public at 7.00 pm, the guests have drinks, canapés, beverages, and so on. When the store closes, they are then released into the six other floors and there is plenty to be doing on each floor. Most corporates gravitate to the basement where you have the 22 computer interactive games, you have the PlayStation, you have got the Xbox, you have the dance machines, giant games, Scalextric set. We are trying to make it experiential for them.

We actually did a party a while ago for some corporate bankers, the average age was about 57 (baby boomer age), very male dominated. The theme was "back to school," back to our Customer Experience of nostalgia. Quite a few of them came dressed in school uniforms. The food they wanted was mini burgers, mini hot dogs, jelly and ice cream, they didn't want fancy canapés. Whilst some of it is about recapturing your youth, I also think it is about the fact that the lives people lead nowadays are a lot more stress oriented. No matter what job you are in, there are pressures, there are deadlines. It is great to go to a place like Hamleys and just let your hair down.

The Customer Experience to Hamleys is critical. Many organizations sell toys, but Hamleys differentiates itself on its Customer Experience. As the story above indicates, consumers crave experiences as they have become more affluent. Further evidence of this is the BBC TV survey of 20,000 people, which asked people what they wanted to do before they died. Here is the top 20:

The ultimate wish list:

1. Swim with dolphins.
2. Dive on the Great Barrier Reef.
3. Fly on Concorde.
4. Whale watching.
5. Dive with sharks.
6. Skydiving.
7. Fly in a hot air balloon.
8. Fly in a fighter jet.
9. Go on safari.

10. See the Northern Lights.
11. Walk the Inca Trail.
12. Climb Sydney Harbour Bridge.
13. Visit a paradise island.
14. Drive a Formula 1 car.
15. Go whitewater rafting.
16. Walk the Great Wall of China.
17. Bungee jumping.
18. Ride the Rocky Mountaineer train.
19. Drive along Route 66.
20. Fly in a helicopter over the Grand Canyon.

They are all about doing things and having experiences – not about owning products.

Red Letter Days[7] is the company that devised the concept of providing gift "experiences" in the UK – either through its brochure or, more recently, by providing "experiences in a box" through major high street retailers. It was founded 15 years ago and its first year's turnover was £10,000 ($16,000); this year it will be £20 million ($32 million). When we met with Rachel Elnaugh, Founder and Managing Director of Red Letter Days, she told us how well experiences were selling in the UK:

> *In a retail environment the profit return per square foot is going through the roof. People said we couldn't push the price of our experiences to more than £49 ($80) because their average gift purchase is something like £5 ($8). But in reality we can comfortably sell a Ferrari driving experience for £250 ($400). It is not an issue of cost because when it comes to special occasions, special birthdays, and special gifts the customer is incredibly flexible when it comes to price. If you want to give your wife a 30th birthday present the price is simply not an issue. You will easily know if she wants to do something – for example, perhaps she's always wanted to go to Milan and see the catwalk show; you'll pay £1000 or £5000 ($1600–$8000). It won't matter because you're giving her something she will remember and talk about for many years to come.*

Customers buy experiences. That is why 95 percent of senior business leaders believe the Customer Experience is the next competitive battleground.[2]

Ellen L. Brothers, President of American Girl, a direct marketer, publisher, and experiential retailer for girls, told us how important the Customer Experience is to her company:

> *Our roots are very much in Customer Experience. This has always been a corner stone from day one. I think any time you can engage the customer in a broad experience you connect with them in a much more meaningful way.*

13

So let us pull some strands together:

- All markets are commoditizing.
- Profitability is being put under severe pressure.
- As the baby boomers are getting older they are looking for new experiences.
- The bad news is they are not going to be around forever and the next population is smaller in number which will mean greater competition.
- The good news is that organizations who change quickly can achieve an advantage over their competition.

So how does this all apply to you? You don't sell experiences like hot air ballooning. Nevertheless, every organization has a Customer Experience. Whether it is talking on the phone with a customer, in a shop, over the Internet, or even an ad in a paper – these are all Customer Experiences. What is yours like? Are you proud of it?

Concern for the Customer Experience is not the exclusive domain of business. Our visits with officials in No 10 Downing Street have convinced us of the UK government's commitment to improve public service customers' experience. Wendy Thomson of the Office of Public Service Reform is responsible for leading customer-driven reform:

> *Within government, the Office of Public Service Reform has advocated for services to be customer driven. Ultimately the judgment about successful public services will be made by the people who use them, and who vote to agree to taxes to pay for many of them. The vision of a customer-driven Whitehall department is to bring the "customer" to the heart of policy makers and deliverers.*

Other public services around the globe are also striving to improve their Customer Experience, as we discovered in a conversation with Waynn Pearson, City Librarian, Cerritos Library in California.[5]

> *Around 1995/96 I became aware of two developments that suggested that libraries were in a great deal of trouble. The first was the dot com craze. The Internet was poised to replace the library as the primary source of information, and like it or not, that is now the reality. The second development was summarized in a report from the Benton Foundation, which found that an overwhelming majority of 18–24-year-olds said they saw the library as something of the past, not something of the future. As we prepared to remodel and expand the Cerritos Library, we decided to address these issues and build the world's first "Experience Library." If young people regard libraries as passé, we reasoned, what do they connect with in the contemporary world? Theme parks and movies were two answers. So, in planning the library, we began, as*

would a theme park designer or a movie director, with the development of themes and storylines. "Traveling Through Time" was a major storyline. To give you some idea of how an "Experience Library" differs from the library you grew up with, we have a full-size authentic cast replica of a T. Rex in the kid's library, a 15,000 gallon salt water aquarium in the lobby, and a series of carefully designed themed spaces that carry our visitors through time, from the Gothic era through the 21st century.

We have a population of about 52,000 in the city of Cerritos, but our core user base comes from a radius of approximately 25 miles. Our library is open seven days a week and somewhere between 3000 and 3500 people visit the library everyday. This kind of foot traffic is equivalent to that generated by a medium-size Nordstrom. A number of developers have visited the Cerritos Library because they think it might be possible to use a library instead of a cinema as the anchor in some of the smaller malls.

These are just a few examples of the many organizations we have to share with you. Every organization has a Customer Experience, whether it is in the public services, B2B, B2C, B2B2C, or any market for that matter. If you have something to sell or if you provide a service of any kind, you have a Customer Experience as you rely on a dialogue between your organization and your customer.

So we need to explore further what makes up a Customer Experience; what are the ingredients to success? We need to provide a frame of reference to help you define your relative position in your market. We want to help establish:

Where are you today?

How customer oriented is your organization?

How well placed are you to deliver a great Customer Experience?

Over the last seven years, we have been fortunate to think about nothing other than the Customer Experience. We have been privileged to discuss this with many fellow experts, renowned academics and senior business leaders. We have been engaged by many brand-leading organizations such as Microsoft, Dell Computers, T-Mobile, TNT, and so on to help them in strategy and tactical implements of the Customer Experience. In addition, we decided to call our company Beyond Philosophy™ as we believe it is appropriate to have a thought or a philosophy, but this means nothing unless you go beyond the philosophy and actually do something. So this is a very practical guide as well, which has been born from our experience and from conducting research, on both sides of the Atlantic, with organizations and consumers alike. All this has led us to discover a previously unidentified trend of how an organization is "oriented" around the customer to enable it to deliver a great Customer Experience.

> *We can't solve problems by using the same kind of thinking we used when we created them.*

Albert Einstein

To represent this discovery we have devised a ground-breaking model that enables organizations to understand where they are, and what they need to do to deliver a great Customer Experience. If the organization recognizes its current position it can clearly understand what it needs to do to Revolutionize Its Customer Experience™.

Our research[2] shows there are four distinct orientations organizations go through on their journey to enable them to deliver a great Customer Experience. We call this:

The Journey from Naïve to Natural™

The four orientations are:

Naïve – Transactional – Enlightened – Natural

The dictionary describes the word orientation as a "relative position." We call them "orientations," as we are defining how organizations are centered or oriented. For example, you will have heard people say they are "family oriented." This means that people have their family at the heart of everything they do. Their action is predictable because they are "family oriented." We are therefore talking about how your organization is oriented to deliver a great Customer Experience. This is from an *internal* perspective. In other words, it considers how customer-focused or customer-centric an organization is. This orientation is made up from nine orientation areas. Each area was outlined in our best-selling book, *Building Great Customer Experiences*,[16] which also introduced our Seven Philosophies for Building a Great Customer Experience.

Great Customer Experiences are:

1. A source of long-term *competitive advantage*.
2. Created by consistently exceeding customers' physical and emotional *expectations*.
3. Differentiated by focusing on stimulating planned *emotions*.
4. Enabled through inspirational *leadership*, an empowering *culture* and empathetic *people* who are happy and fulfilled.
5. Designed "*outside in*" rather than "*inside out*."
6. *Revenue* generating and can significantly reduce *costs*.
7. An embodiment of the *brand*.

Therefore our orientation areas are:

1. People.
2. Culture and leadership.
3. Strategy.
4. Systems.
5. Measurement.
6. Channel approach.
7. Customer expectations.
8. Marketing and brand
9. Processes.

Figure 1.1 outlines, at a top level, the Naïve to Natural Model™. The model enables an organization to holistically understand which orientation it is in and to provide an answer to *Where are we?* The next layer down, the orientation area level, enables organizations to understand why they are in their orientation and answer the question, *Why are we here?* The indicator level enables organizations to understand the detail of what is happening in each of the 259 individual indicators that make up the nine orientational areas, and which ultimately make up their overall orientation.

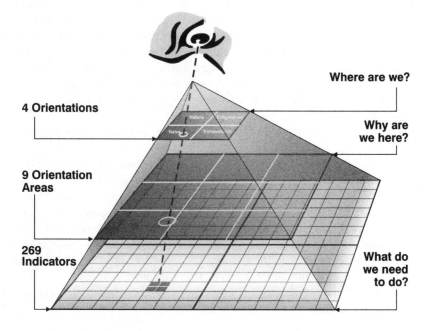

Figure 1.1 The Naïve to Natural Model™: holistic understanding to detailed implementation

At the indicator level organizations can answer the question "What do we need to do?" From that they can then decide what action they need to take to progress on their journey from Naïve to Natural™.

Overall our research[2] tells us this is how organizations are distributed across these four orientations:

Naïve 9 percent – Transactional 67 percent – Enlightened 22 percent – Natural 2 percent

So let's give you an overview of these orientations and then later in the book we have a chapter dedicated to each to enable you to understand them in greater detail.

Naïve orientation

> Definition: an organization that focuses on itself to the detriment of the customer. It is "inside out" either through choice or because it doesn't know what it should be doing.

Naïve organizations focus on themselves rather than the Customer Experience. They are reactive to customer demands. They believe the product, processes, or their services are more important than the customer. Their attitude with the customer is one of "Take it or leave it" or "What do you expect from a product at this price?" Their processes are totally focused "inside out," doing things for their benefit, rather than "outside in," which is changing the organization to meet customers' requirements.

The Naïve oriented organization is organized around its products. These products overlap and are uncoordinated. It is typically a siloed organization and infighting between the silos is rife.

The organizations are in this orientation either because they are:

1. Unaware what they should be doing to build a great Customer Experience. They are not deliberately trying to cause a poor Customer Experience, it is simply that they do not know what they do not know. They are unaware of the impact their actions have on their Customer Experience. By definition they have not spent time thinking through the implications of what they are doing. This typically indicates they believe something else is more important than the Customer Experience. Typically, this could be their product or maybe their production capability.
2. Aware of their orientation but simply don't care as customers are a nuisance, and seen as a means to an end.

Naïve organizations typically target their people on sales or productivity, use internal measures, and either do not undertake customer satisfaction surveys

18

or take little notice of the results if they do. Consider a timeshare company, a double-glazing sales representative, or the image we all have in our minds of a traditional used car salesman. Not surprisingly you would hear an employee say, "We are a product company."

Transactional orientation

> Definition: an organization that focuses primarily on the physical aspects of the Customer Experience. It has recognized the importance of the customer. However, its focus is rudimentary, as many aspects of the Customer Experience remain left to chance and are uncoordinated and "inside out." The organization is typically reactive to customer demands.

The Transactional oriented organization understands some of the basics of the Customer Experience but still remains reactive to customer demands. It has recognized that the customer is "quite" important and it has made some changes to reflect this. The core of its operation is primarily around the physical aspects of the Customer Experience, for example, opening times, answering calls in four rings, accessibility through call centers, delivery times. It is, in reality, still "inside out" and its Customer Experience is not deliberate, but just happens. It does measure customer satisfaction but it is fundamentally focused on the physical elements of the Customer Experience. Some employees are targeted on general customer satisfaction but this is, at best, an afterthought, compared to the important measures of sales and productivity. It has established a customer service organization but typically these employees are treated like second-class citizens.

Organizationally it is often functionally siloed, with each silo treating the customer in a different manner. Little information is shared across functions and customers are forced into dealing with many parts of the Transactional organization to get problems resolved. "Solutions" are billed separately, showing the lack of true coordination in the organization.

Typically, senior management claim they are customer focused but the words and deeds do not match. This contradiction is seen by employees who mimic this behavior.

Enlightened orientation

> Definition: an organization that has recognized the need for a holistic, coordinated, and deliberate approach to the Customer Experience. It is proactive in nature towards the customer and orchestrates emotionally engaging Customer Experiences. It stimulates planned emotions.

The Enlightened oriented organization understands the importance of the Customer Experience and has thus achieved enlightenment. It has converted from being reactive to proactive to customer demands. It has understood the critical nature of defining the Customer Experience it is trying to deliver. It has spent time discussing this at a board level and agreed a Customer Experience statement, which has been communicated to all employees. It realizes that over 50 percent of every Customer Experience is about emotions[1] and therefore it has embedded new processes into its Customer Experience, which are planned to deliberately evoke emotions. Enlightened organizations recognize that customers have emotional expectations, as well as physical expectations, and plan to exceed both.

The Enlightened organization has formal methods to ensure that people spend time with the customer. This applies from the most senior members of the board to the janitor. The leadership walks the talk regarding the Customer Experience.

The Enlightened organization has taken actions to coordinate and align its Customer Experience. Typically, it has appointed a coordination point in the shape of a Vice President of Customer Experience or some cross-party group. It employs people who have emotional capabilities whom it then bonuses on the Customer Experience index, focusing around the emotions being evoked in customers. It has recognized that an organization's culture impacts on the Customer Experience. The Enlightened organization appreciates that the employee experience is equally as important as the Customer Experience, and has undertaken actions to align them.

Natural orientation

Definition: an organization where focus on the customer is total. It is very proactive and is naturally focused on the complete Customer Experience. In order to produce memorable and captivating Customer Experiences it uses specific senses to evoke planned emotions.

In this orientation, the Customer Experience is in the organization's DNA. It does not have to consider what to do as it does it naturally. It understands the critical role that senses play and has deliberately built these into its Customer Experience. It understands that customers have sensory expectations and then uses the senses to create captivating and memorable experiences. It involves the customer in the design of the Customer Experience and has defined its own Customer Experience Recipe™. It is totally proactive to customer demands and undertakes many activities, which even the customer does not see, to build a great Customer Experience.

The Natural oriented organization recognizes the amazing power of "stories" and "storytelling," both inside the organization and outside, and it uses these to great effect to build its unique Customer Experience. Its leadership, and everyone in the organization, has been selected to meet its deliberate Customer Experience. Its culture is aligned to the Customer

Experience and is seen as an enabling tool. It uses theater as a method of producing consistency of its Customer Experience. It considers the product or service it sells of secondary importance, as it knows if it gets the Customer Experience correct then the rest will follow. It has aligned the brand and its Customer Experience and one supports the other. It has very sophisticated methods of collecting customer data, which it constantly uses to improve its Customer Experience. Its systems look at the holistic Customer Experience and provide relevant data at points of contact with the customer.

These are some of the headlines of the Naïve to Natural™ orientations. Figure 1.2 shows the Naïve to Natural Model™. The X axis represents the progression of an organization's strategy on differentiation, that is, its source of differentiation. From using traditional product features as the source of differentiation, moving through to differentiating on service, then through the recent innovations of differentiating on Customer Relations (that is, personalization and customization, which have been supported by investments in CRM systems and the drive towards relationship marketing in order to build relationships with customers) and finally then using the Customer

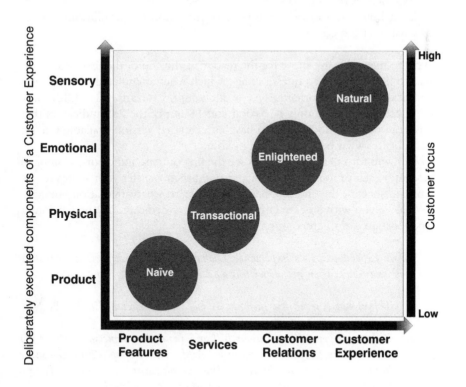

Figure 1.2 The Naïve to Natural Model™

Experience as the primary source of differentiation.The Y axis shows the organization's *deliberate* use of different facets of the Customer Experience, moving from product, through physical, to emotional and finally sensory. The Z axis denotes how customer focused an organization is.

In summary, as you read this book you will:

- understand the benefits of progressing from Naïve to Natural™
- learn why Naïve and Transactional organizations struggle to maintain competitive advantage in the longer term
- understand how Transactional organizations are actually driving the commoditization of their own market places – and the impact this is having on their profitability!
- understand why Enlightened companies have embraced customer emotions as a means of differentiating themselves and increasing customer loyalty
- learn how Natural organizations use theatrical techniques as a key part of their customer strategy
- understand why customers' senses are critical to Natural organizations
- discover why Natural organizations find it easy to build Customer Experiences that improve the bottom line
- learn how you can orientate your organization to Revolutionize Your Customer Experience™.

To try to make this live more for the reader, at the end of the first nine chapters, we have provided a questionnaire which when completed will give you an indication of which orientation you and your organization are in. It is only an indication – we will only be asking you 18 out of the 259 indicators that constitute our full model. We do have an extended version available free on our web site: www.beyondphilosophy.com.

When you turn the page you will see the first of these indicators. Complete these after each of the first nine chapters and then transfer your scores to the summary sheet at the end of Chapter 9 and learn what orientation you are.

We leave you with an extract from the chapter dedicated to the Customer Experience in Tom Peters' book *Re-Imagine!*.

Think Experience. Talk Experience. Look at examples of experience. Analyze those examples. Then get on with it and remember:

1. *This is not a semantic quibble. It is … the essence of life in the New Economy.*
2. *Billions$ upon Billion$ upon Billion$ (and then some more Billion$) are at stake for giant companies. And, relatively speaking, the same high stakes apply to the individual accountant … or to the beaver trapper turned Wildlife Damage Control Professional.*
3. *This is a BIG DEAL!*

Are you missing the gorge?

Do not follow where the path may lead. Go instead where there is no path and leave a trail.

Ralph Waldo Emerson

Naïve to Natural™ self-assessment

Please answer the following questions and then transfer your scores to the summary sheet at the end of Chapter 9.

1. The emphasis of my organization's recruitment process for customer-facing people is on identifying people with:
   a. The right attitude: attitude tests take place with a view to recruiting people who have a generally "positive" attitude.
   b. Specific skills, knowledge of the product, the competitive offering and/or our industry.
   c. An ability to act, role-play, and improvise: people are selected for their ability to evoke deep emotions and stimulate customer senses.
   d. Emotional capability, who are good at evoking emotions: people are rejected because they are not good at evoking emotions.

Your answer [ ]

a = 2 points, b = 1 point, c = 4 points, d = 3 points   Score [ ]

2. The emphasis of my organization's training for customer-facing people is:
   a. Specific in nature, focusing on acting techniques, and stimulating customer senses.
   b. General in nature, focused on dealing with difficult customers providing good service and evoking general "positive" emotions in customers.
   c. Specific in nature, focusing on how to evoke specific emotions in customers.
   d. Primarily product-focused.

Your answer: [ ]

a = 4 points, b = 2 points, c = 3 points, d = 1 point   Score [ ]

2 Please hold, your call is important to us

A year from now don't wish you had started today.

Anon

Steven Hamilton, Theatre Director at Hamleys:

> *As is quite common in a number of stores the escalators at Hamleys were designed to take the customer up one floor and then force the customer to walk around the floor to get the next escalator up to the next floor. The philosophy behind this is quite simple. It forces customers to walk around each floor with the possibility of an impulse buy. A great idea if you are coming from a perspective of just trying to sell things. Not so good if you are trying to build a great Customer Experience. Our customers told us they didn't like this, especially during busy periods.*
>
> *We took this issue to the board and we decided to change the way the escalator worked. This entailed literally taking the escalators out of the six-storey building into the street, turning them around and then refitting them again. A massive task in the heart of London's shopping district. Over a period of two nights, we gained special permission from Westminster Council to close Regent Street to traffic. (The equivalent of closing Fifth Avenue in New York.) The escalators had to be taken out into the street, be turned around and brought back into the store and fitted the other way around. A huge effort, which also cost us a huge sum of money, but it was the right thing to do for our customers.*

As you can imagine this was a massive task and one that must have cost a few dollars. All because customers did not like walking around the floors. This is customer-focused. I wonder how many boards and chief financial officers (CFOs) would have agreed to this expenditure?

This example is interesting for another reason. It is clear previous management thought it was a good idea to make customers walk around the floors, as is common with most large well-established stores. As the market changes, and the Customer Experience has increased in importance, Hamleys has decided to make a significant investment in changing the direction of the escalator. A simple task but one that bears testament to the change in its orientation towards the customer, from doing what was good

25

for the organization to doing what is good for the customer, in other words, from Naïve to Natural™.

Another sign which bears testimony to how an organization is oriented is the way some organizations (the Naïve ones) place their customers on hold for five minutes and at the same time play a message that says:

Please hold – your call is important to us.

Translated, this really means you will need to wait for us, as we don't want to employ enough people to answer your call; our organization's time and resources are more important than yours.

A bit of a difference in attitude, a bit of a different orientation. Unfortunately, the reality is that the Customer Experience in most organizations today needs some attention. We will show the evidence to prove this as we progress through this chapter, where we will examine the current state of Customer Experiences across many organizations and assess where we are.

In association with the Marketing Forum, we conducted research with customers and employees to determine the current state of the Customer Experience across many industries.[1] The results are very revealing. We have broken the Customer Experience into three stages: before, during, and after. Amazingly 51 percent of customers said they felt "apprehensive, nervous, worried, or mistrusting" as they entered a Customer Experience. Why is this the case? We believe that Naïve and Transactional organizations have "trained" customers to expect a problem. Let me tell you about a personal experience of mine:

> *I was in New York recently giving a speech. The evening before I decided to go to the theater. I phoned a ticket agency call center. At the end of the call I asked the agent's name as I was worried I would arrive at the "Will Call" window and they wouldn't have my tickets. To my surprise, the agent replied, "I am agent 287." "What, that's a strange name," I replied. "I am sorry, sir, we cannot give our names out."*

Let's take a couple of steps back. Why did I ask for the agent's name? Organizations, primarily Naïve and Transactional, have trained consumers that if we don't, when we have a problem and call them to sort it out, they invariably deny all knowledge of having dealt with us. Therefore we don't trust them. They have taught us not to trust them. In my example above, this organization's response was to impose a cost on itself and maintain a list of agents and their numbers, rather than fix the underlying root cause of the problem. The issue is simple:

You get the customers you deserve.

26

Organizations effectively train customers how to behave. If your organization always delivers things late, you should expect lots of phone calls into your call center to check if the delivery is planned or not. The evidence we have uncovered is people "prepare" themselves for certain Customer Experiences. Another example:

> *Whenever I am walking through a shopping mall and the man from the AA or RAC (AAA Road Recovery services) approaches me and asks if I would like to join, I always say, "I am already a member." The reality is I am not. I know this is a white lie, but it is just the easiest way to deal with it without being drawn into a conversation I don't want to have and without being confrontational.*

Typically when customers have a serious complaint they tend to gather their facts together and "prepare" themselves for the call. My wife, Lorraine, tells me she mentally prepares herself by adopting an aggressive manner, "to show that she is not going to be pushed around." It is like donning armor and she is ready to do battle! We are not saying this approach is correct, however it is interesting Lorraine feels the need to do this. She has been trained by experience that this is the best approach for her. Less confident customers show their submissive nature in the language they use:

- I am very sorry to trouble you ...
- Is it possible that you could help me ...
- I was wondering if you could help me ...
- Would it be at all possible to ...

These are not the words of confident customers. Our research[1] revealed that only 27 percent of consumers said they felt "confident" before entering an experience. We also found a marked difference between males and females, with only 16 percent of men saying that they felt confident when entering a Customer Experience, compared with 40 percent of women. Whilst this was clearly "generalized" research across all markets, it does beg the question, what is it like for your organization?

What do your customers feel like before they enter your Customer Experience? Is there a difference between men and women? Do you know? If not, we believe you should. Enlightened and Natural organizations can tell you. The Naïve and Transactional cannot.

Rachel Elnaugh, the Founder and Managing Director of Red Letter Days, can tell you how its market breaks down:

> *Our target audience is 70 percent female and typically ABC1s aged between 25 and 55 buying for their partners.*

When we asked consumers about how confident they were during the Customer Experience, we discovered customer confidence declines from 27 percent before the Customer Experience to 18 percent during the experience. What are organizations doing to cause this? Here are some examples:

- We keep customers on hold and give them complex voice menu systems to navigate.
- We talk to them in technical jargon that confuses them.
- We give customers so much choice they are confused.
- The sales assistant's attitude shouts, "You don't know what you are talking about."

The list goes on ...

When we looked at what consumers felt like after a Customer Experience we found 18 percent of them reported feeling "mistrust, disappointment, apprehension, or feelings of being unappreciated," typical of a Naïve organization. So what are organizations doing to leave nearly one in five consumers still feeling some form of negative emotion?

It starts with advertising. Advertising sets customer expectations before they have even interacted with an organization. In 2003, $248 billion was spent in the United States[17] and some £17.2 billion ($29 billion)[18] in the UK on marketing. £4.3 billion ($7.5 billion) of this UK expenditure was spent on TV advertising to create, support, and promote brands, and effectively create a brand promise in the market.

We were told by 82 percent of consumers that when they saw an ad on TV they did not expect the actual Customer Experience they would receive from that organization to match the Customer Experience portrayed in the ad. Unsurprisingly this evoked feelings of disappointment or mistrust. So think about this:

> **Billions of dollars are being spent on building**
> **disappointment and mistrust.**

Here is a customer view from our research[1] that sums it up:

> *Mostly it is unbelievable and I guess it's a function of age that when you reach 38 you realize that they [organizations] are projecting a message that in the majority is far from the truth.*
>
> Consumer interview

Of those consumers who thought the TV advertising and the Customer Experience would be the same, 97 percent said that they felt conned and disappointed when they were not. The level of disappointment was much higher in younger people. A sad indictment, then, of the lack of coordination between the marketing and delivery functions within an organization.

In general, our research revealed that 82 percent of consumers do not trust organizations. Why is this the case? Simple, just think of what happens on a daily basis:

- "I'll phone you back in 30 minutes" ...and they never do.
- "Yes, the engineer will be out tomorrow" ...and he/she does not appear.
- "We'll have it delivered next week" ...and it's not.
- Sales assistant: "Yes, that is our best price." Customer: "Oh, no thanks then." Sales assistant: "Hold on, give me one moment ... I have just spoken to my manager and she says we can give you another 5 percent off." Why did they lie to me in the first place?

You don't have to look too far to see the latest scandal besetting the corporate world, with misstating of company accounts or regulators chastizing organizations for poorly treating or misleading customers. The last word on this goes to an employee from a focus group conducted as part of our research[1]:

> *Most companies are built on so called trust ... it's not about trust at all, it's about getting them in, getting it fixed, getting them on their way, and taking their money. That's what it's all about; it's far from trust.*
>
> Employee focus group

It is these very employees who interact with customers who have a massive effect on the Customer Experience. They remain one of the most important moments of contact for customers. Therefore, it is surprising that we found that under a third of organizations had a strategy for ensuring brand values were met at all moments of contact. Also only 33 percent of employees said they were briefed on their company's advertising and marketing before it went live. How can organizations purport to give their customers a great Customer Experience when this happens?

Just over one in ten employees said that he or she did not enjoy his/her job. What is the likely impact of this on the Customer Experience? This figure more than doubled for certain roles, with 24 percent of customer service staff in face to face roles and 25 percent of call center staff saying they did not enjoy their job. It was clear from the employee focus groups those who did not enjoy their job were not motivated to provide an engaging Customer Experience.

The real surprising evidence was from our new research[2] which shows that 68 percent of organizations believe that people are very important. However 41 percent do not measure employee satisfaction, therefore how do they know how engaged they are?

These are unfortunately common issues, and are telltale signs of the manner in which organizations view customers, particularly Naïve and Transactional organizations. Customers are not stupid; they see and take note. Organizations may say they are customer-focused but their actions betray what they are really like. As a consequence, our research[1] shows 44 percent of consumers say that at *best* their Customer Experiences are "bland and uneventful." *At best!* In addition, 15 percent say they are "frustrating and extremely annoying." This is a sad indictment on the quality of Customer Experiences organizations are providing today. More importantly for these organizations, having a bland Customer Experience is not a good idea in a commoditized market. To prove the point we asked consumers how many Customer Experiences they had yesterday. Worryingly most consumers frequently couldn't remember how many Customer Experiences they had had the day before! Only 6 percent could recollect having more than ten Customer Experiences the previous day, when the reality is that we are bombarded with 2500–3000 messages every day, each of which is a Customer Experience in itself.

In our experience of being involved with many of our clients' customer research programs, it is clear that most of their customers would be happy for the organizations to provide a Customer Experience that simply met their expectations, let alone exceeded them.

You can look at this in one of two ways:

1. Let's aim low, reach our goals, it avoids disappointment!
2. My goodness, what an opportunity to get this right!

Faced with this evidence, and many other factors, we have constructed the Naïve to Natural Model™ to truly enable organizations to understand what they are doing now and to establish what they need to do to Revolutionize Their Customer Experience™.

The evolution of the Customer Experience

In the middle of last century there was no need for organizations to be customer-focused. This doesn't mean that they all weren't – some were – but as products became more available, they needed to provide differentiation and companies realized they needed to become more customer-focused. The easiest thing to do was to fix some of the problems that were creating a poor Customer Experience. The simplest and most obvious problems to fix were based around the physical side of the Customer Experience: reliability, responsiveness, quality, and so on. For instance, it used to be considered acceptable that shops closed on a Sunday. At first some shops decided to open on Sundays and others didn't, but eventually most shops have been forced into responding to this demand.

As everyone followed a similar path, with some being in the vanguard of the change and some being the laggards, eventually the market equalized again and that differentiation was lost. Due to increased pressures on price that a commoditized market brings, organizations have focused internally on cost-cutting programs to maintain profitability. However, this cannot be sustained. When you finally reach the point where the pain of change is less than the pain of staying where you are, you are forced to Revolutionize Your Customer Experience™. In our last book, *Building Great Customer Experiences*,[16] we revealed that 85 percent of senior leaders believed that emotionally engaging with customers would increase customer loyalty. Two years later this has now increased to 98 percent.[2] Two years ago, only 15 percent were doing anything about it;[1] this has now increased to 31 percent.[2] Many organizations are now engaged in the process of Revolutionizing Their Customer Experience™ and providing an emotional engagement. This would indicate we are just about to see a mass move towards the emotional Customer Experience. A number of leading organizations are already there. Disney, Virgin Atlantic, Harley-Davidson, Ritz-Carlton, and other organizations are talked of all the time as delivering a great Customer Experience. These organizations provide an emotional engagement; in fact, they have moved through the enlightenment orientation into the Natural orientation.

All organizations can fit into the Naïve to Natural Model™ and are in one of our four orientations: Naïve, Transactional, Enlightened, Natural. The change of orientation is where the revolution in their Customer Experience takes place. Organizations normally have decided to change for one of a number of reasons:

- The competition have improved their Customer Experience and they are being left behind.
- Their profitability is being squeezed and they realize they have to change.
- As an organization, particularly public services, they are measured against what is happening in the general market and therefore customer expectation forces a change.
- They can see a market opportunity in improving their Customer Experience.
- They realize their organization is not aligned and they wish to reduce costs.
- Survival.
- A new, visionary leader shows them the path.
- Because everyone else is!

In the business context, there is an economic cycle that occurs. See Figure 2.1.

Stage One: It starts with companies identifying a market opportunity. As they move into this market they enjoy a high level of differentiation and can on occasions enjoy high profitability.

Stage Two: As more companies see the market opportunity, they follow the first company's lead and enter the market. Therefore competition increases.

Stage Three: More and more organizations are now in the market and this is affecting profitability. Differentiators are hard to find, and to maintain profitability the company starts to cut costs. It realizes that an increased focus on the customer is also required.

Stage Four: The pain of companies staying where they are is now too great as profitability is really being affected. They now look around for other markets. Hopefully they then move into Stage One again in the new market.

As these cycles increase we have seen a number of organizations being forced into becoming more customer-focused. It is at these points of change that you Revolutionize Your Customer Experience™. Consider what has happened with direct banking and direct insurances. The first movers in these markets enjoyed these differentiators until everyone started to copy their offering.

Over the years, this cycle has resulted in organizations becoming more and more customer-focused.

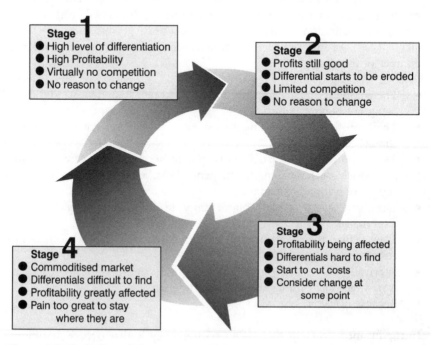

Figure 2.1 Evolution of Naïve to Natural™ orientations

For a change to happen clearly your *understanding* of what you want to change has to increase. You then need to take *action* to change. Finally you need to consolidate the change by *embedding* the action. Let me give you a practical example:

If you smoke cigarettes you may "understand" that smoking is bad for you, but you may continue to smoke despite this knowledge. Therefore, to put a label on it, we could say that you are in a "smoking" orientation.

You may decide to take "action" to stop smoking. Maybe you use nicotine patches or see a hypnotist. After a few weeks you return to smoking as these actions didn't work. Therefore despite your "understanding" and the "action" you have taken, your "orientation" has not changed. You are still in the "smoking" orientation. The vital ingredient that is missing is you did not *embed* the actions to force a change in orientation. If you had managed to "embed" these changes than you would have stopped smoking. Only then can you say you have changed your orientation.

The same applies in business. You may understand what you need to do to improve your Customer Experience, you may even be running some pilots, but your orientation hasn't changed until you embed those changes. Therefore let us give you an example from our latest research.[2]

Forty-eight percent of organizations' levels of understanding are the same as their orientation. In other words they are doing what they know. In 52 percent of organizations, understanding is higher than the orientation. In other words 52 percent of organizations know more than they are doing. Why? Why are they not doing more to become more focused around the Customer Experience? The killer statistic is that overall *only 11 percent* of organizations are taking action to move into a higher orientation. This is despite the poor state of Customer Experiences in many organizations, as we articulated earlier in this chapter. At the moment 89 percent are effectively remaining with their current orientation! To remind you this was:

Naïve 9 percent – Transactional 67 percent – Enlightened 22 percent – Natural 2 percent

This shows that there is a massive opportunity to start improving your Customer Experience and following the lead of the 11 percent.

We will go into understanding, action, and embedding in Chapter 10. If you now overlay this with the orientations, you will see that these economic cycles are happening at each stage of each orientation. Your understanding of the Customer Experience increases; you take some action. This becomes embedded in your organization. At the same time, this economic cycle is in operation. The market you are in commoditizes and you realize that being in your existing orientation is no longer acceptable.

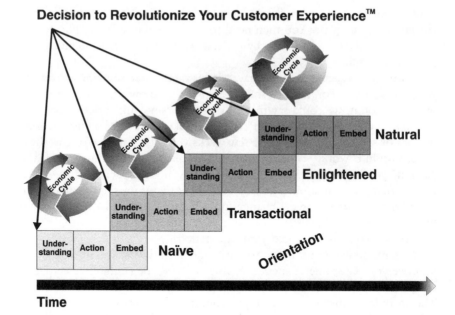

Decision to Revolutionize Your Customer Experience™

Figure 2.2 Economic development of orientations

What makes up the orientations?

Over the last 30 years, I have worked in a number of blue chip companies, getting my hands dirty and climbing the ladder of success. I finally reached the exalted heights of Vice President, Customer Experience for one of the world's largest companies.

I have been blessed with two careers. The first of over 20 years in blue chip companies and I believe that enables me to talk with some authority about life there. I started life a humble salesman but then spread my wings to learn more and worked in sales, marketing, training, and customer service before becoming Vice President of Customer Experience. I had responsibility for 3000 people and led programs that increased our Customer Experience index by 36 percent, saved 17 percent of costs, and increased customer-facing time by 200 percent. I say this not to impress but instead to impress upon you that I am not coming at this from a theoretical point of view. I am coming at this from a practical, pragmatic standpoint. I know what it is like, from working at the shop floor to sitting in board meetings. There is one piece of feedback I am proud of: our clients saying, "We like talking with you, Colin, as we know you have been there, you understand what it is like working in a big organization, you understand the problems and issues we face." I now look back in horror as I recall the lack of customer focus in some of the companies I worked in. The customer was effectively treated as a means to an end.

Let me give you a typical example of a lack of customer focus from one of my previous employers and how all nine orientation areas of the Naïve to Natural Model™ are involved.

Over a three to four year period, we had received feedback from customers, which told us that the lead time of one of our key products was a major issue with customers. This deficiency continuously featured in all our market research and customer satisfaction surveys. I proposed to change this to increase our customer satisfaction. This meant quite a dramatic change, but was by no means impossible. Given that the lead times of this product hadn't changed for some time it didn't take a rocket scientist to know there was a problem and a good overhaul was required. We did further market research to define exactly what the customer expected and we then produced a business case for the change. We identified the key stakeholders, did the politics, and lobbied for support.

All was looking good. We presented our case. It was rejected! Why? Despite our protests, they were not convinced it was worth doing. We were asked to prove that improving customer satisfaction would increase our bottom line. Ironically, the company's first value was "The customer comes first."

My team was distraught. This demonstrated in a single action how customer focused the company really was. Actions always speak louder than words.

Being a tenacious sort of chap I thought, "OK so they do not like that. What is important to them? Cutting costs! There are more accountants here than you can shake a stick at!" Could this be justified on cost savings? We started to investigate. It turns out that the lead times were so unacceptable to customers that 45 percent of all orders were entering the official procedure to escalate urgent orders. 45 percent! Escalation means the management chain became involved at a huge cost. Some customers were insisting that all their orders were escalated at the point the order was placed, as they knew that if they did not it would never be delivered on time! As you can imagine this was imposing a massive cost on the business. We re-cut the business case and justified it solely on the grounds of cost savings. I told the powers that be that as a "byproduct" of this change we would also increase customer satisfaction. They rejected it! Why? Other projects were deemed more important. You could have knocked me over with a feather! At this point I realized we were ideologically different and it was time to leave that company.

These, I now realize, are the actions of a Naïve organization. It had effectively decided to stay Naïve. This story displays all of the orientation areas that affect the Customer Experience. For instance:

Table 2.1 A story displaying all of the orientation areas affecting the Customer Experience

Organization aspect	Orientation area
Despite the rhetoric of "we put customers first," the customer was the last thing they considered.	Culture and leadership
The culture was cost cutting.	Culture
The process hadn't been touched for years.	Process: customer expectation
The customer satisfaction survey was ignored.	Measurement, culture, leadership
Limited or no bonus for customer satisfaction.	Measurement
The leadership didn't spend time with customers.	Leadership
There was no customer strategy. The people didn't care about the customer.	Customer strategy People
The systems didn't highlight the problem of the 45% escalation rate.	Systems and measurement
Many departments involved.	Channel approach
The brand advertising depicted the organization putting the customers first.	Marketing and brand
They had also employed the wrong people, as they were not customer focused.	People: recruitment

You will see that this one case encompassed the nine orientation areas that make up the Naïve to Natural Model™. We dedicated a whole chapter to each of these in our last book *Building Great Customer Experiences*[16] and therefore we would recommend that you read this.

In this chapter we give you a brief explanation of each of these orientation areas and back this up with statistics from our research. You will then see that Chapters 6–9 are dedicated to each of the four orientations, and in these we will give specific examples of how these areas apply to that orientation.

In each of the graphs below you will see we are looking at any two of the four aspects from our research:

1. The current orientation.
2. The "understanding" of what needs to be done in each orientation area.

3. The "current action" in each of the orientation areas.
4. What "previous initiatives" have been undertaken in each of the orientation areas.

Figure 2.3 shows how the Naïve to Natural Model™ is taken down into the orientation areas. It is entirely possible that an organization's overall orientation may be Transactional. However this does not mean it is necessarily Transactional in each of the orientation areas.

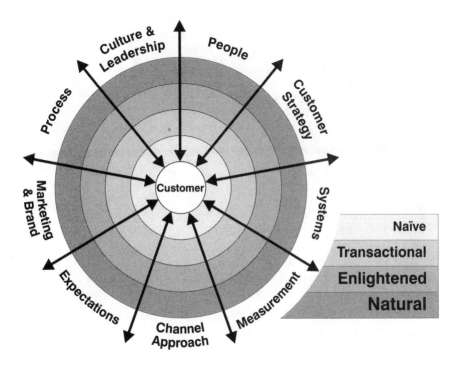

Figure 2.3 The Naïve to Natural™ orientation areas

Figure 2.4 shows the Naïve to Natural™ orientation report for a financial services organization. Overall the organization is Transactional. You will note that its understanding for systems, measurement, channel approach, and customer expectations is Transactional. For marketing and brand, process, people, and strategy its orientation is Transactional, but its understanding is in advance of that, being Enlightened. In one of the areas, culture and leadership, it is in a Naïve orientation, and its understanding is Transactional. We will go into what we recommend for this organization in the Transactional chapter. At the moment we just want you to understand the concept.

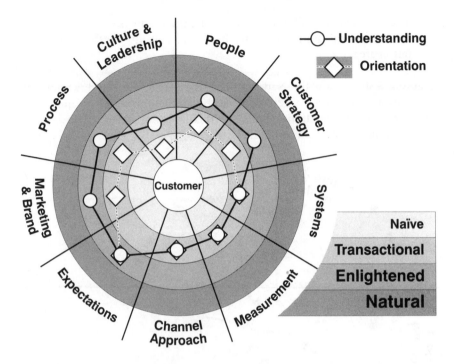

Figure 2.4 A Transactional financial services organization

Although we will be outlining the impact of each orientation area in more depth as we journey through the book, let us explain a bit more about what the orientation areas are and how they affect the Customer Experience.

Naïve to Natural™ orientation areas

1. *People*

   People play a vital role in creating a great Customer Experience. The type of people you recruit, the way you train and treat them, will greatly affect your Customer Experience. Therefore how you recruit people and the training you give them is critical. Our research discovered only one in five organizations is in the Enlightened orientation for people. In contrast 52 percent of organizations understand what they should be doing to progress into this area, but few are doing much to bridge the gap. Surprisingly 35 percent of organizations still only recruit people based on skills and knowledge. Given the importance of emotions in the Customer Experience it is worrying that only one in five senior business leaders realizes recruiting people with emotional intelligence is essential to create a great Customer Experience. However, the good news is that 20 percent of organizations do understand they should be recruiting "emotionally intelligent" people. Are you one of them?

Eighty-five percent of organizations are only training people on products or how to deal with difficult customers whereas two-thirds understand this limited focus is inadequate and that they should be providing training on how to evoke specific emotions.

Figure 2.5 shows the overall scores for the people orientation area and the bell curve shows how, in general, understanding is ahead of their orientation.

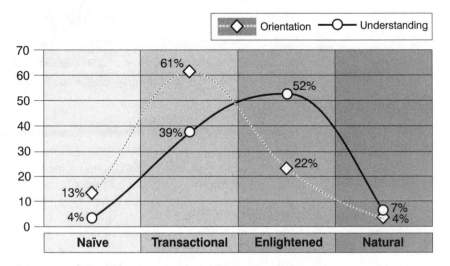

Figure 2.5 The Naïve to Natural™ orientation area: people

2. *Customer strategy*

Having a defined customer strategy is essential for providing a great Customer Experience. Ask yourself this: what is the Customer Experience you are trying to deliver? Do you know? If you don't then you join over half of the organizations we researched who could not articulate the Customer Experience they are trying to deliver. Without defining it, your Customer Experience will come across as being disjointed and uncoordinated. Fifty-two percent of senior business leaders understand that not having a defined experience is wrong, and 54 percent are taking action to develop one. Also, 65 percent of organizations admit that their customer strategy is not aligned with their functional areas like IT, HR, and so on. Over two-thirds recognized they should be. The good news is 54 percent are currently taking action to achieve this.

The overall results for understanding and orientation for the strategy area are shown in Figure 2.6.

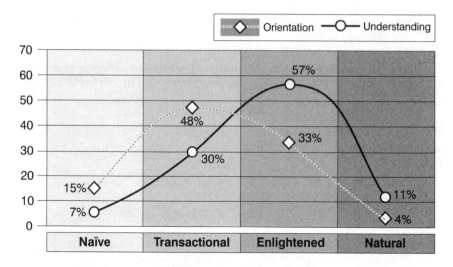

Figure 2.6 The Naïve to Natural™ orientation area: strategy

3. *Systems*

   The systems an organization operates can affect the Customer Experience. For example, if your system requires you to ask the customer for a post-code/zip code or reference number to access his or her details, the customer will consider he or she is being treated as a transaction rather than a person. Do you use a voice menu system ("Press 1 for products, 2 for …")? Clearly this is a system that affects the Customer Experience. Just over one in three organizations now considers whether a voice menu system or a person is most appropriate to answer calls, with 41 percent understanding people are the most effective method. With the many stand-alone systems that have been built over the years it is good news that 57 percent of organizations are now getting a complete view of the customer, probably the impact of the introduction of customer relationship management (CRM) systems.

   The overall results for understanding and orientation for the systems area are shown in Figure 2.7.

4. *Measurement and targeting*

   What gets measured gets done. If you only measure sales and productivity, employees will focus on delivering these, even if this means causing a poor Customer Experience at the same time. You will note this orientation area is not as developed as the other areas. This is the area that needs to be most improved upon by the majority of organizations. The level of understanding of how a Natural orientation would deal with this is particularly low. A total of 78 percent of organizations are still focused on sales and productivity measures, while 54 percent of organizations realize that they should

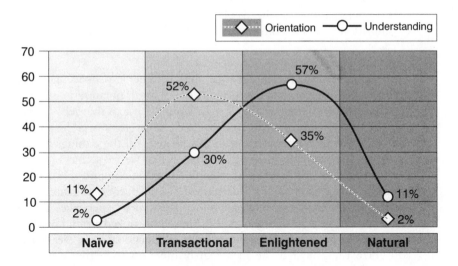

Figure 2.7 The Naïve to Natural™ orientation area: systems

be measuring the Customer Experience and then rewarding people on this measurement, but it's actually not happening. No surprise then that 87 percent of people are still paid on physical measures, which are primarily internal in their nature. The good news is that one in five organizations is taking action to start to pay people on Customer Experience measures.

You will see the data in Figure 2.8 is different. Here we are looking at the understanding against "current action." You will see

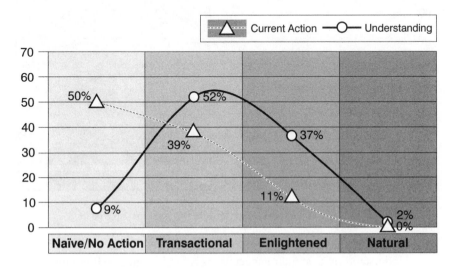

Figure 2.8 The Naïve to Natural™ orientation area: measurement

41

that understanding is ahead of "current action." In other words organizations are not doing what they know they should.

5. *Channel approach*
   The channels that customers use affect the Customer Experience. Do your customers choose the channels they use, or does your organization choose the channels for them? Are they only offered the use of the web? Or can they get the same products and services in a retail store or over the phone? Are the channels coordinated or uncoordinated? All these things impact the Customer Experience. The good news is that we are seeing a growth of organizations that have a dedicated function looking into this coordination. A virtual team has been established by 53 percent of organizations; the more enlightened ones have a VP of Customer Experience. This is needed, as 22 percent of organizations are still organized around product lines, with 48 percent being organized around functional areas. Nearly half recognize they need to be in a matrix function to better serve the customer. The fact that integration of the Customer Experience is a problem is recognized by 50 percent of organizations, and two-thirds recognize that they should be providing a seamless service, but only 31 percent of organizations are taking action to resolve this.

   The overall results for understanding and orientation for the channel approach area are shown in Figure 2.9.

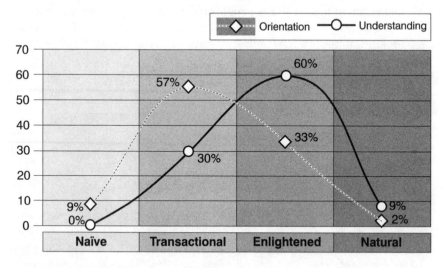

Figure 2.9 The Naïve to Natural™ orientation area: channel approach

6. *Customer expectations*
   Understanding customer expectations is fundamental to building a great Customer Experience. Customer Experiences need to be designed

around these expectations. Having said this, our research shows 65 percent of organizations effectively pay lip service when understanding customer expectations. Eighty-three percent understand that customer expectations should be documented and communicated from both the physical and emotional point of view. Over two-thirds of organizations believe it would be a significant step forward to their organization to simply meet their customer expectations, let alone exceed them! Fifty-four percent of organizations talk in generalizations about customer expectations, with everyone in the organization having their own view of what they are and how they should be met. Also, 59 percent are planning whether they should be achieving or exceeding a customer expectation and 57 percent are taking action to achieve this.

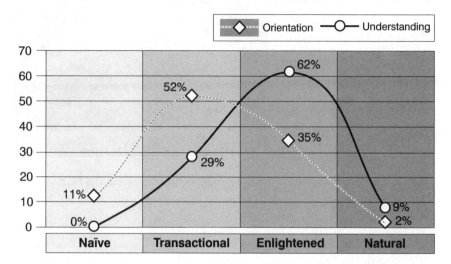

Figure 2.10 The Naïve to Natural™ orientation area: customer expectations

The overall results for understanding and orientation for customer expectations area are shown in Figure 2.10.

7. *Marketing and brand*
   The brand makes the promise in the market; the Customer Experience delivers against the promise. If marketing undertakes advertising that creates a promise, and the delivery unit is unable to keep it, the customer will see the inconsistency. Disturbingly half of organizations make no attempt to align the brand and the Customer Experience. A quarter state that no one outside marketing can articulate the organization's brand values. In our previous research,[1] 45 percent of senior business leaders stated that they knew their organization had brand values, but they personally weren't sure what they were. Nearly two-thirds of organizations realize everyone should

understand the brand values. While 35 percent are taking action to solve this, 65 percent are not. Half of organizations admit that their brand and their Customer Experience do not align, and two-thirds recognize they need to be aligned, but only one-third are doing something about it.

The overall results for understanding and orientation for the marketing and brand area are shown in Figure 2.11.

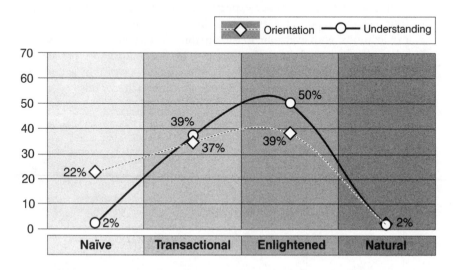

Figure 2.11 The Naïve to Natural™ orientation area: marketing and brand

8. *Processes*

Organizations' processes reveal a great deal to a customer. Is the process designed for the good of the customer, "outside in," or for the good of the organization, "inside out"? You can see from the shape of these bell curves there is a big discrepancy between organizations' orientation and their understanding. Sixty-eight percent of organizations do not have an end-to-end owner for organization processes while 58 percent of organizations recognized they should. Processes are reviewed very infrequently by 74 percent of organizations whereas 61 percent understand they should be reviewed every 6–12 months.

The overall results for understanding and orientation for the processes and brand area are shown in Figure 2.12.

9. *Culture and leadership*

Culture has a massive effect on the Customer Experience. If they live in a blame culture, employees will not put themselves out for the customer. If leaders do not see customers and hide in their office, so will others. Most concerning is that organizations do not seem to

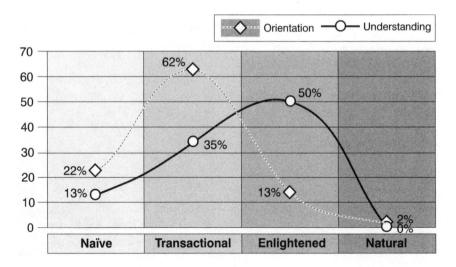

Figure 2.12 The Naïve to Natural™ orientation area: processes

understand what needs to be done to ensure that culture and leader-ship are ready for the Natural orientation. We all know the importance of "role-modeling." Ominously 83 percent of senior business leaders spend little or no time with customers. Just over half understand this is wrong but only 18 percent are doing anything about it. Customer service people are not recognized and are not seen to be as important as salespeople, stated 37 percent of organizations. However, just less than half see customer service people as important and recognize they do generate revenue. There is work to improve this area in 54 percent of companies. Thirteen percent of organizations say that often things are hidden away from the customer when something goes wrong ... in fact the research revealed that these organizations said they would often blame the customer, telling them it was their fault. The tendency is not to believe the customer.

You will see in Figure 2.13 that we have produced the data for "current action" and "previous initiatives." You will see that 54 percent of organizations have not previously taken action in this area, but 30 percent of organizations are taking action in the Enlightened orientation, thus demonstrating the movement of organizations into this orientation.

This gives you an overview of these orientation areas and some of the data from our research. With data of this kind and analysis, you are able to look at what your organization is like. We would encourage you to complete the second phase of your Naïve to Natural™ self-assessment test, so you are not

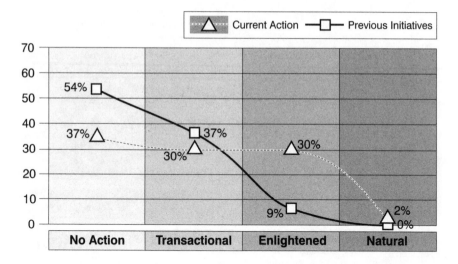

Figure 2.13 The Naïve to Natural™ orientation area: culture and leadership

left behind by those other organizations that are planning to improve their Customer Experience. Remember:

He who arrives late must eat what is left.
                              Yiddish proverb

Naïve to Natural™ self-assessment

Please answer the following questions and then transfer your scores to the summary sheet at the end of Chapter 9.

3. Which of the following best describes the Customer Experience in relation to your organization?
    a. The Customer Experience we want to deliver has been articulated – it outlines the transactional elements and also the customer emotions we want to evoke.
    b. Different groups across the organization look at the Customer Experience in isolation. Nothing is defined. Everyone does what he or she believes is right, so there is no consistency and the Customer Experience is confused.
    c. The Customer Experience we want to deliver has been articulated. It outlines the transactional elements, the customer emotions we want to evoke, and the customer senses that we want to stimulate.
    d. No one in the organization has an overall view of the Customer Experience the organization wants to deliver.

Your answer [   ]

a = 3 points, b = 2 points, c = 4 points, d = 1 point   Score [   ]

4. Which of the following most accurately reflects the degree of alignment between your Customer Experience strategy and other functional strategies?
    a. The organization doesn't have a Customer Experience strategy or there is no alignment – strategy is developed in isolation by product managers.
    b. There is alignment. This has been achieved by the establishment of a recognized infrastructure (such as a Customer Experience council) with members from each function looking at transactions and emotions.
    c. There is no alignment. There are many siloed customer strategies, with each function or department developing and implementing its own strategy in isolation.
    d. There is alignment. This has been achieved by the establishment of a recognized infrastructure (such as a Customer Experience council), with members from each function looking at transactions, emotions, and senses.

Your answer [   ]

a = 1 point, b = 3 points, c = 2 points, d = 4 points   Score [   ]

3 The guiding principles

Out of intense complexities, intense simplicities emerge.
Winston Churchill

Duane Francis, CEO, Mid-Columbia Medical Center, Oregon:

We encourage the patient to choose the decoration of their rooms. We are trying to create a very nice home. For instance, we have bedspreads, which are not common in hospitals. The appointments in the room are very non institutional. The patients can pick and select the artwork. We have completely redesigned our patient gown so that a patient can feel comfortable and feel like they are not being put on display as they amble around their room. We pay particular attention to bed linen so that what they feel and what they see there is not just the traditional drab institutional colors. We use soft earth tone colors and indirect lighting as opposed to harsh fluorescent lights. We have carpeting rather than stark tile floors so we create a warm and inviting environment. We use furnishings and fixtures that are very non institutional in look and feel. We have designed the place with plenty of storage. We know this is very important so that when the hospital equipment is not in use it is put away and not visible. So it is put out of the mind of the patient and they are not constantly reminded that they are in hospital. We place as much information at the disposal of our patients and their loved ones as we possibly can, as we believe that everyone has an inalienable right to have as much information as they possibly can about their illness, so they can make informed health care decisions. We believe obsessively that this is your body, these are your decisions, and you can determine alternative treatment in concert with the medical professionals, so that you feel that you have as much control over the process. Regarding the spiritual aspects of health we have no visiting hours in our hospital. If you want a loved one or friend to visit you any time, night or day, we don't just allow it we encourage it.

A great Customer Experience that is a lot different to the hospitals I am familiar with. This story encapsulates a number of aspects of the Customer Experience. It is well thought through, deliberate, and the Medical Center has planned how it will use the senses to stimulate emotions.

I have found in life, if you understand how something works this gives you the ability to get the most from it. This applies to many areas. For example, we all attend management training courses that teach us how people are motivated. By improving our understanding of people we learn to manage them to make a more valuable contribution to the workplace. What we have found surprising is that not many organizations understand what a Customer Experience actually is; how it is made up and how to positively affect and influence it. Our Naïve to Natural Model™ shows that:

Only 2 percent of organizations know how to reach
the Natural orientation.

Naïve and Transactional organizations tend to look at the subject from a very superficial perspective. The result is many people make sweeping statements and take actions that do not maximize the power of a Customer Experience.

Let me give you an analogy. If you had something wrong with you, you would not expect your doctor to just have a superficial understanding of your problem and provide you with treatment without understanding what is happening to your body, would you? Of course you would not. In fact if the doctor did not understand your ailments he or she would refer you to a specialist, an expert in the field. To Revolutionize Your Customer Experience™ you need to be a specialist. You need to understand the detail, the underlying root causes of what is happening in your Customer Experience so you can diagnose the problem and recommend suitable treatment, to gain competitive edge.

One sweeping statement we hear about the Customer Experience is that creating entertainment or using the principles of theater is the answer. We disagree. Theater and entertainment are *methods* for implementing a Customer Experience. They are not the answer in themselves. If they were the answer you would never see a bad play, but we do. I have seen plays that were boring, with bad actors. Therefore, it cannot just be about theater and entertainment. We concur they are an effective method and that they provide a useful framework from which effective Customer Experiences can be built. We will discuss this in the next chapter. What we should be examining is why, when undertaken properly, these are effective methods. Why are theater and entertainment attractive to human beings? Natural organizations understand why this is the case and exploit it to their advantage.

We believe you should *deconstruct* your Customer Experience into its constituent parts. Having understood what is happening you can *reconstruct* the Customer Experience in the manner that is most effective for your organization and beneficial for your customers.

In this chapter we are going to investigate some of the basic elements of a Customer Experience and reveal our latest thinking about what a Customer Experience actually is.

To help organizations on the journey from Naïve to Natural™, we have established three guiding principles. These reach the heart of how a Customer Experience is constructed. Understanding these principles is the foundation to Revolutionizing Your Customer Experience™ and will help you move from Naïve to Natural™. Before we explain these, let us put these into some context. Let us start by asking you a question that we have now asked thousands of people:

What is the best Customer Experience you have ever had?

Was it on holiday, maybe at a restaurant, or in a shop? Stop and consider this for one moment. Thought of one? Now think about what happened. Consider the situation. What made this Customer Experience your best? The person you dealt with? The surprise it gave you? Remember the setting. What did the place look like? Do you remember what it smelt like?

The first thing you will have noticed is how difficult it is to think about your best Customer Experience. Why? *There are not many of them.* However, if I asked you to tell me about a bad Customer Experience then you would have hundreds.

Now stop and think back to yesterday. I would like you to count how many Customer Experiences you had yesterday. If you are like most people your answer will be between zero and ten. The reality is that you had thousands. There are so many we actually filter most of them out. Did you watch TV yesterday? Did you see any ads? Each one of them is a Customer Experience. How did you travel to work? Did you look at a magazine or read a paper yesterday? That in itself is a Customer Experience, but within it there will have been many ads. Each of these is a Customer Experience. Some you may have ignored and others you were oblivious to. Therefore you might have read the first tag line before being distracted and moving on. Did you go onto any web sites yesterday or receive any emails from organizations? Each of these is a Customer Experience. Yet your mind ignored all of them.

In a commoditized market, is it a good idea or a good use of money to have a Customer Experience that people can't remember and in fact ignore? No! Therefore to ensure that you can Revolutionize Your Customer Experience™ we need to understand what a Customer Experience is. What makes it up? How does it work? Once we understand how it works we can then start to fix things.

Guiding principle one: what is a Customer Experience?

In our last book, *Building Great Customer Experiences*[16], we offered a definition of a Customer Experience. Since its publication we have spent a further two years working in this area, discussing it with senior business leaders, academics, business commentators, and conducting our own research. We now believe this definition needs refining. Therefore here is our new and enhanced Customer Experience definition:

> *A Customer Experience is an interaction between an organization and a customer. It is a blend of an organization's physical performance, the senses stimulated, and emotions evoked, each intuitively measured against Customer Expectations across all moments of contact.*

It is important to understand the detail of this definition, as this calibrates all the Naïve to Natural™ orientations. In other words, if you are deliberately planning to achieve all of this in your Customer Experience and you are doing it in a Natural manner against the nine orientation areas we outlined in Chapter 2, then we would describe you as a Natural oriented organization.

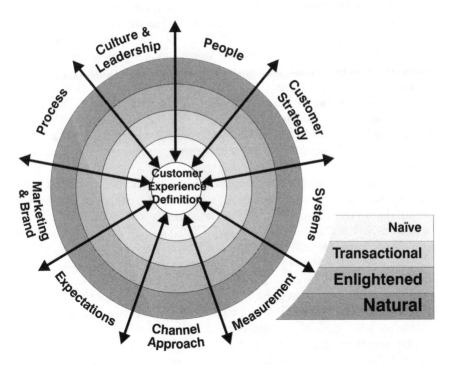

Figure 3.1 The Naïve to Natural™ orientation areas

Therefore it is important that we understand the detail. So let us take each of the key words, one by one. So a Customer Experience is an *interaction*. It is an interaction between an organization and a customer. When this happens, by definition, you are communicating. This interaction can last weeks, like a holiday, or just for a split second, for example a fleeting look at an ad. In any interaction the organization is trying to attract your attention to convey a message; you, in turn, are receiving a message and processing it. Again, this may only take microseconds but it is an interaction nonetheless, as information is given and processed by your brain. In that split second you make a judgment to read the ad or to move on to another page, to stop and look at the shop window or move on. It is therefore important to an organization to construct an interaction that engages individuals for long enough to convey the entirety of the message. Ideally this engages them sufficiently that they want to move onto the next stage, maybe calling the organization to ask about its offering. What are both of these situations doing? They are trying to gain your attention. The longer an organization can hold your attention, the more likely their message will get across.

This interaction is conducted with a *customer*. This refers to potential and existing customers.

The Customer Experience definition then uses the word *blend*. This is critical. In our view a Customer Experience is not just the physical, or just the emotional, or just the senses, it is all these blended together. One of the important aspects of the blend is an organization's *physical performance*. What we mean by physical performance is factors such as product, price, and quality: for example how quickly the calls are answered, the opening hours of a business, its location, and the reliability of their product. Naïve and Transactional organizations believe this is the "be all and end all" of the Customer Experience. To Revolutionize Your Customer Experience™ they need to realize that emotions and senses play a massive part in a Customer Experience.

This is because it is critical to understand how human beings take in information. We gain it by using our *senses*: sight, sound, taste, touch, and smell. In our day-to-day existence we use our senses to gather data about the world around us. *What does the product look like? What does the restaurant smell like, pleasant or unpleasant? What does the product feel like, rough or smooth? What does the food taste like, sweet or sour? What does the music sound like, quiet or loud?* Therefore a Customer Experience is about the senses that are being stimulated. The important point to understand is that we absorb information from our senses. Organizations can control what senses to stimulate, and this is exactly what Natural organizations do. They define how and when to deploy senses in their Customer Experience. Therefore, organizations can control the data the individual collects, which emotions to evoke, thus helping to control the Customer Experience.

Liam Lambert, Director and General Manager, Mandarin Oriental Hyde Park, London:

> *It is a very sensual experience when you stay at a Mandarin Oriental. I have been asked, "What is a scent of luxury?" and I think the scent of luxury is probably a mixture of tanned leather, cigar smoke, and Brasso (metal cleaning polish)! In very luxurious clubs the leather is wonderfully tanned*

and there is a leathery squeak on the seats and a leathery scent like a per-
fume. Somebody was perhaps having a very good cigar and then the
attention to detail is that somebody has been in this club polishing all the
brass just before you got here so you manage to have all these attributes
working together.

In Hong Kong we had a suite called the pine suite. All the wood was pine.
Every day we would spray pine into the corner of the room and after a
period of time after two or three weeks of doing this the whole room smelled
of pine as soon as you walk in. We use some of those things here in the
Mandarin suite. We use cherry blossom or apple blossom spray so when you
walk in the scent is as if you were in China.

Another example would be when you come back to the room in the
evening, it hopefully attacks the senses. When you enter your room we have
turned on the lights by your bed. The bed is turned back and we have the
radio playing quietly, tuned to classical music. The scent is musky, so when
you arrive "home" the room is welcoming – the bed is open and you are ready
to dive into it.

The combination of these physical aspects, the data received by your senses
and your expectations all contribute to evoke *emotions*. For example
remember your best Customer Experience of earlier. How did it make you
feel? Think back. What was the emotion you felt? Have you ever felt frustrated during a Customer Experience: maybe waiting for the call to be
answered or standing in a long line in a bank? We found in our research[1] that
69 percent of consumers said that *emotions* account for over half of every
Customer Experience they have.

Peter Scott, Customer Service Director, T-Mobile:

The fundamental thing about emotions is that we all have them, it's in our
make up and it's emotions that build memories and relationships between
people. Our strongest memories are linked to those things we get emotional
about, whether they are positive or negative emotions. Shared emotions build
relationships, which in turn build loyalty.

If you think about your best Customer Experience then you will realize that
it is not just about the physical aspects, as Naïve and Transactional organizations believe. Enlightened organizations understand half the Customer
Experience is about evoking emotions, and they plan how to evoke specific
emotions. Natural organizations use the senses as a tool to achieve this. Here
are some views from leading organizations:

Rachel Elnaugh, Founder and Managing Director, Red Letter Days:

One fascinating thing we have found through research on experience
giving is that there are actually two emotional highs. The moment of

giving is just as important as the moment of experiencing the gift. So, for instance, when the wife gives her husband the Red Letter Days envelope and he discovers he has been given a Ferrari driving experience, that moment is almost as powerful as the day itself when he goes Ferrari driving. It is an important consideration that we believe is crucial to the success of our business.

Kathryn M. Haley, VP, Client Experience, RBC Royal Bank of Canada:

We realized if we knew the rational indicators and the emotional indicators of client loyalty, and were able to identify the root causes of why people stayed or left, then we could create programs designed specifically to help us retain customers. Some of the areas of dissatisfaction are fairly standard across many organizations. They are price, service, and convenience related. All these rational indicators drive emotional responses.

Ellen L. Brothers, President, American Girl:

On a scale of one to ten the importance of the emotional connection with our brand is a 12. It is the emotion of the little girl wanting this doll called Molly; it's the emotion of giving it to her and seeing her face light up when she opens that box on Christmas morning. It's the emotions of the little girls as they walk into one of our stores for the first time and they jump for joy because they are finally there. It's the ultimate destination for girls, and the emotional bond is a huge component of what this brand is all about.

These are great examples. It is also about the emotions you feel. Think of getting married, getting divorced: decisions driven by emotions. The reality is that human beings are emotional animals.

We do everything based on how we feel. For instance, I am sure you must have heard news items saying:

There is a lack of confidence in the stock market.

What does this mean? What is "confidence?" Confidence is an emotion. Take a moment to consider when you last "lacked confidence." What did it feel like? Perhaps you felt nervous or tentative, you were not sure what to do, and maybe you even felt embarrassed or self-conscious. How does that "lack of confidence" manifest itself? You may decide that as you "lack confidence" you won't go to a party on Saturday night as you don't want to walk into a room full of strangers. Another example is when you "lack confidence" in one of your team. You therefore start to take a more active interest in what he or she is doing, to ensure that things are being performed correctly. Consider this question: would you invest your money in something that you lacked confidence in? No. This is what happens on the stock market and many other places in our everyday lives. When people lack confidence they do not invest their money.

The stock market is run by emotion.

If you look at much of the research[1] you will recall a lot of this was emotionally based. We discussed confidence, disappointment, and trust. To expand this idea let us look at what happened after Enron. People could not "trust" that the balance sheets of large companies were accurate. Trust is an emotion. The lack of trust drove down the value of stock markets across the globe. Emotions are all around us. As I sit here and write this, the latest virus is attacking many of the world's PCs. I have just received a promotional email from my antivirus vendor entitled "Afraid of the virus?" It is playing on my emotion of fear!

Although emotions run our lives they have almost been totally ignored by most organizations. The good news is 28 percent of organizations across the Naïve to Natural Model™, over a quarter of them, are researching specific emotions on a company-wide basis; over half understand they should be.

When customers have a Customer Experience they subconsciously process this information and make some judgments about it. Was it good or bad? How do they make that judgment of whether something was good or bad? Against what terms of reference are they using?

Perception is reality framed by the past.

We review and judge it against the past, against what other people have told us, against similar experiences and what we have seen on TV or read in books; in many different ways.

All of these are wrapped together, so that we make a judgment about what we *expect*. What we then expect is based on all those thoughts going through our mind. Each of us has an expectation about everything: how long it takes to make a cup of coffee, how long it takes to park the car, how loud a rock band will be at a concert. All this feeds our expectations, which are constantly being updated or confirmed as we go through life.

Ellen L. Brothers, President, American Girl:

> *Our products are carefully packaged inside each beautiful box. Inside each box is colorful tissue paper and always a little something extra – something you don't expect. When you're in the direct business you can't touch or see our product up front, so it's important to always exceed customers' expectations.*

We believe that the quality and the presentation of our products plays an integral part in everything we do.

These are also all measured *intuitively*. In other words they are within us. Your view of the quality of food may be different from mine. Your view of how long it takes to park a car may also be different from mine. We all have personal measurement yardsticks inside us.

Twenty-four percent of organizations deliberately plan to exceed customer expectations and have proactively built this into business processes, while 48 percent realize they should be but are not today. Customer Journey Maps (including emotions) should be plotted at both strategic and tactical levels. Emotions have been intrinsically designed into processes by only one in five organizations.

Finally, these are measured *across all moments of contact*. The customer can touch your organization from the Internet, via direct mail, a sales person, customer service, ads: all these are "moments of contact" or as Jan Carlzon[19] said, "Moments of Truth." All these are Customer Experiences in their own right, but together they make up a complete Customer Experience that a person will have with you. They may start by visiting your web site, then your call center and then visit your store or branch.

So as you can see there is a great deal of detail behind the simple question of what is a Customer Experience. But our next challenge is, why bother? Why have a Customer Experience? What is the purpose of a Customer Experience?

Guiding principle two: what is the purpose of a Customer Experience?

In our view the purpose of the Customer Experience is to:

1. *Create an interaction between an organization and individual.*
2. *Conduct a transaction between an organization and an individual.*
3. *Create a desire for future interactions and transactions.*
4. *Create value.*
5. *Create advocates.*

As we stated in our Customer Experience definition, the first purpose of a Customer Experience is to create an interaction. This means there is communication between the organization and the individual. Ideally this interaction moves on to conducting a transaction, providing the individual with the service the organization is offering. At the same time the organization should be looking to create a desire within customers for future interactions and transactions. Customers will only come back if they perceive value in the interaction. Also the organization has to see value in this interaction for it to continue to offer it. For example there is little point in advertising on the web if no one contacts the organization. Finally, the Customer Experience should be such that the individual wants to tell others how great it was. This all can happen over weeks or a few seconds. Pulling this all together, ideally, this is what you want customers to say when they are talking with their friends:

> *I had a great holiday, we are planning to do it again next year, and you should go there.*

Or an example of a Customer Experience that takes a few seconds:

> *Did you see that ad in the paper? It was really good, look out for it. Next time I see it I'm going to give them a call.*

This is the purpose of a Customer Experience. So, having deconstructed a Customer Experience, how do we reconstruct our Customer Experience in order to Revolutionize Our Customer Experience™?

Guiding principle three: how do you Build Great Customer Experiences?

> *Great Customer Experiences are consistent, captivating, and memorable by design. To achieve this, organizations must seize and retain their customers' complete attention by deliberately planning a defined Customer Experience that stimulates customer senses and deeply engages them emotionally.*

It is comparatively easy for an organization to provide a great Customer Experience occasionally. It is vital that you do this every time, like Natural organizations can do; in other words *consistently*. In my experience the only way you can consistently achieve this is if the experiences are *designed*. To design something means that it is deliberate. *Deliberate* is my favorite word. Ask yourself, is your Customer Experience deliberate? Do you mean to do it? Is the outcome of the Customer Experience one that you have proactively designed? In most organizations that we deal with, the Customer Experience is not deliberate – it is something that just happens.

Let me give you an example. Recently my broadband connection stopped working at home. After a few local tests of my own, I phoned the ISP technical support number. Table 3.1 shows the conversation. In it I have captured my thoughts and feelings during my Customer Experience so we can decide if this was good or bad and to what extent this was deliberate and designed.

Table 3.1 A Customer Experience with an ISP technical support agent

	Conversation	My thoughts	My feelings
Colin	I dial the number and wait for ages for a reply. During my wait, I am asked to reboot my cable modem and PC, which I do.	I hope I am not on this call for hours. A sensible reasonable request.	Apprehension. Satisfaction that this is using the time efficiently.
Agent	The agent answers: "Can I have your name, address, and phone number?"	Sensible and understandable question.	A little annoyed at having to wait so long to be answered. No apology offered. I am just a number.
Colin	I give my details, but there is no conversation.	I am a transaction.	Ambivalence.
	I hear clicking of keys	They must be entering the details?	Being ignored.
Agent	"Is that name correct?"	What? I don't know my own name?	Amazement – incredulity
Colin	"No, I always get my name wrong," I said sarcastically. (I am annoyed as a result of being kept so long and then being confronted with a stupid question.)	A chance to get my own back!	Fulfillment.
Agent	"Could you reboot your PC and modem?"	You must be joking!	Annoyance – surprise
Colin	"I have already done this, as instructed, whilst I was waiting to be answered. Why do I need to do this again?"	You are wasting my time.	Annoyed.
Agent	"You may not have done it properly so we would like you to do it again."	You are saying I am stupid!	Resentment, indignation.
Colin	I reboot and nothing happens.	See I told you so!	Contentment and annoyance.

Table 3.1 continued

	Conversation	My thoughts	My feelings
Agent	"Can you wait a minute as I need to speak to an expert?"	What? Are you a trainee? Why wasn't I talking to an expert in the first place?	Resentment, very annoyed.
Colin	I notice that I am listening to the same music on hold as I was when I called in.	Goodness, I hope I am not lost in some queue and will need to begin again.	Exasperation.
Agent	Five minutes later, he comes back. "Can you tell me how much you pay a month?"	What planet is this person on? He goes off to talk to an expert and this is the only question they ask me!	Indignation.
Colin	"What?" I say, "How much do I pay per month? What does that have to do with the fact that my broadband does not work?"	Now tell them what idiots they are.	Anger.
Agent	"We were doing some work in the area" he goes on to explain, "and they disturbed the cable modems and lost a number of customers' details. We have been waiting for the customers to phone in."	Therefore, you do not care that none of my family have had a connection for two days. Why didn't you phone me and tell me?	Indignation, resentment.
Colin	I give him the details. He presses more buttons.	What is he doing? Why will this help?	Annoyance.
Agent	I am asked to reboot.	I hope this works.	Hope.
Colin	It works!	Thank goodness it works. What a poor experience.	Relief, annoyance.

I am sure that you will have had similar experiences. This is typical of a frustrating experience. Do you think this Customer Experience was deliberate? Was it designed purposefully to be annoying? Do you think if I contacted the CEO and informed him of my call that he/she would be pleased and say, "Yep that's great, that's exactly what we planned to do, we want all our customers to feel annoyed and frustrated"?

I would suggest this Customer Experience would horrify the CEO. The organization did not mean to do this. Nevertheless, that raises an interesting question. If it didn't mean to do this, what did it mean to do? What is the deliberate Customer Experience it is trying to deliver?

Think of the word *deliberate*. This comes from the word liberate. When something is liberated it is set free. To make something deliberate means to think about it, and it means you are being specific, constraining something, not trying to be everything to everyone. If someone has a deliberate Customer Experience the organization has carefully thought it through; it is doing something on purpose. Arguments will have been made in favor and against. If the Customer Experience is deliberate, it means all options have been considered, the good and the bad, and then a decision has been made weighing up the pros and cons. The organization has decided what to do and how to do it.

The next challenge is what terms of reference have been used to determine how to create the Customer Experience. What is good and what is bad? Surely this can only be determined if you have a clear picture of what the Customer Experience is that you are trying to deliver? Naïve and Transactional organizations have not thought this through. Enlightened and Natural organizations have, and furthermore have communicated this throughout their organization.

By definition you should be able to answer the following question.

What is the Customer Experience you are trying to deliver?

Do you know? Do your people know? If I came into your organization and asked people, "What is the Customer Experience you are trying to deliver?" would they be able to tell me? Would I get a consistent answer? And as emotions account for over half of a Customer Experience, a follow-on question would be:

What are the emotions you are trying to evoke?

And if you are to evoke emotions you need to determine how you are going to achieve this, therefore another question:

What senses are you going to use to evoke these emotions and how are you going to do this?

Michael Edwardson is a leading consumer psychologist based in Australia[20]. From a study[21] he recently co-authored for the Society for Consumer Affairs Professionals he has determined the following:

We found that at the top end the words people used to describe their best Customer Experience were "contented," "appreciated," "happy," "reassured," "delighted," and "valued." In the middle – the zone of indifference as we describe it – are feelings of "indifference" or "being emotionless." In the worst situation we found customers who felt "disappointed," "frustrated," "angry," "neglected," "annoyed," and "insulted."

If you are a company and you say you want to satisfy customers, it's not going to do anything. In my view the word "satisfied" itself is quite mean-ingless. It is not a good measure for businesses to be using. It's a kind of "Goldilocks" word … it's not too hot and it's not too cold. It doesn't capture the real human emotional experience. What we have shown is that people want a company to make them feel appreciated, happy, respected, and maybe, if possible, even delighted. In most instances it is much more pow-erful to say what we actually want to do is to make people feel valued. People simply want to feel secure and appreciated. These are called self-referent emotions, which come from a feeling that one's sense of self has been regarded and recognized. In many ways it's the easiest emotion to elicit. If you go to the other end, if you go to negative self-referent emotions which is where the company really loses it, this is where people feel "neglected," "insulted," "cheated," "disgusted" – that's worse than anger although it could be linked to it. These emotions are unrecoverable from; because once people feel that way it violates their sense of self. We find that these emotions are the ones that leave you with a customer who is definitely going to defect. Disappointment is especially insidious because, unlike anger, customers don't let you know, they just defect silently and never ever come back.

Have you considered Michael's points in deciding which emotions to evoke? Without having considered what emotions you are trying to evoke, your Customer Experience can't be deliberate. How, therefore, can people deter-mine what they are meant to be doing and what is good or bad? But don't worry, you are not the only person or organization that cannot answer. We spend much of our lives asking clients this question, and 95 percent cannot answer these questions. This is one of those simple questions that does not seem to have been asked before. A massive hole in an organization! In fact we stumbled on this question when I was Vice President of Customer Experience. The president asked me to "improve the Customer Experience and do it at least cost." I accepted the challenge and went back to my office to consider how to do this. To improve something means you need to know where you are today and where you want to be. We had considerable data on what we were doing, but then I asked myself a simple question: "What is the Customer Experience we are trying to deliver?" I didn't know, my team didn't know, my colleagues on the board didn't know, the people in the front line didn't know, no one knew. So what did everyone do? They all did what they thought was the "right" thing. And as they were all working from their own terms of reference regarding "the right thing," everyone was doing something different and therefore the Customer Experience was confused and contradictory to the customer.

As we outlined in our last book, without answers to these questions how do you know what you are trying to do? What happens in organizations is that they have not decided what their Customer Experience is and therefore everyone does what they think is the right thing, but by definition it is different. Most organizations have not given any thought to the emotions they are trying to evoke or the senses they will use to achieve this. It is vital in building a great Customer Experience that you have defined your Customer Experience, one that everyone understands. Creating and delivering a Customer Experience that is *defined*, *deliberate*, and *designed* is key to business effectiveness.

Craig Spitzer, General Manager, The Library Hotel in New York tells us of its deliberate Customer Experience:

> *We came up with this idea of categorizing each room with a different subject. For example on the eighth floor, which is our literature floor, you have fairy tales, poetry, and erotic literature. On the seventh floor, which is the arts, you have paintings, architecture, and so on. At the hotel we actually have 60 unique subjects that guests can choose. Upon arrival the agent may well tell customers that on the third floor we have ancient languages or on the fifth floor, astronomy. The thing that we've learned is when you are able to give people the option to make a decision on which room they are going stay in, that positively impacts their stay. They feel empowered and they are more likely to be more comfortable and enamored with the property as a result.*
>
> *We have built a deliberate Customer Experience. For example on the social sciences floor one of the rooms is on the subject of money. The graphics above the bed are these really neat old copies of a Japanese yen and there's a US dollar and there's a German mark, to enhance the theme. On the shelves you'll have books relating specifically to the topic of the room. Each hall way is adorned with a light stenciled projection onto a wall. So when you arrive on the fifth floor, which is math and science, as the elevator door opens you will see this light projection, which welcomes you and it says math and science so as you emerge you know exactly which subject you are in.*

The development of a Customer Experience statement is critical. This is a clear definition of what the Customer Experience is that you are trying to deliver. We have worked with many clients on defining the Customer Experience statement. Opposite is an example. The important aspect here is the words you can see in italic and underlined – these are the important words. These have been suggested by the customer, and put through our Beyond Philosophy™ process whereby they are approved by the executive board to determine if delivering them is commercially viable. Once it has been decided the Customer Experience statement can be communicated in a number of ways.

In a paragraph:

We will be renowned for our *reliable* service. Our people will be *knowledgeable* and *respond* and *resolve* all customer queries promptly, therefore making customers feel *assured*. This will be delivered in an *enjoyable* and *caring* way that will ultimately make our customers feel *special* and *valued*. Our customers will *trust* us and believe we provide *value for money*.

As a series of words:

Our Customer Experience is:

caring
knowledgeable
reliable
resolving
responsive
assured
special
valued
enjoyable
trusted
value for money.

Or in what we call a Customer Experience Hierarchy of Needs™: see Figure 3.2.

We have discovered, in helping a number of organizations to define their Customer Experience, that there is a Customer Experience Hierarchy of Needs™, very similar to Maslow's hierarchy of needs. In other words, there are basic elements of the Customer Experience people wish to have in place before they can move up the hierarchy. You will see in Figure 3.2 that the bottom two layers of the triangle are fairly common across all industries. When we were working with a train organization its customers told it that they wanted to have an enjoyable journey, which for them was at the top of the Customer Experience Hierarchy of Needs™, but the first thing the organization needed to do was to ensure the trains were "reliable."

It is therefore difficult to obtain differentiation in the bottom two layers. It is in the top two levels that you are able to differentiate yourself and provide a deliberate Customer Experience. In most cases, the top two levels

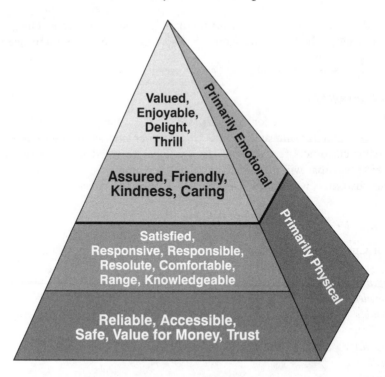

Figure 3.2 The Customer Experience Hierarchy of Needs™

are emotional elements. Moreover, it is the customer who should determine what these elements are and if they are important. You will be able to read in Chapter 11 how Yorkshire Water has been using this and the results it has achieved.

Since the data for creating a Customer Experience statement is provided by the customer, you can thus make your Customer Experience *captivating*. That means that you have your customers' full and undivided *attention*. It is critical to have your customers' full attention so that they can focus on the interaction they are having with you. We have therefore developed the concept of:

Share of Mind™

What is your share of your customers' mind during a Customer Experience? We have discovered that there are different levels of customer attention:

- oblivious
- distracted
- engaged
- captivated.

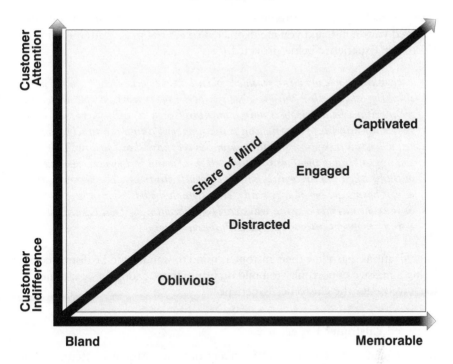

Figure 3.3 Share of Mind™

Oblivious Customer Experiences

There are many organizations that try to grab your attention as a consumer, and yet you are 'oblivious' to their advances. You haven't seen their ads, you ignore their sales representatives in the street, and you do not pick up their product. For example:

> *I read the newspaper every day. It is packed with ads and yet the vast majority of these ads do not even register with me. I am oblivious to them. They clearly have not engaged my senses. The organization has not targeted the ad well enough to attract me, assuming I am the target audience it is trying to attract.*

Giving someone an oblivious Customer Experience costs a lot of money for nothing in return!

Distracted Customer Experiences

When you are distracted you are not focused on the Customer Experience. For instance, you are in a shop and as you wander around you are thinking of other things. You do not see the special promotions. You just go into the aisle and pick up the item required. The organization has not captivated or engaged your mind, and you are distracted so are not paying attention to the Customer Experience being provided.

> *Like many people my mind wanders when I start to get bored. I am normally thinking about other things, what's happening at work, people watching, wondering why a person is doing something in a certain way. Like many people my mind is processing and thinking about things constantly. You can tell when this is happening with someone as they have that "vacant" look when you are talking to them and you can tell their mind is elsewhere. An example of this is when you are waiting in line for a train ticket. The person in front of you hasn't got her money ready, even though she has been in line for three or four minutes. Her mind was clearly on other things. That organization is losing an opportunity to engage with the customer.*

Organizations that allow their customers mind to wander and be distracted are losing a massive opportunity to build on future transactions, as we outlined in the purpose for the Customer Experience.

Engaged Customer Experience

In the engaged stage you have 95 percent of your customers' attention, but it is not captivating, and therefore customers can be easily distracted. There is, then, a danger that their minds may wander and you may lose them. For example:

> *It was recently Lorraine, my wife's, birthday and I was looking to buy a present for her. I was looking on a web site. I was quite engrossed in seeing all the things they are now selling. The web site was "good" and I was engaged but then my son, Ben, asked me a question and I immediately started to talk to him. I never returned to the web site, and then had to buy a present in a panic the day before her birthday!*

I was engaged until the point where something else was more interesting.

Captivating Customer Experiences

As the goal is to create a captivating Customer Experience, you want to capture your customers' whole minds and thus ensure they give you their full and undivided attention. It is the stimulating of their senses to such a degree that positive emotions are evoked, rendering them captivated. Nothing stops them from focusing on your Customer Experience, and importantly nothing can distract them from it. They are so engrossed in your Customer Experience that nothing will pull them away from it. Your "share of mind"™ is total. For example:

Andrew Akers is CEO and inventor of the Zorb. This is a great new experience. I will let Andrew explain what Zorbing is and how they have created a captivating Customer Experience.

A Zorb is a very large translucent ball, which people ride in. Outside it is 3.2 metres (approx 10 ft) in diameter and inside it is 1.8 metres (nearly 6 ft). The Zorbonaut, the rider, is strapped in across their waist and across their shoulders and they have hand and foot straps and then when they are rolled down the hill they are actually rotating head over heels as they go down the hill. The closest description I can give is when kids used to ride inside tire tubes, rotating around as the tire rolled down a hill. Once the Zorb picks up a bit of speed the whole issue of inertia starts kicking in and the centrifugal force starts kicking in. You get pinned to the outside and have a feeling of weightlessness. The Hydro Zorb is a little bit different. In the Hydro Zorb you jump in and there is no harness. We throw a bucket of water in with you, so when you then get pushed off the hill and start going down, the water on the bottom makes it very slippery and you actually slide on the bottom and the whole Zorb rotates around you. They are great fun!

The most common reaction for people at the bottom of the hill is they can't stop laughing, yelling, and screaming. They are laughing because they have had a fantastic, bizarre experience; it is a humorous, exciting, and fun experience. The most common reaction, and this is just so fantastic for a business model, is people get out at the bottom of the hill, where there are maybe a hundred people waiting all thinking about whether to have a go or just watch. Then people get out, and they are laughing so much they can hardly talk ... usually the first words they say as they look towards all of these people is, "You have got to have a go!" For us that is just a fantastic sales model. The second thing they do say is, "I have got to do that again!"

As you can imagine, this is a great Customer Experience where customers are totally captivated and which they give 100 percent attention to.

As you can see, in Figure 3.3 we have outlined the four stages of Share of Mind™. The X and Y axis represent customer attention and how *memorable* the Customer Experience is. So, how captivating is your organization's Customer Experience?

Ellen L. Brothers, President, American Girl:

American Girl Place is all about creating memories. We know a girl's outing to the store is a very special one-for her and her family and, of course, for her favorite doll. While shopping is always a top priority, it's the overall experience that has made American Girl Place such a phenomenal success. For example, girls and their families can watch an unforgettable live musical based on our historical fiction series at American Girl Theater, and then head to the store's café for a delightful lunch, tea, or dinner. And no visit is complete without stopping by the Doll Hair Salon where a girl can have her doll's hair done for the big day. It's the entire experience that elevates American Girl Place beyond an average retail store.

Kathryn M. Haley, VP, Client Experience, RBC Royal Bank of Canada:

We want customers to remember that we provide a great experience and tell other people about it. Word of mouth is really important. It is probably the most important indicator of spreading news. You need advocates. You need ten great experiences to make up for that one bad experience, so people have to remember it. They need to recollect it was a pleasant happy experience, that they felt a certain way. We want it to be memorable, consistent, deliberate and differentiated.

Captivating Customer Experiences are also memorable by nature. Creating a memorable Customer Experience is key in a commoditized market. If your Customer Experience does not stand out, you are part of the blandness of this world.

Organizations must *seize* customer's attention. This is imperative if they are to *retain* their existing customers. As we have also already stated organizations must stimulate customer *senses* to create a captivating Customer Experience, thus helping to *evoke deep emotions.*

These are the basics of the Customer Experience. These are the levers you can pull. In the next chapter we will look at the enablers we can use to constrict this and Revolutionize Your Customer Experience™.

We leave this chapter with the words of Tom Peters from his book *Re-imagine!*

Experiences: I have seldom, if ever, been so affected by a single word. I now view ... positively everything ... through a new lens. "What is this experience like?" That's ... so, so ... very, very ... different from "Were you satisfied with the service?"

I lament what may be my inability to transmit my enthusiasm of this idea to you. I dearly want to inflame you about "all this" as much as I have become inflamed. I want you never to view any transaction through any other lens other than ... Experience Magnification.

Prepare: the time to win your battle is before it starts.
Fredrick W. Lewis

Naïve to Natural™ self-assessment

Please answer the following questions and then transfer your scores to the summary sheet at the end of Chapter 9.

5. Which of the following best describes the degree to which your systems have given the organization "a complete and holistic view of an individual customer?"
    a. Every function has an in-depth complete view of the customer: all products, all sales, and full service history and customer preferences.
    b. Every function has a basic complete view of the customer: all products, all sales, and full service history.
    c. Each department only has a view of its own products, the sales of those products, and the revenues resulting from those products.
    d. Each department only has a view of its own products, sales of the products, revenues from those sales, and the service history.

Your answer [   ]

a = 4 points, b = 3 points, c = 1 point, d = 2 points   Score [   ]

6. Which of the following best describes your organization's approach to call routing/answering?
    a. Customers can talk to a person but it usually requires lots of transfers of calls to get to the right person. A directory of telephone numbers is given to customers to call different parts of the organization for different requirements.
    b. Dialogue is discouraged by extensive use of call routing and many levels of menus to "direct callers to right person." Typically there is music on and "how much we value your call" messages. Typically sales lines are answered quicker than service lines.
    c. A considered appraisal of whether human or machines should answer the phone has taken place. Call routing and the amount of menus have been minimized.
    d. Humans answer the telephone. Videophone contact is also encouraged.

Your answer [   ]

a = 1 point, b = 2 points, c = 3 points, d = 4 points   Score [   ]

4 The enablers

You cannot build a reputation on what you are going to do.
                                                    Henry Ford

Why was Declan's story, "Are you missing the gorge?", so engaging? If there was one person who should know about stories it is a librarian:

Stories are very powerful and are very compelling instruments that enable people to get information across and provide a learning experience. Stories make a subject much more exciting and can be used to describe or create an experience. Our Experience Library is a story in itself, and each of our areas conveys its own story to create a learning environment for our customer.

Wayn Pearson, City Librarian, Cerritos Library, California

Stories can be very engaging. We fill our lives with stories. When we tell our friends what happened to us on holiday, what we said to our boss during the last team meeting, talk about who danced with whom at the office party, or what happened when we took back the TV that didn't work, then we are storytelling. Stories are very powerful methods of communication.

Organizations in the Enlightened and Natural orientation realize stories are engaging, and use them to convey messages and meanings to customers and employees alike. Stories evoke pictures in the mind, and create memories and emotions. They have intrigued human beings since the beginning of time. In the olden days the elders used to sit around the fire and tell tales of their tribe's great deeds. They had been taught how to do that by their ancestors and this is how information was passed down from generation to generation before people learnt to write. This is where the word history was derived from: "his story."

In his book *Story: Substance, Structure, Style, and the Principles of Screenwriting*, published in 1997 by HarperCollins, Robert McKee argues that stories "fulfill a profound human need to grasp the patterns of living – not merely as an intellectual exercise, but within a very personal, emotional experience."

The power of stories and anecdotes should not be underestimated. When a new person starts in the job, to put them at ease, you tell them a story about what it was like the first day that you started. When, in business, we use a "case study" to help demonstrate to a client how the proposed solution has been used with another client, we are telling a story. This story is to give your company credibility and to give the client organization some confidence that it is not alone in doing this. In essence you are trying to evoke emotions of "confidence" and "trust" in your organization.

Robert Stephens, Founder and Chief Inspector (CEO), The Geek Squad:

> *We have no documentation. We imply our expectations through stories. For example, Bestbuy had this store they were opening in the 1990s. They were expanding so huge that the store outside Chicago was due to open up at noon. It was a grand opening, they had painted the parking lot lines the day before but they hadn't dried yet. They were worried that they were only two hours away from opening, so they had to think quick and somebody decided to hire a helicopter to fly over the parking lot 10 feet above the pavement to dry the paint. What I love about this story is that it fosters innovation; it proves it can be done and shows others you can do it.*

Soap operas tell people stories, people want to be involved in other people's lives. Fables tell stories with morals in and are a great way to get the point over in simple terms, and these are even used with children today. Remember the story of the "boy who cried wolf." I can remember telling that story to my children. Even the great religions of the world use stories to get over a message.

The power is that stories are very captivating. When you are sitting down and watching a good film you can become "captivated" as we discussed in the previous chapter. A film and theater are just stories in another form. I bet you can remember the story line of your favorite film? We all remember the stories for Snow White, Alice in Wonderland, Peter Pan, and so on. As you remember your best film you can even remember how you felt: the film captivated you, you were laughing and crying with the characters, you *were* the characters, you were in the film.

You feel the emotion they do. People talk about being "on the edge of their seats." Films and theater evoke emotions; Lorraine my wife is always crying at films and TV programs, because she is either happy or sad! But this is what we are buying: a story, an emotion, and an experience. It is an experience that enables us to escape into another world, we want to be *captivated* and escape into another world for a while.

So ask yourself this:

What are the stories that your customer would tell about you?

Would you be proud of what they would say?

How does this apply to the Customer Experience? Simply either the whole of your organization can be one story, like The Geek Squad or Hard Rock Café, or you can embed stories into the way you deal with customers as Cerritos Library has.

But these stories, films, and theater don't just happen. They are planned and scripted. Natural organizations spend hours planning their Customer Experience. Every detail is considered and the senses are used to evoke emotions. They know that if they combine sad music, a love scene, and a great dialogue, this will have the effect of evoking emotions in the audience. That is exactly what you need to do if you are to Revolutionize Your Customer Experience™.

Doug Stevenson was a professional actor working in Hollywood, he has been a stand-up comedian, and has acted in stage, movie, and television productions. In short, Doug knows about the industry. Doug is recognized as being an expert on "storytelling." He now makes his living as a professional speaker and trainer, teaching people how to tell stories in business. He is the author of the book *Never Be Boring Again – Make Your Business Presentations Capture Attention, Inspire Action and Produce Results.*[22] I attended one of his excellent courses and Doug helped me use the power of stories in my conference speeches. Here's Doug's view on the subject:

> *When you listen to a good storyteller, you hear the story with your head, heart, and soul. You're not a passive listener – you're an active participant. As the storyteller is relating his or her experience, you're experiencing it as if it were your story. You feel what the storyteller feels, and see what the storyteller sees. You memorize and retain the chunks of information contained in the story because you see the images, hear the sounds, and feel the emotions. The story engages your attention on many levels, for a sustained period of time, so when the storyteller makes the point, the learning sticks. Storytelling transcends an intellectual experience.*

Let's look back at the "Are you missing the gorge?" story in Chapter 1. I hope you found it engaging. Maybe you even thought about your own situation, and whether you are missing the gorge. Did you feel any emotion? Maybe you could picture Declan sitting by the stream. I hope this story has spurred you into action.

If you read a good story you are engaged, if it's a great story you are captivated. "I couldn't put the book down" is a commonly heard expression.

Let's again learn from the expert as Doug continues to share his view with us:

> *For a story to come alive and captivate an audience, the content, structure, and performance must be crafted strategically. The story itself is only a*

beginning. Storytelling is an art and the storyteller, the artist. And all artists need tools. The actor needs a stage, props, and costumes. The musician needs her instrument. The artist needs his brushes and paint. And the storyteller needs form, content, and presentation skills and techniques. The great storytellers distinguish themselves not just by their talent, but also by their dedication to their craft. They think about their stories constantly. They structure the sequence and flow of the story, and experiment to find the right words that are genuinely theirs. They work on a gesture or movement until it is just right. Then they rehearse it over and over until it becomes second nature – the line and the gesture effortlessly married together. They incorporate acting skills and turn their stories into little theatrical events. In order to have an end result that is amazing, you will have to spend many hours working on your story. Your story must be worked and re-worked, formed and re-formed. You'll want to find the drama and comedy of your stories and let them shine.

Now you may be sitting there and saying to yourself, "This is all very interesting but what has it got to do with Revolutionizing Your Customer Experience™?" It is quite simple. As previously stated in the last chapter, the Customer Experience is made up of many basic elements, physical elements, senses, and emotions. Typically Naïve and Transactional organizations have not yet recognized this. Natural organizations recognize that stories and theater are a great *method* of delivering the Customer Experience.

In their excellent groundbreaking book *The Experience Economy* Pine and Gilmore say, "Work is theater and every business is a stage." Pine and Gilmore rightly challenge you to define your organization's props and consider the show you are putting on.

So let us take Doug's last section and replace the word "story" with Customer Experience and see how it applies.

For a Customer Experience to come alive and captivate an audience, the content, structure, and performance must be crafted strategically. The Customer Experience itself is only a beginning. Customer Experience is an art and the designer of the Customer Experience, the artist. And all artists need tools. The actor needs a stage, props, and costumes. The musician needs her instrument. The artist needs his brushes and paint. And the Customer Experience designer needs form, content, and presentation skills and techniques. The great designers of Customer Experiences distinguish themselves not just by their talent, but also by their dedication to their craft. They think about their Customer Experiences constantly. They structure the sequence and flow of the Customer Experience, and experiment to find the right words that are genuinely theirs. They work on a gesture or movement until it is just right. Then they rehearse it over and over until it becomes second nature – the line and the gesture effortlessly married together. They incorporate acting skills and turn their Customer Experiences into little theatrical events. In order to have an end result that is amazing, you will have to spend many hours working on your Customer Experience. Your Customer Experience must be worked and re-worked, formed and re-formed. You'll want to find the drama and comedy of your Customer Experiences and let them shine.

Therefore, essential enablers of the Customer Experience are stories. And these stories are most effectively implemented through theater. Stories and theater have a beginning, middle, and an end. As you will have seen from the research we summarized in Chapter 2, so does a Customer Experience. Treating it as a show or a production can enable the Customer Experience. So what is your organization's story? What are the props you use? What is the show you are putting on, how have you structured your Customer Experience? Does it flow? Are you using the right gestures and movement at the right time to evoke the right emotion? How much attention to detail are you paying?

We recently took a group of clients around a tour of the BBC television studios. This was part of a Customer Experience safari we undertake to show people what is happening on the Customer Experience in many industries. If organizations are to use the method of theater to deliver their Customer Experience, attention to detail is something they need to learn. For instance, they will need to go into the minute detail of making the performance as lifelike as possible. At the BBC TV studios we were shown a model of a human brain that was to be used in a detective program. The designers had not only made the human brain to look like a real brain, but they had also made it the same weight as a human brain so it "handled in the right manner." Does your organization go to this level of detail? Another example is when the pop music show Top of the Pops *is filmed. When the audience all dance in front of the stage at the end of the performance, the producers ask the audience to applaud the artist over the top of their head and not in the usual way. Why? Because when they are filming from the back of the studio, if the audience claps in the normal way viewers cannot see them clapping and so it doesn't look like they are enjoying themselves. Clapping above their heads shows the viewer at home how much fun they are having.*

Do you put this level of detail in designing your deliberate Customer Experience?

It is this attention to detail that differentiates the Enlightened and Natural organizations from the Naïve and Transactional organizations:

Rudy Tauscher, General Manager, Mandarin Oriental, New York:

If we know that you like music, maybe you enjoy Mozart, Beethoven, or country music, then we can program that into the room entertainment system. If we know that you enjoy spas then we can ask immediately if you want to make a reservation when you arrive. It is the tiny details that make it a memorable experience.

Ellen L. Brothers, President, American Girl:

A lot of our catalogue photography is shot on location. Clearly this is more expensive, but the attention to detail is key. The same goes for our stores. When customers visit the American Girl Café, they immediately notice the beautiful white linens, sparkling silverware, and real china on the tables. We also created an intimate theater, which seats about 140. Like the catalogue and café, we never compromise our theater experience. For instance, we use state-of-the-art equipment along with live musicians. It would have been easier and much less expensive to have taped music, but the attention to detail is too important – it is part of the overall experience.

A number of organizations in the Enlightened orientation are now catching on to the fact that their Customer Experience needs to be entertaining. We hear words like "entertainment" and "entertaining" as a way of educating people: real entertainment. Disney talks about their people "being on stage" and they call them "cast members" to engender a culture of entertainment.

Waynn Pearson, City Librarian, Cerritos Library, California:

We felt that it was essential not to shy away from the idea of creating an entertaining library. Within the library profession this was a radical departure and was greeted with some skepticism. However, we were also committed to making the library sustainable from a learning point of view. We wanted to blend entertainment and learning, to use entertainment and emotional appeals to draw people in and encourage them to learn. From the beginning, we involved consultants who had worked on theme parks and movies, and at the outset we asked, "What is our storyline?" "What do people want from a 21st century library?" We had been charged to create the "Library of the Future," but what was it like? How do you convey a sense of the future? We concluded that the best way to convey a sense of the future is to travel through time, and our major storyline became "Traveling Through Time." This storyline really drove our whole approach to learning, library services, and collections. Our theme became "Honoring the Past, Imagining the Future." I should note that we developed a number of secondary storylines and themes, most notably in the children's area, which is devoted to "Saving the Planet."

Andrew Akers, CEO and inventor of the Zorb:

> *One way we want to develop our Customer Experience is the way we take people back up the hill. At the moment it is in a four wheel drive van. We want to make that more part of the experience, to become more like you were a NASA astronaut, and you are about to take off on the space shuttle. The ride that you get to the space shuttle is in a specific vehicle, you are wearing specific clothes, and you are hearing specific instructions on the way to the launch.*
>
> *At the moment, we are pretty much launching by hand. One thing we are thinking about doing is using a great big throw switch that mechanically launches the customer. Maybe when a family comes along the little kid gets to launch his father, or the mother gets to launch her family, so there is a real sense of ceremony. We are looking at using sound, and some sort of visual triggers, as well as including people at the bottom of the hill because it is very important to make sure that the people who have come to support the Zorbonaut are also included within the whole process.*

Organizations sell memories...

These are memories and I am sure you have many memories of your own. Surely any organization's aim is to help people to have these memories; and these memories are priceless and have a great value. What we are talking about is evoking the feeling of nostalgia. The reason we buy memorabilia is that it helps us connect to that event. In all the research we have conducted the one word that consumers consistently say they all want in their Customer Experience is *genuine*. For instance at the end of the day a ticket or a program from the Beatles in 1966 is only a piece of paper with printing on it. This can be replicated; but we are only interested in the genuine article, the ticket that allowed someone into the concert that night. In selling an experience, if the experience is good you are also selling a memory. In addition, if that memory is a good one then people want mementos and souvenirs to remember it by. They want to look back and re-live the feelings. They want nostalgia.

We recently spoke with Delia Bourne, from Group Marketing, and Steven Hamilton, Theatre Director at Hamleys in London.

> Colin: *Delia and Steven can you tell me a bit about how you have been Revolutionizing your Customer Experience™?*
> Delia: *I think from the start we need to say the two elements of our Customer Experience for Hamleys are "fun" and "magic." Really that encompasses everything that we do.*
> Colin: *So what does retail theater mean to you?*
> Delia: *It encompasses everything, from the moment that customers walk*

through the door, even before they walk through the door, the windows, the look of the store, the color, the excitement. As they walk through the door we have demonstrators and make sure we have things flying through the air, hopefully it is an exciting journey from the moment they walk through that door. There's excitement, mystery, surprises at every level.

We use the analogy of theater because we believe we are about showmanship, telling a story, taking them on a journey.

Steven: *Yes that's right, but let's not forget the end result is what all businesses are about and we want them to put their hands in their pockets: quite simply, happy people put their hands in their pockets more often than miserable people. But if we can get everyone happy then that is a plus for the staff, it is a plus for the managers; it is a plus for the customers. Happy people spend more and have a better time and so do the people that serve them. Everyone wins.*

Delia: *An example of our theater and our investment in our customers' Customer Experience is our Harry Potter success. We worked closely with Warner Bros to achieve a unique attraction with our flagship store featuring station platform 9¾, the flying car, and the staircase under the stairs where Harry lived at home. We have the sounds of the trains as you walk up the staircase and many more things. All this is about creating a Customer Experience, and evoking emotions with something that the kids and grown-ups the world round know. We are the only departmental toy store in the whole world that has got a Harry Potter staircase.*

Colin: *I can see the conversation at the boardroom table where someone suggested that you create a Harry Potter staircase. I am sure, like in most businesses; the costs would have been a consideration. There are lots of organizations that would say, "What return are we are going to get from investing in this staircase?" How do you deal with that?*

Delia: *Something like the Harry Potter staircase, or a lot of the retail theater that we do, you can't put a value on what we get back. You can't say that has pulled in an extra 20 percent of customers today, you can't always define it to that extent. So a lot of what we do and the emotions are something that is intangible. We are now considered as a tourist attraction, we are up there on the map along with Madame Tussauds and other London attractions, a Customer Experience in itself. We have moved onto a new plane. We are not just a shop, it is a day out, it is a day visit to come here.*

Steven: *Another example is that we have a jungle theme with a nice beautiful jungle on the ground floor. We could leave it like that but now we want to hang things from the ceiling, we want little bursts of smells, sound effects on the ceiling and water spraying in your face to stimulate people's senses. We are constantly striving for new innovation.*

Colin: *Steven, you were talking about the retro aspect and nostalgia. How does that work as part of your Customer Experience? You were talking about parents enjoying toys when they were younger and then wanting their children to enjoy the same kind of toys. This again is something that fascinates us. Everything seems to go round in stages, so could you tell us a bit about that?*

Steven: *The prime example is yo-yos. The yo-yo is a seven-year cycle on average, and yo-yos have been going for hundreds and hundreds of years. We had our 1760 day last year, the first one to promote the fact that we have been around since 1760. I did a lot of work on what toys were around in 1760, like kites were, wheels, roller skates were actually around, and yo-yos were around in 1760. For whatever mysterious reason, yo-yos were big three years ago, huge. We had yo-yo champions coming into the store, and that was three years ago. Last year we didn't sell any yo-yos, but you can bet your bottom dollar that they will be back. I have been in the toy trade for 12 years or so now, and I have seen them twice.*

Delia: *It's emotions again isn't it? It's all about nostalgia.*

This is the theater Customer Experience in action. By focusing on the Customer Experience, in the manner Hamleys do, it has moved through Naïve to Natural™. Hamleys has invested significantly in "attractions" with "Crazy Chris" and the "Harry Potter staircase," which stimulate senses, and the company uses this stimulation to evoke emotions of "fun" and "nostalgia," because quite simply; happy people buy more products.

So what are the ingredients of this great Customer Experience? The analogy of cooking is a good one. Look at any recipe that you would find in any cookbook. Here is a recipe for haggis, a traditional meal in Scotland:

1 sheep's paunch (stomach)	*½ tsp cayenne pepper*
2 lb. dry oatmeal	*½ tsp black pepper*
1 lb suet, shredded	*1 tsp nutmeg*
1 lb. lamb's liver	*1 tsp mace*
1 large onion	*½ tsp salt*

What has always fascinated me about cooking and recipes in particular is how they originated. Who invented the recipes? Who was the first person to say, "Here's a good idea, if we were to get a sheep's stomach and combine that with a lamb's liver, some nutmeg and combine cayenne pepper and the rest, then cook it … it will taste really nice!" And *surprisingly enough it does taste nice*! But these are not obvious things to put together.

Think of the experimentation that must have been gone through to get to the final result. The cook must have experimented with each of the ingredients, the quantities, the quality, how to mix them, at what stage, in which order, and how long to leave it on the heat to cook. It must have taken a great amount of time and effort to get to the finished product. And the same applies to creating a Customer Experience. In the last chapter, we detailed the ingredients that you are going to use to create your Customer Experience recipe.

So what is your Experience recipe? What is in your organization's cookbook? What ingredients do you have? What ingredients do you need to get? What is the desired outcome?

The challenge is that again you need to experiment, once you know what your customers want. You need to mix all these variable ingredients until you come up with your version of haggis. When you do and you have recorded it, then it becomes your recipe and you can repeat your recipe every time to ensure consistency.

The delivery of this recipe through the medium of theater and stories will see you progress into the Natural orientation and you will be able to Revolutionize Your Customer Experience™ and be ahead of the pack.

Most people give up just when they're about to achieve success. They quit on the one-yard line ... one foot from the winning touchdown.

H. Ross Perot

Naïve to Natural™ self-assessment

Please answer the following questions and then transfer your scores to the summary sheet at the end of Chapter 9.

7. Key performance indicators (KPIs) and targets are used to ...
    a. Drive sales and manage production volumes. Our main KPIs are product-related (for example, product returns, time to market, and so on).
    b. Appeal to customer senses. Profitability and Transactional performance account for about 50 percent of our KPIs/targets. Depth of emotions and senses are measured at each moment of contact and account for a significant percent of bonus/pay.
    c. Drive the CE. Profitability and Transactional performance account for about 50 percent of our targets. Defined emotions are also measured across each moment of contact and are a growing percent of people's bonus/pay.
    d. Drive sales and Transactional performance. Main KPIs are revenue and Transactional performance (for example, achievement of stated lead times, punctuality, and so on). Customer satisfaction accounts for a small percentage of bonus/pay.

Your answer [   ]

a = 1 point, b = 4 points, c = 3 points, d = 2 points   Score [   ]

8. Which of the following best describes the mix of internal and customer measures in the organizations overall Key Performance Indicators?
    a. 50 percent internal – 50 percent customer.
    b. 75 percent internal – 25 percent customer.
    c. 100 percent internal – 0 percent customer.
    d. 30 percent internal – 70 percent customer.

Your answer [   ]

a = 3 points, b = 2 points, c = 1 point, d = 4 points   Score [   ]

5   Sensory experiences

Opportunities are disguised by hard work, so most people don't recognize them.

Ann Landers

Duane Francis, CEO, Mid-Columbia Medical Center, Oregon:

We want to create a non institutional environment where patients can feel more like individuals and valued as a whole human being, rather than just a diagnosis in bed three, or the injury in bed two, and being treated as a transaction. Therefore we have created an environment that is susceptible to healing. For example, we use a lot of water features in our facility. We have a waterfall in an open-air atrium: there is open-air access from all of the floors of our hospital, where you can hear the sound of cascading water. We also use salt-water aquariums because we know it creates a soothing and a calming environment. We have fully stocked kitchens on every patient floor where we invite the volunteers, loved ones, or community members to come in and bake cookies or fresh baked bread because the smells wafting down the hall create a "homey" environment and a sense and feeling that is not stressful, and is actually designed to reduce stress. We spend a lot of time on those environment issues, what the patients see, taste, touch, and smell.

A great example of how a Natural organization use senses to create a great Customer Experience. The stimulation of the senses is planned and thought through. Maybe the customer does not consciously understand what is happening but subconsciously it has a dramatic effect. For instance:

When my Personal Assistant, Joanna Kelly, started with Beyond Philosophy™ I wanted to explain to her what we did. During this explana-tion, I showed her a brochure from an organization we were doing some work with. I asked her a simple question, "Do you think this is a quality organization?" Despite the fact that she looked at me as if I was mad, Jo picked up the brochure and looked at it. As she did so, I saw her subcon-sciously rub the pages of the brochure between her thumb and index finger. Although she didn't consciously know she was doing it, she was subconsciously

81

"feeling" the quality of the brochure by using the power of "touch." Jo believed it was a quality organization and proceeded to explain to me why she thought this was the case.

This happens all the time. Jo's sight enabled her to see the brochure, the images, the logo, and to read the copy. However Jo, without realizing it, was also using some of her other senses as another input for her assessment of the quality of the organization. She made the subconscious connection between a quality organization and the quality of the paper they use. This is what your customers do on a daily basis, but in the main, they don't realize they are doing this. So consider this: if you send out direct mail or bills to your customers your customers literally "touch" your organization. When they do, what is the "feel" that represents your organization? Smooth, rough, silky, bumpy? Do you know? Who has decided it? Is it consistent across all moments of contact in your organization: do Marketing and Finance use similar paper or something different? In other words:

Are you deliberately stimulating the senses you wish?

In the same way your brand design is deliberate and specified, is the quality of the paper on which it appears also specified to a similar degree? In most organizations the answer is no. Our research reveals that only Natural organizations proactively use *all* senses – not just sight and sound – to create a memorable Customer Experience. They recognize the power of senses and pay such attention to detail that the use of each sense has been thoroughly thought through.

In this chapter we will look at what we call the "sensory experience," the power behind this and why Natural organizations use this to provide a great Customer Experience. We will also examine what you would need to do to further Revolutionize Your Customer Experience™ from a sensory perspective.

Give me data!

Just stop and think for a moment. We have all seen films on TV where people are tortured through sensory deprivation; this is where victims are cut off from all ability to sense the world around them. They cannot touch, taste, see, hear, or smell. This is a form of torture. Why? Because human beings gather information about the world around them through their senses. Is the drink hot or cold? Is the object dry or wet? Does it look bright or dull? Is it pleasing to the eye or not? Does it smell good or bad? Does it taste sweet or sour? Does it sound loud or quiet? We all take our senses for granted, but they are one of the primary ways we gather information. We do not even think about it, we do it automatically. Senses are a primary ingredient of the Customer Experience recipe.

Kathryn M. Haley, VP, Client Experience, RBC Royal Bank of Canada:

At RBC, we wanted to translate our deliberate Customer Experience into the branch environment. We are creating a much more uplifting friendlier, inviting, welcoming environment. We are changing the colors, the fabrics, and the floors. We are bringing in lighting and lamps and flowers and plants. We are deploying music and we are experimenting using smells. In essence, we are experimenting with different combinations of senses that evoke certain responses.

The Natural organization has realized that the Customer Experience happens within the person. You touch something and receive data, which is then converted into a feeling, which is then converted into an emotion. From our Customer Experience definition, we can infer this feeling will be intuitively measured against Customer Experience expectations. So let us explore each sense in turn and discover how these apply to the Customer Experience.

Sight

Organizations use sight a great deal in their Customer Experience. What does the logo look like? What does the ad look like? Does the reception desk look tidy? Does the branch or shop look pleasant? In fact sight is potentially overused as the other senses can be ignored. One important area for sight is the whole idea of "space."

John Clayton, Operations Director, Richer Sounds:

When we bought our store in Hull it was huge. The floor space was so massive and we actually made it smaller. We put false walls up and actually made it a small shop to create that friendly atmosphere. This means that customers are always close and you can talk to them. The other thing is, when we are quite busy it can be a bit of a pub atmosphere with customers all talking to each other. It makes it easier to have a bit of a fun and banter because of the small size.

We take in the majority of our information through sight. We make judgments on whether things look attractive or unpleasant. We make initial decisions about other people from the way they look. We can also be repelled by the way something looks: some people don't like the look of spiders, insects, and so on. With sight we can tell if something is moving or stationary. We then coordinate that with hearing to see if that gives us the same information.

Andrew Akers, CEO and inventor of the Zorb:

Although the Zorbs are clear and you can see through them, once you actually start going down the hill, your attention is actually pretty much on the

> *inside of the Zorb. So while you are rolling down the hill you get down to the bottom and people say, "What did you see?" and you reply "I don't really know!" So there are all these little bizarre experiences depending on which sense you are concentrating on – which are all quite different from what we are normally used to.*

Sights also evoke emotions, bring back memories, and provide us with context in our world. Think of the photographs you have in your office or at home: visual images that embody an emotion within them. You recall where they were taken, who is in them, and what they mean to you. Even now you can feel those emotions and memories come flooding back.

Sound

Andrew Akers, again:

> *Another part of our experience is the acoustics, which are very bizarre inside the Zorb. We have a phrase, "When you are inside the Zorb, no one can hear you scream," because the sound coming out of the Zorb is muffled. It is almost like you are inside this kind of aural vacuum where sound can't come in and sound does not come out. So it gives a strange sort of experience in terms of your hearing. It is also bizarre as your sight is distorted by the Zorb.*

Sound brings things to life: when silent movies were replaced by "talkies" early in the last century, they had a revolutionizing effect on the industry. We have a great ability to detect different sounds and voices. When a friend calls, you can normally tell who it is within one word. I can tell which member of my family is walking up the stairs in our house; by the speed of the pace and the kind of sound the person is making as he or she walks. I can tell which door is opening by the sound of the hinges, which cupboard is being opened by the sound of the "clattering around." All of these sounds are distinguishable. The movies use this a great deal, and talk about "sound effects." The sound effect of a door creaking open, the echoes of footsteps in the distance as they come down the corridor, a darkly lit corridor; all signifying something scary is about to happen.

Duane Francis, CEO, Mid-Columbia Medical Center, Oregon:

> *We have a full time musician (music thanatologist) on staff who creates a healing environment by playing a harp and by participating with patients in a musical healing process.*

What people say and how they say it is important. A person who has been told to say, "Have a nice day" is totally different from someone who means it!

Music is used a lot; in shopping malls, music on hold, in lifts and lobbies of hotels, at conferences as "walk in" music. Music has a profound effect on us. Think of the great music for the *Jaws* films. The music started off slowly signifying the shark was on its way and then sped up as the shark went in to attack. That was very scary! Therefore, music can have a big impact on the way we feel. Upbeat happy music cheers us up, whereas slow music can make us feel sad. Certain music can evoke deep and significant memories and emotions. For example:

> *A few years ago I went on holiday with my family to the Florida Keys. We had a great holiday. When we were traveling in the car we were playing "Fine Line" by the band Hootie and the Blowfish. We would all sing along and, in fact, we even went on the Internet to find the lyrics to create song sheets. Every time I now hear the record I remember that time and can see us driving down the highway in Key Largo with all the family singing along. A special time, a special memory, and, even as I think about it now, it evokes emotions of pleasure and love and being free with my family.*

In the morning, when you enter a Disney theme park, the music is upbeat and happy, contributing to an atmosphere of excitement. By contrast in the evenings as people leave the music is slow, reflecting the fact that people are tired after a full day in the park. Here are some other examples of how music is being used and the effect is has:

> *"Music has a very strong impact on emotions, depending on the tempo, the volume and the musical genre," says retailing professor Jean-Charles Chebat of Montreal's Hautes Études Commerciales (HEC.)*[23] *"People make inferences to music. [They think] if it moves me then [retailers] understand me."*
>
> *A study conducted by the professor reveals that fast music played when shoppers are browsing or waiting to ask for advice from a sales clerk enhances good feelings and creates a perception of good products, while the same music played while shoppers are standing in line at the cash register makes them nervous and even aggressive. Soothing music at the checkout, it seems, calms people down.*
>
> *In 1999, Montreal-based real estate firm Ivanhoe CDP Group commissioned a one-week study. It found that slower music played at a Quebec shopping mall made for a brighter, livelier and more relaxed atmosphere, with shoppers lingering longer in stores and paying more attention to products and advertisements.*
>
> *Music also has a positive impact on customers' relationships with salespeople. In a recent article published in the* Journal of Business Research, *Professor Chebat describes a week-long study conducted at a Montreal-based travel agency in which four scenarios were examined: no music playing;*

slow music playing (60 beats per minute); moderate tempo music playing (90 beats per minute), and fast tempo music playing (120 beats per minute). The results? The professor found that slow music produced the most desired outcome for sales. Customers were able to recall more precisely what was said to them, thus creating a positive attitude towards the product and increasing their decision to buy.

So what is the sound that your organization is recognized for? What piece of music would sum up your Customer Experience? Are all the "music on hold" systems in your company playing the same piece of music? Who decides? *Is it deliberate?*

How do you use sound effects? What accent is the most trusted in your industry? What is the optimum tone that your people should be using with your customers? Language is essential.

Natural companies have thought this through. They ensure that the music they play in their TV ads is the same across all their moments of contact.

Touch

We all feel the need to "connect" with each other by touching. It is seen as a sign of affection: holding hands, hugging each other, stroking a dog, or holding a baby. Humans love to make a connection. Don't worry, I am not going to suggest that you hug your customers, but I am going to ask you to recognize that people love to touch things. For instance, at Sea World they have "petting pools," people form a line to "touch" a stingray or a dolphin. They are surprised when they find the dolphin has a rubbery skin. It provides them with more data about a dolphin and it slightly changes their perception of it. A number of people have pets. But consider the word "pet" for a moment. This means that you are touching or petting the animal. Let me give you another example:

I support my local soccer team Luton Town FC. At one of the matches, before kick-off, they paraded the soccer World Cup. Everyone was very excited to see this, as it was a complete surprise. As the man carried it around the pitch my daughter Coralie ran up to the edge of the pitch and asked the man if she could touch it. The man was happy to let her. The crowd, upon seeing Coralie touch the World Cup, all started to move from their seats to do the same. I am sure the man regrets letting Coralie start this trend as he was there for 10 minutes! To this day when we look at the World Cup on TV we proudly say, "We've touched that."

Touching something makes it more real. There is a connection being made and the object feels more a part of you than before.

Lush produce handmade cosmetics and a sensory experience. In discussions with Mark Constantine, Director, he gave us an example of how it has created products to provide a sensory experience:

> *We actually do something called the ballistic that whizzes around in the bath like a whirling dervish and generally puts a smile on your face. Not just highly scented and colorful, it gives you an extra experience when you drop it in the bath since the oils we put in the product often have specific effects on the body and senses. All our ingredients are chosen very specifically for their effects and benefits and when we are formulating and inventing we work very hard to produce amazing products that our customers know work and they will get maximum pleasure from using. For example, our massage bars are solid blocks of Fair Trade cocoa butter that literally melt on contact with the skin so there is less mess and, because cocoa butter is more lubricating and emollient, it is thus far better than oil.*

Naïve organizations do not understand this and instead of encouraging people they have big signs all around that say, "Please do not touch." By contrast, Natural organizations encourage customers to touch their products. For instance the Natural organization recognizes that when people are looking on the Internet for products they still like to visit the store and see and touch the product before buying; despite there being a perfectly good description on the web site.

Smell

There are whole industries focused on aromas and smells; the perfume industry, fragrances industry, air fresheners, and so on. Smells have a powerful ability to evoke emotions and senses. Recall the smell of seaweed – it reminds you of the seaside. Think of the smell of baby lotion, reminding you of your children when they were young. Think of the smell of onions and burgers frying at the sports game. Recall the smell of a barbeque reminding you of summer. Recall the smell of coconut suntan lotion reminding you of holidays.

Duane Francis, CEO, Mid-Columbia Medical Center, Oregon:

> *We use a lot of aromatherapy. We try and make sure that the sensation of smell is used in the Customer Experience. We understand how aroma impacts the senses in terms of creating either a calming or, conversely, an anxious environment. There are obviously sterilizing liquids that we use to maintain cleanliness, but using different aromas, we try and put the smells from these into the background as much as we possibly can so that they assault the senses as little as possible.*

Smells can evoke deep memories and emotions. I love the smell of freshly cut grass, the aroma of coffee, and the smell of bacon cooking early in the morning. We all know that when selling your house the aroma of baking bread or cakes creates a "homelike" feel and makes the buyer find your house more agreeable. In our experience, though, not many organizations use smell very much in their Customer Experience.

Aroma is being used in several exciting applications in places like museums. For example, the Tenement Museum in New York pipes smells of coal fires into the museum to replicate the past. The UK Natural History Museum uses the smell of boggy swamps to recreate the environment for its T. Rex exhibition. Here are a few more examples of how people are using smell in their Customer Experience and the effects it has:

> *One factory-marketing specialist proved the commercial value of smell with a recent experiment in a Montreal-area shopping center. Jean-Charles Chebat,[23] from the University of Montreal's HEC Management School, pumped discreet traces of a sweet citrus fragrance (a combination of lemon, orange, grapefruit, and tangerine) into the mall's air for a week. "The shoppers didn't even know the scent was there because the airborne dose was so tiny," Chebat explains. Merchants, however, certainly smelled a difference: Purchases that week were up by $55 to $90 per customer. Even though the experiment was conducted during a traditionally slow business period and the stores had been instructed to offer no special sales or promotions, Chebat speculates that the fruity fragrance changed the entire feel of the shopping center despite the fact that the decor had remained untouched. The scent worked like magic. "With the citrus aroma, customers felt that the space was more comfortable, happier, more stimulating," says Chebat. "They seemed to think the products and services were better quality, even though they were the same as the week before."*

The technique can be pushed beyond the natural associations with smell, according to a recent study conducted in a Las Vegas casino. Dr Alan Hirsch, of the Chicago-based Smell & Taste Treatment and Research Foundation,[24] says that by scenting the area around slot machines with a custom aroma, he generated a 45 percent increase in the number of coins fed into the one-armed bandits.

Taste

Taste is clearly the most challenging sense to stimulate for most organizations, other than for supermarket food stores where food sampling is now common. The experience of food retailing is quite complex. You will see the counter where a new product is being offered to customers. It is cooked in store and therefore you can smell the food being cooked, you can hear the food being cooked, and what the person is saying about it. You can also see and touch the texture of the food and finally you can taste it.

What is the taste that would describe your organization?

The sensory experience is vital when looking at the entire Customer Experience. It is the combining of these senses that enables you to have a dramatic effect on your Customer Experience, just as the way that you communicate with your customers does.

Kathryn M. Haley, VP, Client Experience, RBC Royal Bank of Canada:

> *The way we communicate with our clients is changing. Language and behavior are key to building relationships. We use words that are more cus-tomer-friendly. We are also taking great care to recognize key life and business events as opposed to getting right to the task and going through the transaction. Customers feel much more important to us … just as they should!*

You can either take action, or hang back and wait for a miracle.
Peter Drucker

Now carry on with your self-assessment.

Naïve to Natural™ self-assessment

Please answer the following questions and then transfer your scores to the summary sheet at the end of Chapter 9.

9. Which of the following best describes the structure of your organization? The organization is ...
    a. Matrixed – functions are pulled together to face the customer.
    b. Siloed and organized around different functions.
    c. Organized around the customer.
    d. Organized around our products and product lines.

Your answer [   ]

a = 3 points, b = 2 points, c = 4 points, d = 1 point   Score [   ]

10. Which of the following best describes who owns and is responsible for the Customer Experience in the organization?
    a. No one generally owns or is responsible for the Customer Experience. The Customer Experience ends up being done for each individual product – usually this happens by default as no one thinks proactively about the Customer Experience.
    b. There is a group, comprised of representatives from all functions, who have been given responsibility for owning the (transactional and emotional) Customer Experience *or* a vice president/director of Customer Experience has been appointed.
    c. No one generally owns or is responsible for the Customer Experience. Customer experience ends up being done by silo: all activity is by silo (this can be done proactively by some silos and by default for some silos).
    d. There is a group, comprised of representatives from all functions, that has been given responsibility for owning the sensory Customer Experience *and/or* an experiential vice president/director has been appointed.

Your answer [   ]

a = 1 point, b = 3 points, c = 2 points, d = 4 points   Score [   ]

6 Naïve orientation

People can alter their lives by altering their attitudes.
William James

As we start to look at some of the detail behind the Naïve to Natural Model™, let us remind ourselves what the orientations actually signify. An organization's orientation is its "relative position" against how deliberately it is implementing its Customer Experience against our definition, which is:

> *A Customer Experience is an interaction between an organization and a customer. It is a blend of an organization's physical performance, the senses stimulated, and emotions evoked, each intuitively measured against Customer Expectations across all moments of contact.*

As a reminder, an organization's orientation is made up from nine areas, which contribute to its overall orientation, as shown in Figure 6.1.

An organization can be in the Naïve orientation for all nine areas, although in our experience, this is unusual. Often an organization is in two or three different orientations across the different areas. Again you should note that these areas are based on what an organization actually does *internally,* which then critically shines through in the Customer Experience it provides.

It is also critical to appreciate we are discussing what an organization does, not what its people understand, or should be doing, or what its intentions are. As you will see in Chapter 10, it is entirely possible for "understanding" in the organization to be in advance of their actual orientation. In fact our research shows that in 52 percent of cases an organization's understanding is ahead of what it is doing. We are not talking about your knowledge but the impact of what you do; what actually happens.

Naïve oriented organizations

We choose to call this orientation "Naïve" because this word potentially offers an explanation as to why an organization is in this orientation; why it is not very focused on the customers and their Customer Experience. By calling it Naïve we are giving these organizations the benefit of the doubt. Here are three options for why organizations may be in this orientation:

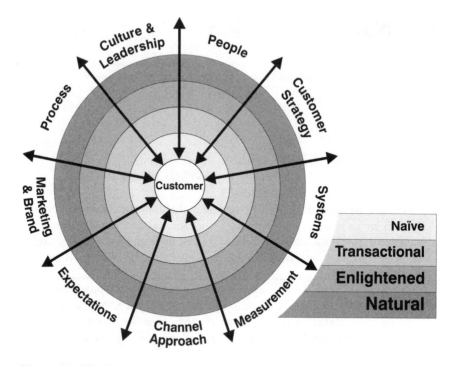

Figure 6.1 The Naïve to Natural™ orientation areas

1. They "don't know what they don't know." They don't know what they should be doing to provide a great Customer Experience.
2. They have chosen to be. It is a deliberate act. They have looked at the market conditions and determined this orientation is the right fit for their business model, or the prevailing market conditions. For instance, they may have determined that they don't want to be focused on customers and their experience as no one else in their market place is; or if they are in a monopoly situation; or if they provide a product or service that is in such high demand. Perhaps they have decided they can reduce costs by not being focused on the Customer Experience.
3. Finally an organization could also be in this orientation "by default." What we mean by this is it knows it should be focused on the experience it gives its customers but something always gets in the way; by definition something else is deemed more important. Therefore it never actually changes its orientation. Like our analogy, it knows it should give up smoking, but it's never quite the right time.

As you can imagine we would not advise any organization to be in the Naïve orientation. We believe that being focused on providing a great

Customer Experience is vital for any organization. This is because it is either potentially missing an opportunity to gain further business, or resting on its laurels and will have to change when competition increases. Here is a Naïve to Natural™ report from an organization in the manufacturing sector:

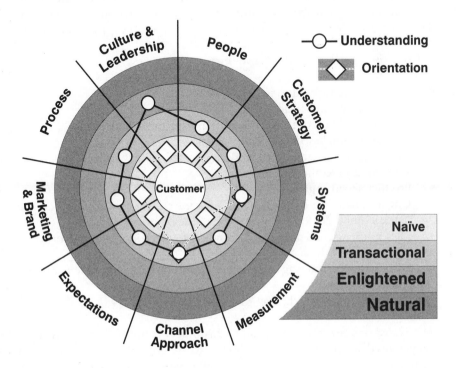

Figure 6.2 A Naïve manufacturing company

Orientation area	Orientation	Understanding
People	Naïve	Transactional
Strategy	Naïve	Transactional
Systems	Transactional	Transactional
Measurement	Naïve	Transactional
Channel approach	Transactional	Transactional
Expectations	Naïve	Transactional
Marketing and brand	Naïve	Transactional
Process	Naïve	Transactional
Culture and leadership	Naïve	Enlightened

You will see that in all areas, except systems and channel approach, this organization is in Naïve orientation. Its understanding is primarily Transactional, with the exception of culture and leadership, which surprisingly is Enlightened. So, the organization knows what it needs to do that would have a marked difference. Our advice to this organization is to capitalize on the cultural and leadership understanding and set in place an action plan to move from Naïve to Transactional in this area. Then the next area it should tackle is customer strategy, to define where "north" is.

Let's look at the traits of a Naïve organization:

- Very product-focused: price and features-led.
- Reactive to customer demands.
- So product-focused it does not measure customer satisfaction.
- Very physically based Customer Experience.
- Not focused on employees who are treated poorly and not given any authority to recompense customers.
- Product-siloed organization.
- Uncoordinated in its approach to customers, who are asked to call on separate numbers for different parts of the organization.
- Sales, efficiency, and productivity-driven. Most important: key performance indicators (KPIs).
- Focused on rewarding employees based on sales, productivity, and efficiency measures.
- Dictatorial in which channel the customer uses.

The Naïve organization's attitude to customers is normally poor. A word people used a lot during our research to describe this orientation was "arrogant." Customers are seen as an inconvenience and as a means to an end. This attitude drives the very core of this orientation. If the customer complains, the Naïve organization's automatic attitude is that the customer is wrong. The customer complaints process is quite basic, and people typically stick to the letter of law when dealing with complaints, providing no more than the law requires. Our research[2] across the Naïve to Natural Model™ shows:

13 percent of organizations "treat complaints with distain."

We asked, "Which of the following best describes the basis on which customers are managed when something goes wrong?" 13 percent of organizations demonstrated a Naïve orientation by answering: "Everything is hidden and kept away from them – we often blame customers, telling them it went wrong because of something the customer did or didn't do." The tendency is not to believe the customer.

Naïve organizations normally have a great deal of "small print" which they hide behind when they are dealing with customer complaints. They are also quite aggressive in nature. Refunding money is not a typical activity and it normally takes them a great deal of time to respond. All this, as you can imagine, provides a poor Customer Experience and the customer starts to build up a resentment of the organization.

Naïve organizations provide a Customer Experience that is entirely physical. They have either failed to realize that they are evoking emotions or don't care that they are. But certainly all their actions do evoke emotions, and not normally positive ones! By nature, Naïve organizations are very reactive to customer demands. To try to make this live a bit more for you, let us give you an example of an organization that, at least from the outside looking in, we would class as being in the Naïve orientation.

In undertaking research for this book we came across a web site called *Skytrax*.[25] The web site states that Skytrax are "leading research advisors to the world airline and air transport industry." It ran the following editorial article about an airline.[26] We have decided to remove the name of the company from the article, as the purpose of reviewing this is to learn not to cause embarrassment.

Do "A.N. Airline" believe in Customer Service?

The criticism of "A.N. Airline" for its growing, poor record of customer service continues unabated. Alas, turn to many media pages, and the airline is praised in many corners – it is profitable, it enables the "common" person to savour the pleasures of air travel.

In reality, "A.N. Airline" is an airline offering the lowest possible quality of product and service, at the lowest cost to the company.

Free seat giveaways and other mass publicity do not conceal the fact that you simply cannot give away airline seats for nothing and expect to turn a profit.

There is of course the argument you can attract customers with special promotions – and hope to impress them to want to return and fly "A.N. Airline" again. If that were the objective, you would provide a proper level of service in the first place.

Try to follow up a customer service complaint with "A.N. Airline," and you will have a long and probably pointless task. This is an airline that simply does not care about you as an individual, and your chances of either a reply, let alone an apology are more or less zero.

Low cost airlines can be good – as witnessed by the industry's best of jetBlue in North America. Southwest Airlines is the world's original model for low cost, and still the largest, but even they cannot claim to offer a level of customer care and customer service to match jetBlue. If you want service and some proper element of reliability then it pays to invest wisely. In this instance, we cannot see any reason for selecting to travel with "A.N. Airline."

But what do this airline's customers think? To balance this we have taken two views: one good view and one bad.

Customer 1: the good news:

> *8 February 2004*
> *Flown "A.N. Airline" without any problems – service is OK and might not be of Cathay Pacific quality, but I like "A.N. Airline" because of the unimaginably low price, which has made it possible for a student like me to travel a lot more.*[27a]

Customer 2: the bad news:

> *22 January 2004*
> *Cheap flights maybe, but God forbid you ever have a problem that needed resolving! This company has no scruples and makes up its own rules, fees and then more charges on top! If you ever have to deal with their customer services forget it, total waste of space! They are only contactable in writing or by fax and even if someone died would begrudge you any remorse!*[27b]

Quite strong opinions and you can sense the emotions behind these. The accusation of "no scruples" is very emotive. This organization is focusing on its market differentiator – its price. Some customers like this; some don't. To deliver its product it has stripped away all of the "normal" customer functions expected of a large company. So what is normal? Well, normal is defined by the individual. In our Customer Experience definition we state, "intuitively measured against customer expectations." However with 11 percent of organizations admitting their people don't talk about expectations within the organization and 24 percent not researching and documenting expectations, it is little surprise that expectations are often not met. The person who wrote this article clearly has a view about what "normal" large company functions should be. We assume one example would be that the company communicates with individuals over the phone about complaints rather than only in writing. We would suggest this airline's belief is that the market conditions are such that it does not need to be focused on the Customer Experience as it is providing a cheap price and that is good enough. It is also seeing a massive growth in the market place, with people attracted by the price. So perhaps it concludes that it does not need to bother with all this Customer Experience stuff? Its Customer Experience is a cheap price. There are clearly sufficient customers, at the moment, who accept or tolerate this. On the other hand there are a group of customers who expect to receive some form of customer service, and this article and the other customer example shows they are not happy.

Let's look at a few sentences in the article that highlight a few key points about Naïve organizations.

> *If that were the objective, you would provide a proper level of service in the first place.*

This comment indicates that the writer has in mind what a "proper level of service" looks like. The writer has an expectation that the airline is not fulfilling, even at these low prices. The writer of this article had appreciated the price of the ticket but still expected a "proper level of service," which was not being provided.

> *Try to follow up a customer service complaint with "A.N. Airline", and you will have a long and probably pointless task.*

On the face of it the complaints process is not good. Again, this is probably a strategic choice by the organization. It costs money to deal with complaints and if a person wishes to complain, the company's view is, "What do they expect when they are only paying $$$?" Well the answer for this person is clearly a lot more than this company is providing. Dealing with complaints in a poor manner is typical of a Naïve organization.

> *This is an airline that simply does not care about you as an individual, and your chances of either a reply, let alone apology, are more or less zero.*

The airline does not care, another symptom of a typical Naïve organization. It is interested in productivity, profit, and its product, not the customer. Customers see that, hence the comment about "this company has no scruples." However, the other interesting bit is that the writer is referring to "care," which is, of course, an emotion. The customer is articulating that emotionally he or she does not feel cared for as a result of this Customer Experience.

This attitude starts at the top; here are the views of Robert Stephens, Founder and Chief Inspector (CEO) of The Geek Squad, which is definitely *not* a Naïve organization:

> *What you tend to find is that what is important to the boss is important to the employee. After all, employees are doing what they are paid and told to do. So the leader is the catalyst, it is not as though they are the dominant force, but they are the spark. I would definitely say when the leader stands up in front of people and jumps around and talks about the importance of customers, the people are not going to get it the first time, they are not going to get it the second time, they might not get it until the 16th or the 32nd time. But they will get it over time. The leader has to role model what they want their people to do. They say it takes a human 21 days to form a habit and that is doing it repetitively, so it takes time.*

Rudy Tauscher, General Manager, Mandarin Oriental, New York:

> *Providing a great Customer Experience takes an entire mindset and it has to come from the top. It has to come from the top of the company and I think that when these people talk about service they give a lot of lip service and it is not really part of their strategy – they think it is but it is not.*

In my experience people will follow what the leader does, both good and bad behaviors. Of senior leaders in organizations, 13 percent[2] do not spend time with customers. What signal does this send to their people? Do you think they will spend time with customers? No. The result is that if people do not understand what customers want at first hand, they are likely to deliver a Customer Experience that is poor: cause and effect.

In summary, our view is that the subject airline is a typical Naïve organization. The Customer Experience is questionable and in many cases does not meet customers' expectations. This drives negative emotions such as frustration, annoyance, and anger. Due to market conditions the organization will remain profitable until the market has reached saturation. Once this happens, our predication is that this type of Customer Experience will not continue and the organization will be forced to Revolutionize Its Customer Experience™. It will be forced to change its attitude to customers and move out of the Naïve orientation into the Transactional, or even the Enlightened, orientation. We shall wait and see.

This has already happened in the mobile (cellular) industry. In Europe over the last ten years this market has been expanding rapidly. Every year companies in this industry achieved exponential growth. They did not have to focus on their Customer Experience as they had more than enough new customers joining. A couple of years ago the market started to become saturated. This has driven companies to change their orientation. All the mobile companies have shifted from a customer acquisition strategy to customer retention. They have moved from a key performance indicator of customer growth to one of customer retention and lifetime value. How do you retain customers? One way is by providing a great Customer Experience! Over the last year we have undertaken work with a number of the big mobile companies across Europe because of this fact. All are looking to improve the Customer Experience. They are all taking actions to do so and achieving some great results! The race will be who can embrace the Customer Experience orientations and embed the Customer Experience in its organization the quickest. Here is Peter Scott, Customer Service Director, T-Mobile, talking about the excellent work it has undertaken to improve its Customer Experience:

> *Since undertaking the focus on improving the Customer Experience from an emotional perspective, we have seen a whole series of significant improvements.*

For example, customer satisfaction with regard to interaction with our customer service advisors has shown significant improvement, our problem resolution in one call has improved, sales results have increased in teams that have been trained, and employee engagement has risen. This all goes straight to bottom line profitability.

This is often an issue for all organizations that have enjoyed quick growth. You find to your cost that if you have mistreated your customers in your growth phase, it will take some time for customers to forgive you.

Here is a further example of a Naïve organization taken from a UK web site:

We paid £6000 ($4000) to have a kitchen [cabinets] installed in our new home. The survey was carried out by an unprofessional fitter [engineer], who derided the company he was working for, but because we had no kitchen we decided to go ahead. On the day it was supposed to be delivered, it did not turn up. It was only when we rang them that they told us it had been cancelled and they could only re-deliver, fit, etc., one month later. They were rude and unhelpful, and told us that the date had been changed two weeks previously; they did not at any time call, or contact us regarding this matter despite several phone calls from us prior to this, letting them know we were okay to go ahead and asking them to have the fitter call us. At this point the matter is still not resolved, and they are unable to give me details of how they intend to sort the matter out, or compensate us for the time taken off work for the kitchen to be installed.

"Rude and unhelpful." Imagine the emotions this Customer Experience drives. In this example there are a number of elements that reflect a Naïve organization. As you can see the fitter "derided" the company he worked for. When this happens it makes the customer lose confidence and trust in the organization. So why does this happen? One reason is the way a person is treated in an organization. Naïve organizations do not treat their people well. As a result they do not deliver a great Customer Experience. Our research shows that Naïve organizations have not made the connection that "happy people give you happy customers." They treat their people very much as a commodity, like their products. This attitude is inevitably passed on to the customer, as this example shows. Naïve organizations typically do not have an employee satisfaction survey, or if they do then the results are ignored. Here is an example of a call center employee[1] who worked for one of the largest insurance companies in the UK. This is her view of what it is like working for this company:

It is constant, you don't get a breath … if you have got indigestion and you want to get up, you can't move from your desk. Basically you have to press a button to go to the toilet, press a button for your break, if you are not back on time it is regimented all the time...

... they decided to put a few pictures up to try and cheer us up but it didn't work, then they were really good, they gave us water for our break, so we didn't have to walk upstairs. It is really like prison...

We asked her if her company were customer-focused:

It is supposed to be investors in customers but it isn't really, it is just getting them on and off the phone, keeping them happy, you can't be nasty to them, you have got to be very nice, smile while you are talking and just get the next one in ...

As a result of this working environment, this woman feels like this:

... I have days where I feel that I could just throw myself out of the window. I am glad I am on the bottom floor! But you have got to keep going; you need to pay the mortgage, you need to pay the bills...

... I have indigestion all day and you just get like a dull feeling in your chest all day and when I come out of there I think thank God for that and when I turn the corner to go into work the pain comes back again.

Do you fancy working here? How does the organization expect this person to deliver a great Customer Experience? It can't. What is important to this Naïve organization? Productivity. Don't worry about the effect on the customer or the employee, what we are worried about is "processing" the customer as soon as we can, and then on to the next one.

Our research supports this and reveals that this is not an isolated incident. As nearly one in ten organizations admits, "people are seen as a commodity and treated as expendable." Worryingly 22 percent of organizations reveal that the notion of employee satisfaction has not been thought about or considered, and in the same number of organizations the concept of the employee experience has not been thought about. The employee experience has a direct relationship to the organization's Customer Experience. Poor employee experiences will result in demotivated employees and a poor Customer Experience. Again, cause and effect.

These are all actions typical of a Naïve organization. It also has always seemed to me that the woman we quoted above from the employee focus group comes across as a caring person. The issue for her is that she is not working for a caring company. Therefore the emotional strain on her is even greater. The reality is that she is working for the wrong company. Naïve organizations give little thought to the types of people they recruit. In fact 35 percent of organizations told us that no thought has been given to the cultural fit of people being employed. As you can imagine the result of all this is a high turnover of staff and a high level of absenteeism. This ironically drives up costs and creates a poor Customer Experience, as new recruits never perform as well as experienced recruits.

This "inside out" attitude continues in how processes are designed by Naïve organizations. Here is an example of a very "inside out" process.

> ### 84? You're too old to buy jigsaw, woman told
> *A mail order company has apologized to an 84-year-old customer after telling her that she was too old to buy a 1000 piece jigsaw. Iris Milne was told by a customer service operator at the catalogue company that she could not buy the jigsaw because she was aged over 80.*
>
> *The company later issued a statement saying that the ban applied only to the over-90s because "they have trouble filling out forms."*
> The Times (London), January 31, 2004

Isn't this unbelievable?! They don't serve people over the age of 90! Consider the conversation which must have taken place in the office. It must have gone something like this:

Table 6.1 Conversation between manager and employee at a mail order company

Who	What are they saying?	The Naïve trait being displayed
Manager	"I have been looking at our stats report and I have noticed that a number of forms are being completed incorrectly. Why is this?"	The manager hasn't looked at customer satisfaction data, as it doesn't exist.
Employee	"Yes we noticed that. We have done some digging and it appears that the problem is because of our customers, in particular older customers, who aren't completing them correctly."	Blaming the customer. Very "inside out." Not even considered it could be the form that is the issue.
Manager	"But our forms are really simple. Are you sure it's just older people, don't other age groups have a problem as well?"	Automatically assuming it is not the company's fault. Showing leadership to the employee that blaming the customer is OK.
Employee	"No it is definitely older people. Maybe we should change the forms? Or even do a simpler one for them? At the moment we are involving ourselves in phoning them back and getting the proper information, which is clearly imposing a cost on us."	Some transactional behaviour being shown by the employee. They "understand" what they should be doing.

Table 6.1 continued

Who	What are they saying?	The Naïve trait being displayed
Manager	"How many jigsaws do we sell to old people? Do we have a breakdown of ages of people we sell too?"	The manager is focusing on the sales, and is not worried about the impact this has on the customer.
Employee	"Not really but we sell about ten per week."	Again no insight to what the customer thinks.
Manager	"That's not a lot; maybe we should just not sell jigsaws to people who are old?"	A totally "inside out" behaviour. No consideration for the customer.
Employee	"You mean tell people they are too old to buy our products?"	Again showing a glimmer of hope that this person understands that this is the wrong "Naïve" response.
Manager	"Yes, why not?"	Challenging in an aggressive manner: I am the manager and I am clever. You are an employee and you are not.
Employee	"OK, that would solve the issue if you are happy that we lose these sales?"	Employee been "put in their place" and said in an "I'm annoyed with you" tone of voice.
Manager	"Yes, I'm happy. What next?"	Does care what employee thinks, doesn't care what the impact will be on customers.

Clearly we don't know if this conversation is accurate, but something like this must have happened for the company to adopt this as a Naïve policy. Now consider the culture of an organization that would make a policy like this. Where does this come from? Again, it comes from the leaders of the organization. If the leaders consider this acceptable, immediately they are setting an example to all their people on how to treat customers.

Naïve organizations design processes for their own benefit and what is important to them. Let me give you a personal example:

We were having digital TV fitted. We booked an appointment that was some time in advance due to the popularity of the product. On the appointment day we waited in for the engineer to call. No one showed up. We contacted the call center, and found that as the previous installation had taken longer than expected our installation had been cancelled. We were told that we needed to reschedule the installation. Rather than being offered a date in the next few days we were put to the back of the queue and had to wait a number of weeks, despite our protest. It was easier for the organization to deal with customers in this manner. As demand was high they couldn't be bothered to devise a process to deal with customers in our circumstances in a different manner.

Naïve organizations do not consider the customer. Nearly a third of organizations admitted processes are designed on the basis of what is good and convenient for the organization. This means the customer has to fit around them; a very "inside out" behavior, which shows contempt for customers. The Naïve organizations consider the customer is always wrong, and feel it is acceptable to just "not turn up" if it suits them. The irony is this causes a number of calls into their organizations to check if the delivery/engineer is coming, thus imposing a cost on them. Naïve organizations can appear quite customer-focused when they are selling you something, but as you again can see from this example, their attitude changes once the order is placed. The onus is then on the customer to chase them. In 28 percent of organizations a list of telephone numbers is given to customers to contact different parts of the organization for different requirements, displaying to the customer a disjointed Customer Experience.

A company's culture also shines through in a Customer Experience. If you live in a "blame culture" where everyone just wants to blame someone else when something goes wrong, then the effect on the Customer Experience is that your people will always stick to policy and never do anything outside these policies, even if they know it's the wrong thing to do.

One of the further telltale signs of a Naïve organization is the job titles people are given:

When I travel to our London offices in Piccadilly I normally travel by train. I noticed the person who inspects my ticket is called a "Revenue protection officer." How did I notice? It's written on his hat!

Now once again stop and think what this organization's attitude to customers must be. This person's job is to "protect" the company's revenue from those evil customers. Why did the company decide to put this title on the hats? Is it proud of this, or does it consider it some form of deterrent? Think about what must happen in this organization. Internally it must refer to this group of employees in daily language; think of the subliminal impact that this must have on the organization. It is focused on "protecting," defending, and stopping these evil customers. This reinforcement must drive other "inside out" actions, as it has been "sanctioned" by the use of these words. This is the type of "inside out" display of what the Naïve organization really thinks of customers.

Mike Gooley, Chairman of Trailfinders, independent travel experts:

> *A number of years ago a sales manager of ours was running a sales meeting when he called our clients "punters." I stopped him and said "David, don't use that word. I know you don't mean any harm, I know it's not in front of our clients but I just don't want to hear it because it's the seed of something else. We call our customers 'clients.'" I think that is important as somehow or other the word "client" feels a bit more elevated than customers, it feels like they should be respected more, and sends an important message to our consultants. Again we call them consultants and not "booking clerks" as that is what they are doing and our clients "consult" them for this advice.*

The words people use to describe customers are important. We have been undertaking some work in the TV industry that calls its customers "the audience." Transport organizations call their customers, "passengers." This to me seems to devalue customers. A passenger is someone who travels. I can pick up a passenger in my car; it doesn't make him or her a customer. I think organizations should give serious thought to how they name their customers.

Typically Naïve organizations are very focused on their products. You will see from Figure 6.3 that the focus of a Naïve organization is on the product. This product focus diminishes as you move through the Naïve to Natural Model™ and the Customer Experience focus increases.

Naïve organizations believe that their products are the be all and end all of their Customer Experience. Market research is primarily focused on product attributes and pricing, and is primarily conducted by product lines; this is the

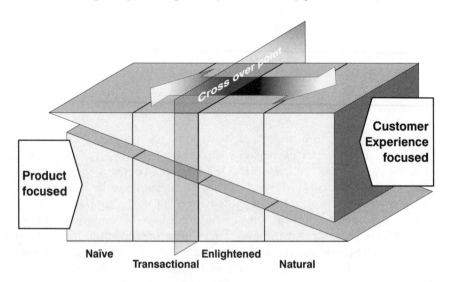

Figure 6.3 The Naïve to Natural™ crossover points

case for one in four organizations. This obsession with products is reflected in the organizational structure and segmentation, which is entirely based around products. In fact 22 percent of organizations are organized in this manner. Product managers are the kings of this orientation. As they are siloed organizations there are conflicting messages sent to customers about competing products from the same company. Typically the customer will be confronted by a number of contact points to deal with. Thirty percent of organizations admit that internal functions and departments only have a view of the products in the company they are responsible for selling and/or servicing, the sales of those products, and the revenues resulting from those products. This is reflected in poor communication internally and therefore in the Customer Experience. Typically front-line people are not all informed of changes.

In the Naïve organizations 100 percent of all measurement is around the internal functioning of the organization, with no customer measures. Typically, productivity and sales measures are prevalent. Incredibly this was the case for a quarter of organizations. Only the physical aspects of a Customer Experience are measured by 33 percent of organizations, leaving emotions and senses unrecognized.

In Naïve organizations salespeople typically have a high commission-based salary and selling products is important. Typically you will see that sales calls are answered a lot quicker than customer service calls. Customers expect that as the sales calls are answered quickly, customer service calls will be answered equally as quickly once they have bought the product. When this is subsequently not the reality, this drives feelings of annoyance, frustration, and disappointment.

Nearly one in three organizations reveal that the predominant driver for the organization's remuneration and bonus scheme is on product performance or achievement of sales volumes. This sales focus will drive behaviors that impact the Customer Experience negatively. For example salespeople are tempted to put customers under pressure to meet targets. Double-glazing, time share and used car salespeople typify this image. Our research[1] showed that many salespeople admitted that this pressure to meet targets, and earn a great deal of money, results in their being dishonest with customers.

Here are some quotes from employees from our research:

- *I think to succeed in life you have to be a bit shrewd.*
- *You can't be too honest.*
- *If you know something is going to take about five weeks or something, you will say we'll have it next week.*
- *Where I'm selling a product for a tenner, £15 or £20 ($20–$30), I mean the ethics don't come into it.*

What gets measured gets done, and what is financially rewarded gets done even more. This problem becomes endemic in the Naïve organization.

Everyone, including management, is collaborating or "turning a blind eye," as they have targets to achieve as well. The effect this has is that customers do not trust organizations, as we heard in previous chapters. The organization may recognize the impact this has on its customers, but it finds it an acceptable method of achieving sales targets. Targeting of this type contributes to the culture of the organization and to its attitude to customers. The effect of this pressure to achieve sales means that Naïve organizations "manage" their targets, which again imposes a cost on the business. Here is another quote from an employee we interviewed.[1]

> *Well, the company is into targets. You know all targets can be massaged through. There is always a way round reaching things if you really need to. Like we've explained there's always someone you can phone up who you can say "I need one more order" to and then you'll get it. So I think all targets can be reached.*

Employee interview

In this example the customer who was contacted would be put under pressure to buy something he or she didn't want as a "favor" to the salesperson. Another example of managing sales is to keep orders back – not have them processed for a month if you have already achieved that month's sales target. Processing orders late results in a late delivery for the customers. This type of measurement drives this type of behavior.

Naïve organizations do not give consideration to how the customer wants to be contacted. They do what suits them. For instance they proactively contact customers either by phone or spammed emails without considering whether the customer would like this. These unsolicited calls have reached such a point in the United States that a new law called "Do not call" has just been introduced. If you don't want to receive unsolicited calls you register the fact on the *National Do Not Call* web site: https://www.donotcall.gov. Since its launch 23 million people have registered. People are sick and tired of companies annoying them at home. The same applies to "spamming" people. Naïve organizations adopt the view that spamming people is acceptable. In both cases Naïve organizations are only concerned with selling their products. They do not care that they are driving feelings of annoyance and frustration with customers.

If you were to look at a Naïve company's organizational structure, it would be focused around product groups. Look at the Naïve company's team meeting agendas – you will not find any mention of the customer on the agenda.

So in summary the Naïve organization is focused not on the customer but on itself. There are a number of telltale signs. If you see your organization in some of these areas, then here are a few things that you may wish to look at to help you Revolutionize Your Customer Experience™.

What do the Naïve organizations need to do to Revolutionize Their Customer Experience™?

- change their attitude to customers
- put themselves in the customers' shoes and see what it feels like
- realize that emotions account for over half the Customer Experience
- define the Customer Experience they want to deliver
- move from reactive to proactive
- understand that all these elements ultimately affect the Customer Experience
- define a plan of how to move forward
- look at all customer touch points and review if these are appropriate
- review customer complaints and define where the biggest problem areas are
- treat their employees well.

The mind is like a parachute, it only functions when it is open.

Anon

Naïve to Natural™ self-assessment

Please answer the following questions and then transfer your scores to the summary sheet at the end of Chapter 9.

11. Which of the following best describes the frequency with which customer expectations are reviewed?
    a.   Done on an ad hoc basis – as required.
    b.   Done on a systematic basis – expectations are reviewed at frequent and predetermined times.
    c.   The organization does not capture and research customer expectations.
    d.   Done on a systematic basis – expectations are reviewed at least annually.

Your answer [   ]

a = 2 points, b = 4 points, c = 1 point, d = 3 points   Score [   ]

12. Which of the following best describes your organization's approach to managing customer expectations?
    a.   Decisions have been made about which expectations, including emotional, will be exceeded and which will be met.
    b.   People don't talk about expectations within the organization.
    c.   People say that meeting expectations would be a significant step forward, but there is little evidence that this is done in a systematic way – it is transactional expectations that are referred to.
    d.   Decisions have been made about which expectations, including sensory, will be exceeded and which will be met.

Your answer [   ]

a = 3 points, b = 1 point, c = 2 points, d = 4 points   Score [   ]

7 Transactional orientation

Good intentions are no substitute for action; failure usually follows the path of least persistence.

Anon

As I was driving down the road a few weeks ago the CD player stopped working in my car. When I took it into the garage the staff informed me it needed a new player and they would order one. The service up to this point was quite good, as you would expect from a Jaguar dealer. They had greeted me nicely and were quite efficient in the check-in. Then some of the telltale signs of a Transactional organization started to show: "It may take some time for the part to come in as Jaguar is not very good at storing this kind of thing," they said. Then they really placed themselves in the Transactional orientation when they said, "Why don't you call us on Wednesday and see if it's in." **I needed to phone them, they would not phone me.**

Over the next two weeks I called them on six separate occasions to find out if the part had arrived. Finally, it did. I took my car to have it fitted and left it with them for a couple of hours. On returning to collect my car I was informed they had ordered the wrong part and I would have to repeat the same process. I was now annoyed. The receptionist made a flippant remark: "Don't worry, we have washed the car for you," as if this was some sort of compensation, but her real hidden message was, "What's all the fuss about? It doesn't take much to come back again." "We'll order the part again; call us next week and see if it's in or not." The process repeated itself ...

I do not tell you this story to impress you that I drive a Jaguar, but to impress upon you a few traits of the Transactional organization. In the Transactional organization the brand and the actual Customer Experience are not aligned. A great deal of time is spent by the Transactional organization in building its brand image, but it has not gone that critical one stage further and defined how it will manifest itself in the Customer Experience. This disparity drives customers to feel distrust and disappointment, as this consumer from our customer research[1] outlined:

Mostly it's unbelievable and I guess it's a function of age and when you reach 38 you realize that they [companies] are projecting a message that in the majority of cases is far from the truth.

Consumer interview

The Transactional organization normally has a well-developed marketing function but it has failed to inform the people who deliver the Customer Experience what the brand values are, what they mean to the organization, and what they should be doing to make those brand values live. Due to this, customers see a disjointed Customer Experience. Advertising is one of the first areas where customers' expectations are set. If they are not set in the proper manner, the Transactional organization's staff will spend all their time in recovering the situation.

The core of the Transactional organization remains "inside out." In the story above about my car, the one simple action of asking me, the customer, to call the organization rather than the other way round, revealed many things about its orientation. It is in essence saying it is very busy, or it is too difficult to arrange a system where it will contact the customer. Instead, it expects the customer to do the work, without consideration of the impact of this on the customer. The culture and the mentality of that dealer are such that this hasn't entered its mind. Finally, the dealer commented on the lack of coordination of the parts stored and their availability, again showing a disjointed approach to the customer.

Transactional organizations do think the customer is important, which is a marked improvement on the Naïve organization. However, they believe the customer is still not *as* important as the organization is. The Transactional organizations remain physically based and do not look at the emotions they should be evoking.

The phase that sums up this orientation is:

"Have a nice day!"

This phrase for me sums up the fact that they know customers are important, they know they should be saying it but they don't *really* mean it, it's not genuine. It's scripted. Customers know this is the case and can see through it.

Figure 7.1 shows a Naïve to Natural™ orientation report for a Transactional financial services organization.

You can see the orientations in each of the areas and how that compares to the organization's understanding.

Overall our algorithm places this organization as a Transactional organization.

You will note this organization's orientation in the systems, measurement, channel approach, and customer expectation areas is the same as its understanding. This indicated to us that this organization was operating at the limits of its knowledge. We therefore recommended it needed to increase its

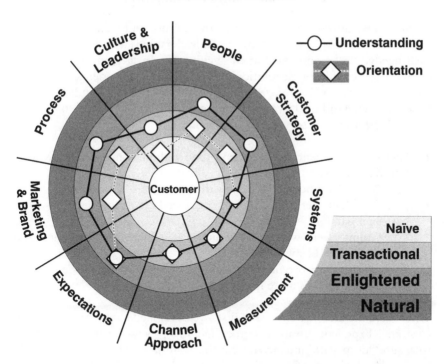

Figure 7.1 A Transactional financial services organization

Orientation area	Orientation	Understanding
People	Transactional	Enlightened
Strategy	Transactional	Enlightened
Systems	Transactional	Transactional
Measurement	Transactional	Transactional
Channel approach	Transactional	Transactional
Expectations	Enlightened	Enlightened
Marketing and brand	Transactional	Enlightened
Process	Transactional	Enlightened
Culture and leadership	Naïve	Transactional

understanding in these orientational areas in order to move forward. At our suggestion the organization invested in some training. In fact it attended our annual Best Practice Study Tour where we go behind the scenes of organizations such as Virgin Atlantic, Dell Computers, Microsoft, Lexus, and Pret A Manger to see what other organizations are doing and gain ideas on how to move businesses forward.

Our main concern however was in the culture and leadership orientation, which is Naïve. Clearly culture and leadership is a critical area and as such needed to be addressed at the beginning. In fact, in our view, this organization could not Revolutionize Its Customer Experience™ without addressing this area. Therefore we need to take a look at the indicator level to see the detail of how it was performing. At the indicator level for culture and leadership, we discovered the following:

- Senior management did not spend time with customers and were very internally focused.
- "Deep staff" did not spend time with customers.
- Only product performance was discussed at team meetings, not customer data.
- When things went wrong, everything was hidden from customers and they were often blamed.
- Customer service people were seen as second-class citizens and salespeople were seen as more important.

These were the areas we addressed first. We developed a senior management Customer Experience awareness program and a process for the organization to ensure "deep staff" interacted with the customers. Thus managers could see first-hand what was happening, and make better quality decisions based on customer feedback rather than in the "inside out" way they had done so before. The organization also looked at the issue of "second-class citizens." It introduced a "service" incentive for the first time, not just a sales incentive, inviting service people to conferences rather than just the salespeople. We worked with the organization to increase understanding, and planned for moves into the Enlightened orientation.

Ironically this organization's orientation on customers' expectations was good. It even looked at customers' emotional expectations. However, this information was not being designed into its existing Customer Experience. Simply it was not using the data it had. We therefore undertook a Moment Mapping® exercise to design in the emotional aspects of the Customer Experience.

The "customer strategy" area indicates that it does not have a defined Customer Experience. This was one of the next exercises we did with the organization. This was helped by the data it already had, as it scored high in these areas on "expectations." Specifically:

- It understood customer emotional expectations.
- These were documented against each moment of contact.
- The physical and emotional expectations were reviewed annually.

This issue here was that this information was not being acted upon. It had the data but did nothing with it.

Here are some of the traits of a Transactional organization:

- Physically biased with a few customer key performance indicators (KPIs).
- Functionally organized and has recognized the need for customer service.
- Provides "800" free phone numbers for customer contact, but has extensive call menus to screen calls.
- Biased towards customers' physical expectations.
- Senior managers spend limited time with customers.
- Does not have a complete customer systems view.
- Has no defined Customer Experience.
- Recruits people with right attitude, rather than just skills.
- Focuses training on how to deal with difficult customers.
- Gives employees some limited authority.

Sixty-seven percent of organizations are Transactional. Over the years, the Naïve organization has improved the physical aspects of the Customer Experience, and evolved into a Transactional organization, which is very good news. We have seen opening hours increase; the web being used more as it is convenient for customers, as well as being a cheap channel for organizations; and more organizations dealing with customers over the phone, as it is convenient. Over this period we have seen banking move from the phone to being online. We have seen the comfort in modes of transport increase and safety levels improve. In addition, the quality of the goods has improved. Organizations are now so confident of the quality of their product that they offer extended guarantees, over and above the legal requirements, as a "feature" of the product; all good news for the Customer Experience. The reliability of products has improved dramatically and prices have reduced significantly. In short, a great deal of work has gone into improving the physical Customer Experience by the Transactional organization. Ironically this works, but its very nature has been a commoditizing force.

All of this is great and a marked improvement on the Naïve organizations. However, the improvements have been limited to the physical side of the Customer Experience. Transactional organizations are very focused on the physical side of the Customer Experience and the transaction itself. They focus on:

- price
- productivity
- internal measures
- quality
- transactions
- customer satisfaction – only physical
- cost.

Take the fast food burger market. When McDonald's first opened its doors everyone was impressed with the cleanliness, the speed of delivery, the taste of the burgers, and the price. Some organizations have moved on from being Transactional organizations, some have not. This focus on the physical aspects of the Customer Experience places them at the bottom end of the Customer Experience Hierarchy of Needs™. Key elements of the Customer Experience here are things like:

- reliability
- resolution
- accessibility
- responsibility
- value
- comfort
- safety
- range
- convenience.

This can leave customers appreciating the physical aspects, but still wanting more; wanting organizations to care for them, help them, make them feel significant, and valued. The Transactional organization does not understand this.

Transactional organizations are more proactive to customer demands than the Naïve organizations, but still not proactive enough. Transactional organizations have recognized the need for, and have invested in, the function of Customer Service – again a step forward for the customer. The Transactional organization is customer-focused enough to recognize the need for customer service departments. However, its "inside out" nature is revealed when these are answered by extensive call menu systems ("Press one for this, two for that, and so on"). These are put in place to distribute the calls in the most efficient way. Efficiency, unfortunately, remains of greater importance to the Transactional organization than the Customer Experience. It accepts that customers don't like call menu systems, but productivity is more important. Another telltale sign of a Transactional organization is the message that is played while you are "on hold." Typically, you hear a message saying:

"Please hold, your call is important to us."

Well, we all know that this is evidently not the case. If it was, we wouldn't be waiting for our call to be answered. What it is really saying is, "We know you are a customer and customers are important, but they are not as important as we are and therefore our time and resources are more important than yours." So, wait.

In essence the Transactional organization treats customers as a transaction. Here is the view of Robert Stephens, Founder and Chief Inspector (CEO),

The Geek Squad, about one of the things a Transactional organization should do to Revolutionize Your Customer Experience™:

> *The telephone interaction is something people hate, waiting on hold, or when nobody gets back to them right away. So one of the things I looked at as a sole person in the company is that I can't always answer the phone. So I decided if I'm going to make you hear a voicemail message then I'm going to give you a chuckle and let you know at the same time that you are chuckling that I'm dead serious about returning your phone call and will also let you know when I'm going to return it. So I would say leave your name and number and I'll call you back within "four to seven minutes" – I calculated that I get the page within 12 seconds and I can finish the current call and then return the call. That worked and people would say, I trust you because you are specific. When people say I'll call you back in five minutes it is a general term, but if you say four to seven then you are being specific. Those are all mundane details but together they paint a picture of what you stand for, and sooner or later customers are able to differentiate through interaction with other companies why they should stick with you.*
>
> *And the great thing about this is that, I did this because I had no money! These things don't cost anything, they are the things you are already spending money on, already spending time and thought doing and if you spend more thought you might get a better investment.*

In Transactional organizations customers are typically asked to perform some form of task by the organization while waiting for the phone to be answered. For instance, "Key in your phone number." This appears then to be totally ignored by the organization when the agent answers. It's as if it does it with the sole purpose of annoying you. A further sign of the Transactional organization is the extensive use of answerphones. Employees put their answerphone on when they are "busy" doing work as they don't want to be "disturbed" by customers as they have important work to undertake: very frustrating for the customer.

As Transactional organizations are focused around productivity, their call centers typically use scripts. This is to try to codify the Customer Experience and deal with it in the most efficient manner. The scripts are written in a way that is customer-friendly but not a lot of room for maneuver is given to the agent to meet customer needs. The customer can recognize when a script is being used and knows it's not genuine. This again drives feelings of distrust with customers and makes employees believe they are robots, which again has a negative effect on the Customer Experience.

The internal structure of the Transactional organization remains siloed, with a bit of customer-focused organizational structure creeping in. For instance, the sales team might be industry-focused. The silo working still causes communication issues between different groups within the organization. Let me give you an example:

A while ago I wanted to buy a laptop computer for my daughter, Coralie, who is at university. I had completed my research and coincidentally as the Sunday papers arrived one morning a flyer popped out from one of the leading PC brands. I picked up the flyer and looked at the front page. There was a good offer on a laptop so I called the company. I was put through to a salesperson. This is the conversation I had:

Table 7.1 A Customer Experience with a PC sales agent

Who	What the company said	My thoughts and feelings (orientational areas in *italics*)
Agent	"Good morning, XXXX company, how can we help?"	
Colin	"I have just picked up your flyer and would like to find out a bit more about your XYZ offer."	
Agent	"What XYZ offer is that?"	They don't know what offers are in the market. Surprise. *Marketing and brand*
Colin	"The one that is in the papers today."	
Agent	"OK, let me have a look on the system … [clunking of keys] … no, nothing here … can you tell me a bit about it?"	They are treating you as a transaction and "processing" the request. The silence indicates that either they don't know that it would be better to engage the customer in conversation or that their systems are so complex it takes all their concentration. Either way emotional expectations are not managed. *Expectations, process, systems*
Colin	"Yep, it says the XYZ PC and a price of XX…"	
Agent	"No, I don't have that, could you fax me a copy of that?"	What?! Surprise, annoyance. I have to do the work! *Expectations, process, culture, systems*
Colin	"What? You want me to fax this to you?"	
Agent	"Yes, that would be very helpful, we haven't seen that, it happens all the time, sounds like a marketing campaign."	Annoyance, frustration.

Table 7.1 continued

Who	What the company said	My thoughts and feelings (orientational areas in *italics*)
Colin	"OK, I'll fax it to you ..." [I fax it to them and then call the person back]	I have to call them back!
Agent	"Yes, I see the offer, we haven't been told about this and in fact this product is no longer available and hasn't been for a number of weeks. They must have been trying to get rid of their old stocks. Sorry about that."	They are happy to reveal the lack of coordination in their business, and reveal they are passing on the blame by using the word "they." They further degrade the organization by revealing their old stock policy. *Culture, channel approach, marketing and brand*
Colin	"So you are advertising on the front page of your flyer a product you don't have?"	
Agent	"Yes, sorry, could I interest you in a GHY model?"	They don't really care they just want to hit their sales target. Frustration.
Colin	"No, thanks."	
Agent	"OK, thank for calling XXXX company, have a nice day."	They are not genuine.

Now I am sure as you read this, this would have sparked off memories in your own mind of situations like this that have happened to you. The sad point is, this is not unusual.

Different groups across the organization look at the Customer Experience in isolation – nothing is defined, everyone does what they believe is right – so for 39 percent of organizations there is no consistency and the Customer Experience is confused. This demonstrates that the left hand in the organization is not talking to the right. In the companies I have worked for in the past, this was a common occurrence. Marketing failed to tell the other customer-facing arms of the organization what it was advertising. This is typical of a Transactional organization.

The real question is, how much did this example cost?

- the cost of producing the brochure, artwork, production, and so on
- the cost of putting the brochure in the newspaper
- the lost opportunity of having a product which it could have sold
- the time it takes for the agent to deal with the enquiries generated
- the time the customer has wasted

- the impression this makes on the customer
- the number of people the customer tells.

This adds up to a lot of money, effectively to provide me with a poor Customer Experience, driving emotions of frustration and exasperation.

Our research[1] shows across the spectrum of Naïve to Natural Model™ only 33 percent of employees said they received briefings on their company's advertising and marketing before it went live. This figure fell to 13 percent when looking at employees working in call centers, who are obviously a key interface for customers! This is a typical comment from an employee:

> *You actually hear more from the local press than you do from the company, and things leak out and you as an employee find out more later.*
>
> Employee interview

Here is another example of a Transactional organization from a Philosophers' Day workshop I was running. This is a workshop for senior executives to understand the concept of the Customer Experience.

> *I was chatting with the VP of Customer Service from one of the attending companies over lunch and he was looking quite fraught. I asked him what the matter was. "One of the marketing managers in the organization has been running low on budget and therefore decided to bundle together a promotional mailing that was meant to be going out over a six-week period, sending it all at once to get a larger discount on one mailing. The mailing reached our customers all at once, and they all responded at once, rather than spread over the anticipated six-week period we had planned on. The result is, the call center is snowed under with calls – 56 percent of calls were abandoned." This is a great example I could share with the board of how its cost-cutting environment had driven a poor Customer Experience and had cost it far more money than it had saved.*

Clearly, it was not just customers responding to the promotional flyer who were abandoning their calls, it was the usual customers for that day. To overcome the problem the organization drafted more people in to deal with the volume of calls, and paid overtime rates. Obviously, this didn't just happen in one day, and the call rate remained high for three or four days before it gradually declined. As the organization's usual customers also could not get through, this resulted in a bow wave of customer complaints, which needed to be dealt with, at further cost. Sales were lost and people in the center were put under a great deal of strain. It destroyed the measurement that they had in place for bonus and incentive schemes, and all because a person in marketing wanted to complete his work and stick within his budgets. No consideration was given to the impact of his actions on the rest of the organization. The Transactional organization has a siloed mentality, and this causes a poor Customer Experience.

This silo mentality is reinforced by systems. Systems have typically been built and designed for functional silos, around legacy Naïve systems. As the organization has evolved, scant regard has been paid to the customer; instead systems have developed around what is good for the company and its products, and channels have been designed with their own integrated systems. Typically, the Transactional organization now has a number of systems that are specific to each silo, and this means that people cannot see what is happening in other parts of the organization. This results in customers being confused as they try to navigate around the silo functions, either to buy or to receive customer service. Over the last few years, customer relationship management (CRM) systems have been implemented with some relish to try to make things better.

As the Transactional organization is more customer-focused than the Naïve, it understands that it can meet customer's needs by bundling a series of products together from the various different product lines in the company. These are presented to the customer as a bundle, as a "complete solution" – a "one-stop shop". However, when the installation of these products takes places the true orientation of the company is revealed. Typically this "bundled" solution is delivered at different times and in an uncoordinated fashion. It feels like a "solution" to the customer, but when delivered is actually a group of products tied together with a bit of string. This is confirmed when the customer is given three or four different points of contact for obtaining customer service or technical support for the various products that comprise the solution, not one place to deal with all problems relating to that solution. Finally, this can extend to the billing. Separate bills for each of the separate products are produced and sent to the customer: not one bill or one solution.

One of the key differences of the Transactional organization from the Naïve orientation is that it recognizes people make a difference to the Customer Experience, although interestingly 24 percent of organizations admitted that this is just lip service and that people are really seen as a commodity – they aren't trusted and have limited levels of authority and empowerment. Half of organizations across the Naïve to Natural™ spectrum give their people some limited authority to act on their own initiative. But generally, management seeks to limit the decisions that individuals can make. Lots of policies exist and scripts are used extensively.

However, this is only from a top level. Typically, the organization recruits people for the "right attitude." It also considers the organization's general culture and tries to recruit people who will "fit."

Employee satisfaction is considered, and is seen as important. Yet our research[1] across all Naïve to Natural Models™ shows that 24 percent of employees in face-to-face roles say they do not enjoy their job. Clearly these people will find it difficult to build great Customer Experiences. A third of employees said they did not feel proud to work for their company. This rises to 50 percent for call center employees. In the Transactional organization, people are given training on providing "good" service. This includes "how to deal with difficult customers" and general training, which is focused on providing good customer service and positive emotions. Emphasis is on tone of voice. This still leaves customers wanting more, as their emotional and sensory needs are not being fulfilled.

Waynn Pearson, City Librarian, Cerritos Library, California would give the Transactional organization the following advice on how to Revolutionize Its Customer Experience™.

Let me give you an example of a transactional environment in a typical library. If you walked into most reference libraries and went up to the reference desk there would be somebody sitting behind the desk reading a book or working on a computer and it would take a while before you would be acknowledged. You would probably feel that you were interrupting the librarian; that's why so many people are reluctant to approach the reference staff. We've changed the environment by requiring that employees pay attention to the public, not stare at the computer screen. They are also trained to get up and walk around the desk to greet people eyeball to eyeball and transact business without the barrier of the desk. Moreover, we have roaming staff who circulate throughout the library and proactively offer service; these staff members are equipped with radio headsets and PDAs (personal digital assistants) to facilitate service.

We talk about the customer and how important they are, but the staff and what they do is just as important. Our staff went through intensive re-training and we re-established how we would handle everything from a transactional basis. We used very straightforward methodology. For each service, we asked, "What does the first-time user want? What does the frequent user want?" Then we turned it around and asked, "What do the staff need in terms of the first time user?" and so on. We established an entirely new approach for customer service training, which we call "WOW!" training.

It wasn't called "WOW!" at the beginning; it became "WOW!" as people came into the entrance of the library and went "WOW!" because they were standing in a huge space that went up three stories and was filled with overwhelming "eye candy."

We took that term and applied it to a Customer Experience training program developed specifically for the Cerritos Library. While it relies on the basic principles of any good customer service, it also includes consideration of the special characteristics of the library. Thus, for example, staff are trained to answer questions about the behavior of the fish in the aquarium.

In the Transactional organization, the culture of the company is considered but the connection between culture and the Customer Experience has not been made. The leadership has recognized that the correct attitude of employees is critical to its success, and therefore it has implemented employee satisfaction surveys and it is recruiting people who have the "right attitude." Mark Constantine, Director at Lush, told us of his experience at other cosmetics companies.

My experience of other cosmetics companies is you have the guys – the scientists – that make the product and you have graduates that check it for quality. Often the guys that make the product hate the graduates, though the graduates are probably unaware of that. The graduates are often upstairs in white coats and the guys who make the products are normally downstairs.

The guys downstairs have samples of the product you are supposed to match your product to. The guys downstairs will do anything to try to trick the graduates upstairs in the white coats. They will send a sample up and have it rejected just to prove that those people upstairs are fools, or they do worse things.

Our research[1] across all orientations showed 100 percent of respondents said leadership was important for organizations, but only 25 percent could give examples of how their leadership was reinforcing a Customer Experience culture in their organization.

Due to the siloed nature of the orientation, the "they culture" is alive and well. The customer is constantly being told "the delivery will not come out today as 'they' [meaning another part of the organization] haven't done their job." Salespeople in particular frequently talk about delivery as being someone else's responsibility. Their job is to sell, and once the product is sold it is someone else's problem/responsibility to deliver and they are not particularly interested from that point on. This leaves the customer feeling that the salespeople don't care and that the organization is disjointed.

This is all to do with the process that the company puts in place. Of organizations across the Naïve to Natural™ spectrum 57 percent state that processes in their organization are owned by individual silos, functions, or departments, and they are generally in the Transactional orientation. Forty-one percent have no overall customer journey map like Moment Mapping®. Some rudimentary mapping by silo/function has been completed – but it is very Transactionally based. In the main they are "inside out." For example, look at the practice adopted by some airlines of overbooking seats. These airlines overbook their seats in the hope that some passengers will not turn up. Whilst this is OK if those passengers don't turn up, when they do, someone is left behind. You can imagine the emotions this causes. The Transactional organization is customer-focused enough to know this will cause a problem and when this happens offer compensation immediately, which is far more than the Naïve organization would. But our question is why you would put yourself in the situation in the first place. The answer is profit. While more customer focused, the Transactional organization still has not truly let go of the profitability/productivity debate. As you can imagine this drives the feelings of lack of trust in organizations that undertake such practices.

Another way that you can identify the Transactional organization is to look at its complaints process. This reveals a multitude of sins. A typical company's process would be something like this:

Table 7.2 Typical complaints process: "guilty until proven innocent"

Activity	Typical characteristics of this orientation	What it says to customer	What it says to employee
Agent answers the phone. The customer wants to complain. Agent listens to complaint in an understanding manner.	They have been trained on how to deal with "difficult customers."	They are listening. This is good. I am quite important.	Customers are quite important.
The agent tells the customer they are sorry for their problems and they will need to speak to another group.	Lack of empowerment. Management doesn't really trust their people. They haven't employed the right people.	I am talking to the wrong person. The organization does not trust this person, so why should I? The company thinks I could be lying. I am guilty until proven innocent.	The company doesn't trust me to make a decision. They must think I am stupid.
The call is transferred to the "complaints team." They ask client to repeat the complaint. They say that they will need to look into this.	Lack of coordination in organizational structure as asked to repeat information. Dealing with customer as a transaction.	There is no coordination in the company. They are just trying to grind me down...	The complaints team are of a higher intelligence than me – I must be stupid.
The organization undertakes an investigation – this could result in an engineer being sent out – to confirm the customer's story.	A process-driven response, which assumes the customer is lying and the story needs to be checked.	They think I am lying. [This can impose cost on the customer in certain industries that may need to send out an engineer to view the situation and the customer may need to be present and take a day off work.]	We are more important than customers. The customer is trying to con us. You can't trust customers.

Table 7.2 continued

Activity	Typical characteristics of this orientation	What it says to customer	What it says to employee
Complaints team call back customer and say they can offer a level of compensation.	Quite customer focused. Some level of empowerment.	I was right, so why didn't they believe me in the first place? Why have I had to wait all this time for this to be sorted? Am I only worth this much? They don't care about my time.	The customer is only worth this much and we need to get away with the minimal possible.
Customer wants more compensation. Complaints team now have to refer to management as outside their remit.	Poor attitude to customer to get to this point.	Always continue to complain as you will eventually get to the managers.	We are not capable of dealing with this.
Management make decision and customer is informed.	Managers think they know best, employees don't have brains.	When I complain in the future I will always ask to deal with a manager.	Why do they waste my time? Why don't managers always make the decision?

When we analyzed the complaints process of one of our clients, its staff confessed that only the day before they had had a meeting with 12 senior managers to decide a £2000 ($3500) customer complaint. Our challenge to them was that the meeting alone probably cost the organization that amount of money. The Transactional organization does not trust its customers or employees. It creates policies for the 5 percent of employees and customers who seek to abuse the system. When training relates to emotions and is focused on dealing with difficult customers, providing good service, and evoking general "positive" emotions in customers, 52 percent of organizations rated their training as being general. This lack of trust is picked up by customers and, in turn, does not incline them to trust the organization.

In the area of measurement the Transactional organization has very physically based targets and measures. Our research across the Naïve to Natural Model™ showed only 26 percent of employees said that their bonuses were linked to the Customer Experience. Over half of organizations confess that the balance between internal and customer measures is 75 percent and 25 percent respectively. The main KPIs of 52 percent of organizations are stated as being revenue and Transactional performance (for example, achievement of stated lead times, punctuality, and so on). This reinforces the "inside out" nature of the organization.

The targets are 75 percent internal and are about productivity and sales. As with the Naïve organization, this continues to drive the wrong behaviors. Salespeople are judged on how many calls they make, the call center is judged on "average call handling time" and "percentage of calls answered within so many seconds." All this drives productivity but doesn't drive a great Customer Experience.

> *Most companies are built on so called trust and what it looks like ... it's not about trust at all, it's about getting them in, getting it fixed, then getting them on their way and taking their money off them. That's what it's all about; it's far from trust.*
>
> Employee focus group[1]

> *If they are really customer focused they wouldn't be concentrating on the number of calls per day you have or the people that you deal with ... it would be satisfactory outcomes at the end of that conversation rather than how many people you have spoken to that day. That is the real measure of how good your services are, how many people you have dealt with satisfactorily, not how many people you have spoken to today.*
>
> Employee focus group[1]

Typically in Transactional organizations, a general customer strategy has been agreed and although this is focused around the customer at the heart of the organization, typically the words and the actions are very different. Transactional organizations cannot answer the question, "What is the Customer Experience you are trying to deliver?" Consequently, everyone in each of the operational silos does what they consider to be the right thing. But in the absence of a commonly agreed Customer Experience, this ends up being different in each of the functional silos. Mark Constantine, Director at Lush, tells us an interesting story of one of his customers segmenting his products.

> *All manufacturing is governed by batch codes. We wanted to use the best people to make the product and for them to have pride in the goods they were making; we wanted them to be craftsmen. If you just put some code that does not mean anything to anyone this means nothing to them. If you put their name and date on it does.*
>
> *So for years we did that. It might have on it "Made by Dave on 01/2004." We wanted to take that one stage further so we got photos of them, drew little cartoons of their faces and shoved those in the middle primarily so their mum or dad could see what they had done and they would be proud. Also it*

means the people working in the shops get an idea of who makes a nice product, the whole thing is a very positive experience.

The really interesting part of this is I spend a lot of time in the stores as I like them. I saw this guy on Sunday looking through some people creams made by one person. I said to him, "Are you looking for somebody in particular?" He said, "I prefer a girl to make my cream." It was lovely; I had never thought of it like that before. You would never think, "Oh, maybe customers would like something girls had made," until they actually point it out. We would never have picked up on this if we hadn't been in the stores.

Finally, the last telltale sign for us of a Transactional organization is spamming. Transactional organizations do not "spam" their customers as Naïve organizations do, but instead they operate an "opt out" policy. They have already ticked the box for the customer to receive information, and usually this is placed at a point where customers won't notice it. Customers are invited to "opt out" if they don't want to receive the materials!

So, the Transactional organization is definitely more customer-focused than the Naïve organization and is typified by the phase "Have a nice day". The Transactional organization is still very prevalent today, and this is why a number of these examples will hit a spot with you. Do you fit into this orientation or have you progressed onto the Enlightened orientation?

What do Transactional organizations need to do to Revolutionize Their Customer Experience™?

- understand that emotions play a key role
- start to recruit people with emotional intelligence
- review processes so that they evoke the right emotions
- implement middleware systems to give a complete customer view
- understand the need to focus on employees' well-being
- align the Customer Experience with the employee experience
- define the Customer Experience
- look at customers' emotional expectations
- build an overall customer journey potentially using Moment Mapping® – this is covered in more details in a later chapter
- increase the time senior executives spend with customers.

To accomplish great things we must not only act, but also dream, not only plan, but also believe.

Anon

Naïve to Natural™ self-assessment

Please answer the following questions and then transfer your scores to the summary sheet at the end of Chapter 9.

13. Which of the following best describes the degree of alignment between your organizations brand and its Customer Experience?
    a. Full consideration is given to aligning the brand and Customer Experience – a formal mechanism exists to ensure this happens.
    b. No consideration is given to aligning the brand and Customer Experience – brand values are developed in isolation from operational groups.
    c. Full consideration is given to aligning the brand and Customer Experience.
    d. Little consideration is given to aligning the brand and Customer Experience – operational groups may occasionally be consulted on the development of brand values.

Your answer [   ]

a = 4 points, b = 1 point, c = 3 points, d = 2 points   Score [   ]

14. Which of the following best describes the primary emphasis of your organization's market research?
    a. It is primarily focused on customers' service requirements and making a general assessment of the experience they have.
    b. It is primarily focused on product attributes and pricing, and is primarily conducted by product lines.
    c. It includes looking at specific emotions and is conducted on a company-wide basis.
    d. It includes looking at specific emotions and senses and is conducted on a company-wide basis.

Your answer [   ]

a = 2 points, b = 1 point, c = 3 points, d = 4 points   Score [   ]

8 Enlightened orientation

When you see a successful business someone once made a courageous decision.
Peter Daucher

Duane Francis, CEO, Mid-Columbia Medical Center, Oregon:

What you need to do is empower your associates and colleagues to be decision makers and to give them the freedom to deliver your philosophy. We have our Mid-Columbia Medical Center University here, where every new employee, every new associate that comes to work for us is schooled for a solid week on what our mission and philosophy are and how we want to put them into practice.

We then give them the authority and freedom to make decisions. We open every meeting with what we call an excellence thought and a core value statement where we tell stories about examples that we have observed where someone did something extraordinary to demonstrate our philosophy of care. Recently, we had someone tell a story of a radiation technician who went to a patient's room to transport him for an x-ray. This was a patient that had been in the hospital for three or four days, and who was going to be in for a number of days further. As they were in the elevator, the patient said, "I miss the ability to just have my favorite food. I love Chinese food and I can't wait until someday that I can have Chinese food when I get out of the hospital again." So this technician took the patient, did the test, took him back up into his room. As he was coming out he saw the patient's doctor and he pulled the doctor to the side and asked if there were any dietary restrictions on this patient. The doctor said, "No he can eat anything he wants." So after his shift, this employee on his own time drove down town and bought some Chinese food. He put it in his car and then took it into this gentleman's room and gave him his Chinese dinner and walked out.

Those kinds of things literally happen every day, I remember I had left the hospital to go to a meeting and I came back about mid afternoon and was parking in the parking lot and the director of our ICU (intensive care unit) was walking in the lot. So I ribbed her a little bit and gave her a hard time and said, "Gosh, are you quitting work already?" She said, "No I am just running an errand." There was a gentleman who was driving across country, he was driving through Oregon on his way to Washington and had ended up with some chest pain and had to come through our emergency room and had been admitted to our telemetry unit to be monitored for heart problems. He happened to mention that his dog was in his camper. So this was a depart-ment director, this wasn't a nurse or an employee, immediately after she dealt with this patient, she took his car keys and came down and made sure that his dog had some water and food and was taken care of.

There are experiences like that all the time. I think in terms of delivering on that and creating an extraordinary experience, we empower our staff to do whatever it takes to make sure that expectations aren't just met but they are greatly exceeded.

One of the big differences between the Transactional and Enlightened orga-nization is the latter has recognized that over half of the Customer Experience is about emotions. It not only recognizes this is the case but plans to evoke defined emotions. It is "Enlightened" hence the name for this orientation. The change of orientation between Transactional and Enlightened is a significant one. It is not because any of the areas are fundamentally different; but because people have changed their perspective on life, their paradigm.

We were working with a Transactional telecoms company. We were con-ducting a strategic debate at a workshop about the emotions the company could be evoking, one of which was trust. As we debated this, we were asked if this meant that they would need "optimization of a customer bill," in other words, making sure the customer was on the cheapest package all the time. Typically in the telecom market this doesn't happen all the time, as it would reduce the profitability of the telecoms company. I made the point that if you want to evoke trust in customers, you need to proactively ensure your customers are on the best discount rate, because if customers discover they are not, this drives feelings of distrust. One of the team said, "But that would cost us $XX." "Yes," I replied, "if you are serious that is exactly what it means." The lights started to come on.

The Enlightened organization has had these debates and made these types of decision. But, be warned, in our experience when faced with the decision to move out of the Transactional and into the Enlightened orientation, some people and organizations are not prepared to make the transition. That is not because they do not understand, in the main they do, but because it is hard to do, which it is. This is why 67 percent of organizations are Transactional and only 22 percent are Enlightened and 2 percent Natural, yet the under-standing is ahead of what they do. People who are in the Transactional organization have spent their lives understanding the Naïve and Transactional orientations and they are scared. They are scared about moving from their comfort zone into something new. They are scared of what they are going to lose. They have made their reputation on being good at the

Transactional orientation, and they question whether they are going to be good at the Enlightened orientation. They are so blinkered they would prefer to carry on "missing the gorge" and rushing toward the precipice.

> *Emotions set our highest level goals, including how much and well we work and buy. By creating the right emotions in employees and customers, the phenomenon of emotional engagement is the next economic force in the highly competitive marketplace.*
>
> Curt Coffman, co-author, *First Break All the Rules*

Our research[1] across the Naïve to Natural Model™ revealed that in 97 percent of cases consumers said they wanted to feel:

- confidence and/or reassurance (44 percent)
- satisfaction (14 percent)
- delight (39 percent).

So what is the emotion your organization is trying to evoke?

A report from an Enlightened orientation organization is shown in Figure 8.1 and in the following table.

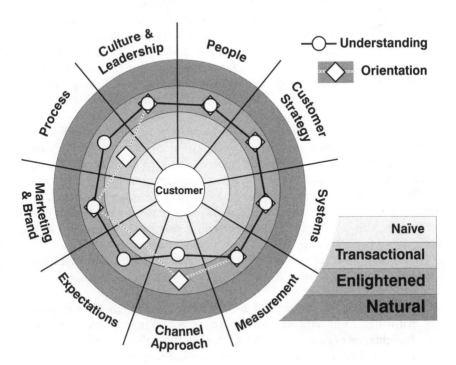

Figure 8.1 An Enlightened high tech company

Orientation area	Orientation	Understanding
People	Enlightened	Enlightened
Strategy	Enlightened	Enlightened
Systems	Enlightened	Enlightened
Measurement	Enlightened	Enlightened
Channel approach	**Enlightened**	**Transactional**
Expectations	**Transactional**	**Enlightened**
Marketing and brand	Enlightened	Enlightened
Process	Transactional	Enlightened
Culture and leadership	Enlightened	Enlightened

You will note in the main that there is a high degree of correlation between the orientation and the understanding. The organization is doing what it knows. Therefore to improve the Customer Experience it needs to improve its understanding into the Natural orientation, to Revolutionize Its Customer Experience™. You will also note that the processes are still in the Transactional orientation, although the organization understands it needs to move into the Enlightened orientation. As organizations' processes touch the customer, this is the area we really worked with them on, implementing our Moment Mapping® solution. You will note that for channel approach, orientation was ahead of the organization's understanding. This may seem strange but not when you again look into the detail: at the indicator level, we discovered that this organization was doing a number of things without necessarily understanding how they affected the Customer Experience it was providing.

For example at the indicator level in the channel approach, its offering to the customer was seamless. This was not a purposeful act but a consequence of the integration of the systems developed; not a surprise when you consider it was a high-tech organization in this environment already.

The challenge for this client was to push the organization into the Natural orientation. Comparatively speaking, in its industry the organization is doing very well. This goes back to the compelling story, "Why change?" as the majority of the competition is not doing anywhere near as well.

When we looked at the detail of this report we found the indicators it needed to focus on were:

- Recruitment: its recruitment process was designed to identify people with the right attitude who have a generally "positive" attitude. Enlightened organizations go further than this – they recruit people with emotional capabilities. Therefore we worked with the organization and developed an "emotional intelligence" assessment procedure.

- Employee experience: it had no mechanism to measure this. An Enlightened organization would have this in place and be creating improvement action plans from its output. This was put in place as well.
- Expectations: the whole orientation area of "expectations" was letting the Customer Experience down. It was not meeting customers' expectations. Following this feedback we established a process to understand customers' emotional expectations and decide in which areas the organization would exceed customer expectations.

Now for some traits of Enlightened organizations. They:

- have defined their Customer Experience
- focus on stimulating planned emotions and build these into the design of their Customer Experience
- recognize customers have emotional expectations and plan how to meet and exceed these
- have started to align the employee experience and the Customer Experience
- employ people with emotional capabilities
- look at the end-to-end Customer Experience
- have appointed a VP of Customer Experience or established a Customer Experience council
- involve customers in the design of their processes
- integrate systems to achieve a "complete view of customer"
- use Customer Experience measures, which account for a large part of people's bonuses.

There are a number of key things that change at the crossover point from Transactional to Enlightened. A number of these are attitudinal, from reactive to proactive, from "inside out" to "outside in," and from physical to "physical and emotions." The latter is the largest, planning to evoke specific emotions. In the Enlightened organization emotions are discussed openly, as everyone knows emotions drive our very existence. Some of the key changes can be seen in Figure 8.2.

Sonia Wolsey-Cooper is Customer Service Director, AXA PPP Healthcare, where employees can clearly become involved in sensitive and challenging conversations with customers when they phone to discuss their treatment for themselves or their family.

> *What we don't want is for somebody to be bright and breezy on every call. We want them to pick up the prompt and do what is appropriate for that call. So, if somebody wants you to be bright and breezy and have a chat before managing that conversation, that's fine.*
>
> *Where it is clearly embarrassing, sensitive, or just a heartbreaking situation we encourage our people to gauge their response, match the customers' tone,*

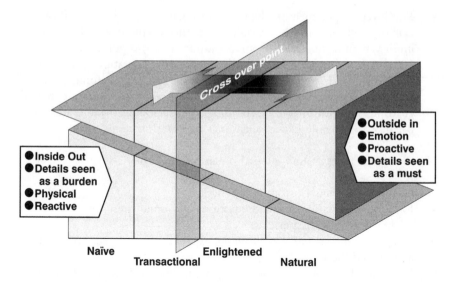

Figure 8.2 Key factors at the crossover point between Transactional and Enlightened orientations

> *making sure the customer would have come away thinking that was the best possible way somebody could have dealt with me in that situation.*
>
> *It is not easy. You are switching all day between having a straight-forward conversation to one where someone's child is seriously ill and they are looking for some support. So it can be a very trying and challenging role as well as one that can be fantastic. Occasionally, I have people come off the phone and be close to tears because they became involved. As much as you can, you counsel to keep a professional distance. But we are all human of course and it can affect you – so we ensure there are a lot of support methods available.*

The Enlightened organization knows what emotions it is evoking at each stage of its interaction with a customer. It has spent time in defining the emotion it wants to evoke, and it has planned these into the design of the Customer Experience. This is at the high end of the Customer Experience Hierarchy of Needs™ outlined again in Figure 8.3. This is not an exclusive list of physical and emotional elements but will give you an idea of the approach.

Emotional expectations: a key attribute of the Enlightened orientation

In Enlightened organizations the new concept of emotional expectations is accepted and built into everything it does, and used as a competitive

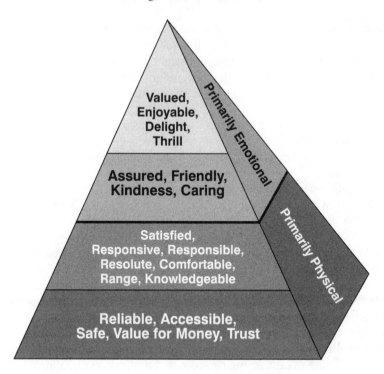

Figure 8.3 The Customer Experience Hierarchy of Needs™

weapon. So what are emotional expectations? We have all heard about physical expectations. However, before we introduced the concept in our last book, *Building Great Customer Experiences*,[16] not many people had discussed the concept of "emotional expectations." Simply put, this means how we expect to feel. Think about attending a funeral: you would expect to feel quite sad or depressed. On the other hand, think about going on holiday: you expect to be excited. To explain this in our workshops and seminars with clients I always use the following example. You may wish to do this yourself.

> *I ask people to raise their hands if they have ever been to India. Invariably not many people have visited this beautiful country. I then ask them to imagine that they are traveling to India. I ask them to imagine they have landed in India and gone though passport control and collected their bags and they are now standing in the arrivals lounge in the airport. I ask them to look around, and describe to me what they see and describe how they feel. People start shouting our words like "hot," dusty," "tired," "colorful," "crowded," "busy," "nervous," "stressed," "lack of confidence." I then ask them to open their eyes.*

The fascinating thing for me is that whenever I do this I am amazed by the level of detail that people go into. But the killer is that they have managed to go into this level of detail and yet they have never been to India! So how do they know? As we outlined in Chapter 3, the answer is that there are many things that contribute to giving us an expectation.

- Our expectations are built from previous experiences.
- We have read things in papers.
- We have had previous experiences that are similar: we translate what they are like.
- We go by what people have told us.
- We go by what we have read in magazines, seen on TV or in films, and so on.

But the really interesting bit is that if you look at the typical expectations that people have, they describe emotion. They describe the emotions they are going to feel! People typically say they are going to feel nervous or stressed, which is understandable if they are visiting a country they have not visited before and they are in a new environment. In our research[1] on the Naïve to Natural Model™, senior business leaders talked frequently about the need to meet and exceed their customers' expectations. However, only 15 percent said that they were trying to capture their customers' emotional expectations. Of these, only 10 percent tried to exceed those emotional expectations. Again this shows a major competitive advantage for those Enlightened organizations.

So what does this mean for the Customer Experience? The first thing it means is that the Transactional organization just focuses on understanding physical expectations. The Enlightened organization recognizes that customers have emotional expectations as well, that these make up over half of the Customer Experience, and it proactively designs the Customer Experience with this in mind.

We conducted some research on this.[1] We broke down the Customer Experience into three parts:

1. Before the Customer Experience.
2. During the Customer Experience.
3. After the Customer Experience.

We asked consumers to inform us of how they would feel going into a Customer Experience: that is, their emotional expectation. Seventy-three percent of customers said they didn't feel confident when they entered the Customer Experience; 51 percent said they would feel apprehensive. As we have discussed, confidence is an emotion and so is apprehension; they go hand in glove. An Enlightened organization knows this and has taken steps to understand this, and critically put in place actions to improve it.

If you break this research down further we started to discover some fascinating facts. For instance, 60 percent of women lack confidence when entering the Customer Experience but this rises to a massive 84 percent for men. Let me give you a personal example of how this manifests itself:

> *Lorraine, my wife, deals with all the finances in our home. She is the one who liaises with the banks and all the credit card companies. I know nothing! So when it comes to the very rare occasion when I have to call our bank, I can't remember the passwords, I can't remember the account numbers, and I am expecting to be embarrassed by my incompetence. As a result I avoid contact with it like the plague, as I don't want to feel embarrassed!*

The Enlightened organization would understand my embarrassment, and undertake activities to sympathize and guide me through the process to build my confidence. Our research showed that 44 percent of consumers want to feel confident and reassured. This difference between men and women is interesting. I was presenting with Tom Peters at a conference in Orlando, Florida. He recommended a good book by Faith Popcorn called *EVEolution*. Tom was wrong, it is not a good book; it's a great book! Faith informs us in the United States, women buy 80 percent of all consumer goods, 51 percent of all consumer electronics, and 75 percent of all over the counter (OTC) drugs. They buy 50 percent of all cars and influence the decision on 80 percent, and so it goes on. The message: women buy loads of stuff! If they buy loads of stuff, then they are more comfortable with doing this than men. The key issue here is that our research was general in nature across many different industries. But the questions I frequently ask our clients are, "What's it like for your company? Are men less confident than women entering *your* Customer Experience? Or is it the other way around?" Naïve and Transactional organizations cannot answer that question. Many organizations in the Enlightened stage have started to understand that they need to segment their market in more sophisticated ways.

But this is only the beginning; the Enlightened organization can clearly articulate its customer emotional expectations and has designed them into the process. One of the first steps is to determine the emotion the organization plans to evoke.

Customer Experience design: Moment Mapping®

There are a few customer journey tools on the market, but to our knowledge the only tool that is available and designed with the express desire to embed emotion and senses into the Customer Experience design is our Moment Mapping®. We named it Moment Mapping® to build on the Jan Carlzon "Moments of Truth".[19] Moment Mapping® is a process for embedding emotions and senses into the Customer Experience. Disturbingly our research reveals that only 17 percent of organizations have customer journey maps, which plot both the strategic and tactical level for the physical Customer Experience; far less at an emotional level. Without this journey map it is difficult to plan a customer journey. It is like traveling from one location to another without a map to see what is the best journey and what to do if there is an accident.

Clients tell us that what they like with Moment Mapping® is that they can break down the customer journey into its constituent parts and then plan to evoke emotions at different points, based on customer emotional expectations. This helps map those moments of truth. We outlined this process in our book *Building Great Customer Experiences.*[16] Since then our thinking has progressed further. We have recognized that during a Customer Experience there are a number of Combustion Points™. These are where customers' expectations are not met and their perception of the experience they are receiving declines rapidly. The identification of these Combustion Points™ and the reason they are happening is critical. Once the reasons for these have been defined, it is possible to plan a way around them. One way is to implement an Emotional Cookie™. An Emotional Cookie™ is just like a "cookie" that gets placed on a computer from the Internet. It is inactive until it is required and then comes to life to trigger an emotional response.

Let me give you an example:

The Beyond Philosophy™ team was doing some work with an insurance company. It was in the Transactional orientation and taking action to move into the Enlightened orientation. As part of this project we were looking at one of its processes for life insurance policies. As is typical of a Transactional company, the process had not been reviewed from the customers' perspective for years. The Combustion Points™ within the process were quite obvious. When the person called in to report the death of his or her partner, this kicked off a great big process, which took some three months to complete.

As you can imagine the surviving partner's emotional state entering the Customer Experience was very high. There were a number of Combustion Points™ in the process. Firstly, the company carried on dealing with that person as if nothing happened, in a very transactional way; it came across as very "matter of fact." It carried on sending promotional letters with both partners' names on the letter. The correspondences were in legal jargon and didn't take into account that the remaining partner was obviously in a heightened emotional state. The organization didn't even say sorry to hear of the person's news! All these items added up to be a poor Customer Experience due to the number of Combustion Points™. To improve this we used Moment Mapping® and our concept of the Emotional Barometer™. Like a weather barometer that goes up or down with the variations in the weather, the Emotional Barometer™ goes up or down with the emotions companies evoke in their customers. Our challenge to this organization was, "How does this action affect customers' Emotional Barometer™?" In addition how did it intend to embed new emotions in this process?

The Customer Experience statement stated that the organization wanted the customer to feel "valued." So together we set about changing a number of items. To evoke an emotion there needs to be a trigger, therefore we placed a number of Emotional Cookies™ in the process. For instance, a large amount of the transaction was completed online to lessen the stress on the customer completing complicated documentation. The team was trained on how to deal with customers in this emotional state. We placed an Emotional Cookie™ at the beginning of the call by asking the call taker to say the organization was very sorry to hear about the death, then spend time talking to the customer about it. We suggested the organization sent a "bereavement card" signed by the person dealing with the policy claim. Part of the problem from the customer perspective was the time it took to process the claim. We found as the process had not been reviewed for a number of years, it could be shortened considerably to enable the money to be paid quickly in case the person was experiencing financial difficulties. So we substantially improved the Customer Experience but also we had reduced the cost of the process from £100 to £20 ($160 to $32) – saving 80 percent of the costs! Improving the Customer Experience can save money!

These Emotional Cookies™ can be many things. If your boss gives you praise it evokes feelings of pride and satisfaction. If your boss shouts at you in front of all your colleagues, this evokes feelings of resentment and embarrassment: a Combustion Point™. In our research,[1] consumers said that combustion points in their Customer Experiences evoked the following emotions: "unappreciated," "mistrust," "disappointment," and "apprehension." I wonder what these companies did to evoke these emotions, and what Emotional Cookies™ they could be placing in the Customer Experience to trigger the desired emotions.

Across the Naïve to Natural Model™ only 22 percent of organizations stated their approach is integrated and seamless in appearance to the customer – but they actually incurred a cost of failure to project this seamlessness to the customer by doublehandling things internally. This is being addressed by 48 percent of organizations who are appointing a group, comprised of representatives from all functions, which has been given responsibility for owning the transactional and emotional elements of the Customer Experience.

Significantly the Enlightened organization has a process to review its end-to-end Customer Experience. The first question is always, "Where is the start and where is the finish?" The Enlightened organization lets the customers decide. Let me give you an example. We were undertaking some work with an airline. They asked us to conduct a "Mirror"[28] review of their Customer Experience; this is when we review the whole experience with a fresh, external pair of eyes. The first debate we had with the client was in determining what constituted its end-to-end process. For example, is it the phone call into the center? Is it the booking transaction on the web? Is it the ad that drove the customer to the web in the first place? Our belief is that an organization should have a view on where the process starts and finishes, but that it is the customer who is the final arbiter. In this case the customers included traveling to the airport as a key part of their airline Customer Experience. The client initially argued that this was nothing to do with it. We disagreed. The Customer Experience does not just occur at the points and places where an organization is interacting with its customers. The Customer Experience of shopping, for example, can be influenced if a person cannot find a car parking space or if the person's wallet or handbag is stolen. Just because an organization does not "own" that part of the Customer Experience it does not mean that customers do not see it as part of the experience, and certainly does not mean the organization cannot affect or influence it. The Enlightened organization understands this.

We undertook analysis with airline customers, and we actually walked the Customer Experience ourselves. Our findings were that the Customer Experience should absolutely include the journey to the airport. So let us ask you some questions we asked the airline's customers.

How do you feel when you wake up in the morning and you are traveling to a business meeting on the first flight of the morning? You would be like most of our respondents if you said that you felt anxious or concerned about making sure you were on time to get on the flight, and not delayed by traffic or something that halts your progress. The evening before, you might have laid your clothes so as not to disturb the family; you might have gone to bed early that evening. During the night you might not have slept very well, as you could have been in that "shallow" sleep where you are constantly thinking, "Is it time to get up yet?" So, before you have even started you are tired and anxious. You jump in your car. How are you feeling now? You are still anxious, so you listen to the radio to see if there are any traffic jams. Any delay gets you more concerned.

In the case of the airline, we discovered that the car park signage on arrival at the airport was poor, so customers became lost or confused, adding to their anxiety. When they finally reached the car park, they discovered that the terminal building for this airport was a lot farther away than they anticipated, again increasing their anxiety. When the customers were waiting for the bus there was no indication of when one would arrive to pick them up. The driver treated everyone with ambivalence and gave no form of reassurance that it would not take long to get to the terminal. Customers were then dropped off at the terminal building with no instructions on how to get to their check-in desk. When the customers reached the check-in desks the signs were not clear, again adding to the anxiety. Finally they entered a long queue waiting to be served. When they finally got to the check-in desk they were nearly ready to explode. The person on check-in would say, "Where are you traveling today? Did you pack the bags yourself?" There was no acknowledgment, understanding, or care about the emotions the customer had been going through to get to that point. And we have all been there: worried we are going to miss our flight! They were treating customers like a transaction. Well, an Enlightened organization would understand all of these processes.

Our research revealed a growing number of organizations, 22 percent, who now look at processes end to end and determine the emotions that happen at different points within the processes. Organizations that understand they should be doing this number 58 percent. In which camp are you? Those who do or those who know they should?

There are a number of Combustion Points™ in this customer journey. We worked with the client to implement a number of Emotional Cookies™ and suggested the following:

- Send the customer an email two days before the travel date informing them of any known road works, how long it takes to get from the car park to the terminal, and where to turn when they come into the airport terminal: evoking feelings of care and feeling valued.
- On the morning of travel send the customer a text message informing them of any delays with the flight or possible road delays, evoking feelings of care, confidence, and significance.
- Improve the car park signs to remove the Combustion Point™ and evoke feelings of being in control.
- With high-value customers offer an alarm call!
- Train the bus driver to inform customers how long the bus takes to get to the terminal: evoking feelings of confidence.
- When people arrive at the terminal, have people combing the queues. These people will understand that customers are feeling anxious, and will have been trained in working out strategies for relieving their anxiety. For instance, they are trained to walk up to the person at the end of the queue and inform them that they have plenty of time, or can take them to another queue for boarding quickly if they are likely to miss a flight: evoking feelings of caring, being valued, and confidence.
- Recruit emotionally intelligent check-in desk people who can empathize with the customer.

This is Moment Mapping® in action. It provides the ability to deconstruct and then reconstruct the Customer Experience to deliver the Customer Experience defined and evoke the emotions chosen.

Another example from Kathryn M. Haley, VP, Client Experience, RBC Royal Bank of Canada:

> *Our people are learning to pick up on certain things like emotional triggers. They are learning to respond with real understanding, empathy, and*

expediency. For example, when customers say, "I have been a client for X years," they want to be acknowledged for this tenure and for the value that they add to the organization. Or if they say, "I just don't know what to do," you know it may have been the third person they have talked to and they need a quick response. You can pick up triggers about people: when they are angry, when they are upset, when they are not feeling valued, when they are not feeling important, when they are not feeling recognized – and so we are encouraging our employees to pause in the moment, to really listen, and to respond with the client's interests in mind.

Another example is with customers who are about to refinance their mortgage. They are coming in with really different emotional states. On the one hand, they are probably excited about the possibility of transforming their home, and on the other, probably quite nervous because they don't know if they can afford the new addition. They need to feel they have come to the right place, that we understand their issues, and we help them to feel confident in the financial decisions.

Peter Scott, Customer Service Director, T-Mobile:

We have reviewed our handling of "lost and stolen" calls to take into account emotional state. With our call routing system, we are able to route these calls to a specific group of advisors who we have specifically trained to relate to customers in a potential state of stress. If someone has lost a phone, with all their various phone numbers or, worse still, been mugged; they will be in an emotional state, so we have focused on different call handling skills, counseling skills, different questions, and ways of opening the call. Our old call style was much more rigid and colder as an experience.

If you've been mugged and you're feeling emotional the last thing you want is somebody saying, "Can you tell me what your cellular telephone network (CTN) is please?" Instead we've taken an approach of, "Are you all right, is there anything else I can do? Have you made contact with the police?"

The customer feedback is very positive. We also found that first call resolution went up because the agent was much more perceptive around the problems facing the customer. An unexpected by-product was we were able to, where it was appropriate, convert a number of those into opportunities to upgrade to a new phone.

Enlightened organizations are, in effect, taking a much more proactive stance and anticipating customers' needs. They are doing things for customers and the customer does not even realize what they have done. In doing this customers will notice an organization is different from the competition, and this attention to their needs will be repaid many times over.

Liam Lambert is the Director and General Manager at Mandarin Oriental Hyde Park, London. Over the last few years we have conducted an annual Customer Experience Best Practice Study Tour. We think that the Customer Experience is so great that we always base our delegates there before we take them on a behind the scenes traveling tour of companies that are good at delivering a great Customer Experience. On the tour Liam invites the delegates to watch him and his team undertake a task he calls "Morning Prayers." This always amazes our delegates. *Each* morning, Liam's management team review the *entire* guest list of new guests that are joining them that day. This means on average some 80 people. Liam personally reviews this with the whole team. He asks whether the guest has stayed in the hotel before, he asks his team what the guest's preferences are, what are the little things that the guest likes when moving in? Liam takes up the story:

> *For instance a guest may ask if they can have a hot drink of milk when they go to bed, therefore my team would ensure that a hot drink is waiting for them. Or, we phone and ask whether they would like one. Something that the guest might normally have to pay for, we often provide for free, not to be recognized, but to improve the Customer Experience in a very subtle way.*

During the "Morning Prayers," Liam says, "Can we gain more preferences on this visit please?" What does this mean? It means the hotel watches the guests to see what they do and what it can do to make their stay better. The hotel takes note of the drink the guests order when visiting the bar after a long hard day, and has it ready and waiting for them the next time. The hotel recognizes what types of food people eat and ensures they have this available. The hotel recognizes that a particular guest is always flying in from overseas and is tired, and therefore the team will do things for the person unexpectedly.

To help provide a great Customer Experience a member of the team also goes onto the web and, if possible, downloads a picture of the guest who is staying at the hotel, which is then printed and put up outside the staff lounge so that colleagues can recognize the guest when they meet in the corridor. This is being proactive. This is the standard. Another key crossover point for the Enlightened organization is the move from being "reactive" to "proactive," which is shown in Figure 8.4. Organizations in this orientation are oriented around doing this as Natural. If you speak to Liam he would say, "I don't see what all the fuss is about. Surely everyone does this?" The answer is, Enlightened and Natural organizations do, Naïve and Transactional don't.

The results of this kind of "proactive" activity are vital. When Liam took over the Mandarin it was fifteenth on the list of luxury hotels in London and 150th *in the world*. Today it is now third in London and sixteenth in the world. Great Customer Experiences pay dividends.

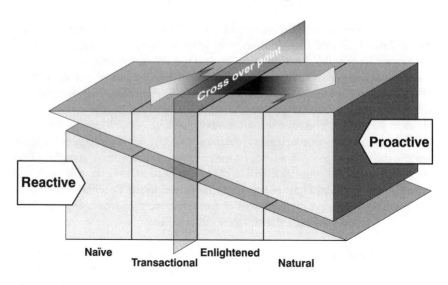

Figure 8.4 The Naïve to Natural™ crossover points

An Enlightened organization has a completely different attitude to the customer from the Naïve and Transactional organization. The customer is very much in the lifeblood of the Enlightened organization. It would not dream of doing something that was not focused around the customer; this would be anathema to the organization. It does things for the customer without a second thought. It intuitively knows what to do. It does not have to produce a massive business case for changes. It knows that putting a bottom-line figure to an improvement in customer satisfaction is difficult but if it feels like the right thing to do then it will go ahead.

When you look at all the companies that really stand out in our economy today – Virgin Atlantic, Pret A Manger, American Girl, Build-A-Bear Workshop – they stand out because of the emotional engagement with the customer.

In the Enlightened orientation *genuine* becomes a vital word. The genuine company is not afraid about what it looks like, it is proud of it. It has aligned its brand and Customer Experience.

Liam Lambert again:

> *We want our colleagues to be natural, not to learn words by rote, not to learn how to answer the phone exactly, but to use their own warmth and their own charm, what comes naturally to them.*

Mandarin Oriental is happy for the customer to see what is happening. As we discussed before, for example, customers can look from the restaurant into the kitchens to see their food being cooked. The organization is making the statement that it has nothing to hide and in fact it is proud of what it does. Customers know when an organization and its employees are not being genuine. They can tell when the employee says, "Have a nice day," whether the person means it or not. It's the inclination in the voice, the tone used. The organization in the Enlightened orientation realizes this and has made the decision to "free" the people to talk in the language and in the way that is natural to them; therefore, they have removed the need to strictly adhere to scripts, as in call centers. They are instead used as a "guide" for what to say.

We described in the Transactional organization how there is a misalignment between the brand and the actual Customer Experience. This has been recognized and resolved by the Enlightened organization. It recognizes that the brand makes the promise to the customer and the Customer Experience delivers against that promise. It has aligned the brand and the Customer Experience, and the advertising does not make claims that cannot be fulfilled by all people in the organization.

One of the key ways that the Enlightened organization has managed to achieve this customer focus is by having a *deliberate* Customer Experience statement that has been defined, as we outlined in Chapter 3. Once this has been established the key elements are then communicated – as you will read in the Yorkshire Water case study in Chapter 11 – and acted upon.

Enlightened organizations realize the customer will not stand for an uncoordinated Customer Experience, and have taken steps to alleviate this situation. Across the Naïve to Natural Model™, one in five has established a "matrixed organization" to ensure functions are pulled together to face customers. Forty-six percent of organizations state that every function has a basic complete view of the customer: all products, all sales, and full service history, again aiding a holistic Customer Experience. In a third of organizations, systems are deployed to drive improvements in the Customer Experience.

A number of Enlightened organizations have created the new role of Vice President of Customer Experience. We provide a free monthly e-magazine entitled *Customer Experience Times*™, the purpose of which is to create a community of interest for people concerned with the Customer Experience. Each month I personally scan who has subscribed. It's amazing how far it reaches. We have seen an enormous increase in people with Customer Experience in their job title. In our talks with clients and people who have been given this function, invariably the job description looks like this:

Role:

- to coordinate the company's Customer Experience
- to work with the functional areas across the company to provide a seamless approach to the customer
- to ensure a unified approach to the customer
- to own the end-to-end Customer Experience.

Invariably such roles do not have a great deal of people reporting into them. They are a centralized function, and to a certain extent you could argue they are a cost of failure.

One of the roles this function performs is to coordinate the organization's approach to the market. In addition, the coordination extends into the fairly boring, but fundamental, area of business planning. In the Enlightened organization the Customer Experience is considered at the business planning stage. In *Building Great Customer Experiences*,[16] we detail a tool for doing this, the Customer Experience Pyramid™. Working with one client we discovered that it had 159 programs it was looking to implement the following year. The challenge we set the organization was to articulate how each would improve the Customer Experience and affect its *deliberate* Customer Experience. From this work, we defined a typical set of decision criteria for the acceptance of programs: For instance:

- How will this affect the Customer Experience?
- Which *element/s* will this affect?
- What is the planned impact of this?
- How will it be measured?
- When will it impact?
- What happens if we don't do it?

Each of the client's functional areas came and presented their programs. Over a third of the programs did not even plan to hit any of the elements from the Customer Experience. Therefore, the key question was "Why run them?" We managed to dramatically reduce the number of programs. We refocused the remainder, thus improving the Customer Experience and saving the money that would have been otherwise wasted on programs that were not focused in the appropriate area.

A typical area that needs to be addressed early by the Enlightened organization is improving its systems, so that a "single view of the customer" can be achieved across the organization.

Mike Gooley, Chairman, Trailfinders:

> *We were delighted to introduce "Matchmaker" – it essentially uses a call line identification system to recognize callers. We are still working very hard to increase the recognition rate. We want to replicate the feeling you have when you go into a pub or a restaurant for a second time and you get recognized. You do feel good about it and it is going to lead you back there. You start the experience off in a happier frame of mind so the experience goes better for everybody.*

Systems are a key enabler for driving emotional Customer Experiences. Let me give you an example:

I was speaking at the North American Customer Management conference with Michael Porter and Tom Peters. As I wanted to make my session inter- active, I asked my favorite question, "What is the best Customer Experience you have ever had?" At this conference a chap called Gary put his hand up. He told the audience a great story. Apparently he was a resident in Florida and therefore had an annual pass to Disney. It was his daughter's eighth birthday and they decided to take her to Disney for the day. When they arrived at the turnstiles they put the ticket in the machine to enter the park. Suddenly it made a sound, which attracted the cast member's [Disney employee] attention. It was to signify it was his daughter's birthday. The cast member made a really big fuss of the girl and gave her a big badge with "Birthday Girl" written on it. That day every cast member that she passed made a point of coming up to that little girl and making a big fuss of her, including the person who was cleaning the streets.

This is a great story and doesn't surprise me as I know, from the behind the scenes tour we have undertaken, that the emotion Disney is trying to evoke is "happiness." It wants to make people happy. This is a prime exam- ple of how they do it. The thing that sparked off this entire experience was the system beeping to say it was her birthday. This means that someone would have had the idea to do this in the first place. Someone must then have specified it to the IT department, which then wrote the code for this to happen. Therefore, systems can be used to evoke emotions. But this is only the beginning: for this to happen it took people. When you ask people about their best ever Customer Experience, invariably people say, "It is about the person." The companies who have reached the Enlightened orientation have recognized this, and have embedded the selection of people with emotional intelligence into their recruitment process. There- fore, they do not just look for skills and attitude; they look at the emotional capabilities of the candidate. The Enlightened organization recognizes that employees are vital, and it takes much more care of them than Naïve and Transactional organizations.

Once these people have been recruited, their training becomes vital. Across the spectrum of Naïve to Natural Model™ we found that 38 percent of employees reported receiving training on how to stimulate positive emo- tions in their customers. Only 10 percent of employees received training on specific emotions. The majority were in the Transactional area for this indi- cator, with 52 percent of employees saying their training focused on how to deal with difficult and angry customers. This is very different in the Enlightened organization, where all employees understand the emotions they are to evoke and how to do this.

One of the things we are constantly being asked by clients is, "Should the internal experience be the same as the Customer Experience?" This is really quite simple. A number of years ago I realized that if you want to get the task done you needed to focus on the person. If you can understand the person and take care of the person, the task gets done. Therefore:

The employee experience should be the same as the Customer Experience.

Our research[2] shows that only one in ten organizations has a defined and articulated employee experience that is aligned with the Customer Experience they want to deliver. The recruitment process is aligned to culture in 37 percent of organizations. The culture is defined and forms part of the selection process. This is vital. For example, if a Customer Experience statement includes the elements of "trust," "fun," and "caring," then the organization needs to trust its people and provide a fun and caring environment for them. The Enlightened organization understands this. Imagine having a manager who is very aggressive with you and is shouting at you to make sure that you have fun with the customer. Is that going to put you in the right frame of mind to do so? No. How can you say you want to have a trusting environment when you limit the amount of money your people can offer a customer to resolve their issue, and do not allow them to deal with complaints properly? You can't: the employee experience and the Customer Experience have to be aligned. This also means that the culture of the organization is aligned. The Enlightened organization has made a major breakthrough in understanding the Customer Experience, and it includes emotional aspects in that Customer Experience. It has defined a deliberate Customer Experience that everyone can use to align the Customer Experience and the organization. But what do organizations need to do to Revolutionize Their Customer Experience™ again, and become Natural organizations?

What do Enlightened organizations need to do to Revolutionize Their Customer Experience™?

- consider the senses they are going to use
- build senses into their Moment Mapping®
- define how they are going to stimulate the senses
- look at using theater and entertainment as a method for providing a great Customer Experience
- provide training in acting techniques
- understand customer sensory expectations
- gain real alignment of the people, the culture, and the Customer Experience
- look to create captivating and memorable Customer Experiences
- review processes regularly
- involve the customer in their design.

Fall down seven, stand up eight.
Chinese proverb

Naïve to Natural™ self-assessment

Please answer the following questions and then transfer your score to the summary sheet at the end of Chapter 9.

15. Which of the following best describes the basis on which processes are designed?
    a. Changes to processes happen to focus around the customer. These are matched against the Customer Experience the organization is trying to deliver.
    b. Processes are designed on the basis of what is good and convenient for the company – usually done by product managers and product lines.
    c. All processes are reviewed to focus around the customer. These are matched against the Customer Experience the organization is trying to deliver.
    d. The customer is talked about but all processes are designed for the convenience of the organization. Design takes place in silo without consideration of the impact on other silos or the customer.

Your answer [   ]

a = 3 points, b = 1 point, c = 4 points, d = 2 points   Score [   ]

16. Which of the following best describes the depth to which "customer journey" maps have been created?
    a. No overall customer journey map exists. However, some rudimentary mapping by silo/function has been completed – but it is very transactionally based.
    b. Customer journey maps (including emotions) have been plotted at both strategic and tactical level – emotions have been intrinsically designed into processes.
    c. Customer journey maps (including emotions and senses) have been plotted at both strategic and tactical level – emotions and senses have been intrinsically designed into processes.
    d. No customer journey map exists.

Your answer [   ]

a = 2 points, b = 3 points, c = 4 points, d = 1 point   Score [   ]

9 Natural orientation

People seldom see the halting and painful steps by which the most significant success is achieved.

Anne Sullivan

Waynn Pearson, City Librarian, Cerritos Library, California:

Within the broad context of our storyline, "Honoring the past, imagining the future," we had to create a sense of place and community. At the beginning, as we sought to create a deliberate Customer Experience, it was like building a city or a village from scratch. What kind of place did we want to create? We always saw the library as a learning destination, a "Club Med for the mind," if you will. We wanted it to be a community gathering place. These considerations helped us shape the library's outside environment as well as the conference center on the third floor.

We considered the different needs – emotional, intellectual, and physical – that people have when they come to public spaces, and we tried to find ways to address as many as possible.

For example, one thing people are looking for is a sense of comfort. Southern California is hot and dry, and many public spaces are large, barren expanses of concrete. The area around the Cerritos Library was designed with numerous water features. This helps to convey an aura of coolness and calm, but also the particular water features around the library are designed to make people stop and interact with them. One water feature involves sculptured dolphins set among fluctuating water jets. My city manager always likes to say, "Waynn, everybody loves dolphins," but it is actually true – they do. Even on cloudy days, there are always kids running among the water jets, either trying to stay dry or trying to get wet, I'm not sure which. We also have a beautiful pond, called the Amaryllis pond, as you enter the Civic Center, by the parking structure. This is a Feng Shui space, with wonderful sculptures of frogs and other water creatures and many koi fish. The sound of the pond resonates around and is very soothing, so people find our environment pleasing before they enter the library. (The Amaryllis pond, in fact, has been the recipient of anonymous "gifts" of koi.) We have used the landscape around the library to adjust customers' perceptions and feelings before they enter the library.

Shortly after the library opened, I was riding up in the elevator with three teenage girls and one said, "This place is really cool isn't it?" The other replied, "Yeah, it's just like a mall"! You can't get higher praise from a teenager!

As you can see Waynn and his team at the Cerritos Library have spent a great deal of time creating a deliberate Customer Experience that recognizes the critical importance of customer emotions, and have also planned how to use the senses to evoke these. Every tiny detail is thought through to deliver the deliberate Customer Experience. These examples embody a number of the traits of a Natural organization.

There is another critical aspect of the Natural organization that must not be ignored. The people, the culture, and how people act on a day-to-day basis. This is always a challenge to explain in written form and it's a bit nebulous, but Robert Stephens, Founder and Chief Inspector (CEO), The Geek Squad, told us a wonderful story, which encapsulates it for me.

There are certain things that I have done as the founder; I like to think that I created the first version DNA. I like the concept of DNA because at some point if you are going to have a good culture, just like a bacterial culture, it has to replicate, grow, but somehow maintain part of its original form, whilst evolving to its environment and I think that is totally relevant to any company. To achieve this my job is all about influence and inspiration. Influencing people is the most effective and efficient low-cost way of affecting people's behavior. You do that through inspiration. Inspiration is the ability to maybe tell a story or do a wacky thing and it sets the tone to the people and they get the message and they go off on their own.

I'll give you an example; we all have badges in the Geek mobiles with names and titles, and so on. One day I came in and I saw a bunch of the special agents standing around some of the new cadets and I asked them what they were doing. It felt like some form of ritual. They were just initiating some other new cadets. I said, "I don't remember telling you or creating a policy for that." They said that they had just come up with this thing and they thought I knew about it.

They explained that, as a sign of loyalty to The Geek Squad, that they asked all the new agents to have their driver's license photos retaken in their Geek Squad uniforms. When I heard this I was blown away, it was like invasion of the body snatchers. I asked to see all of their licenses, and to my surprise every single one of them had photos where you could barely see their neck, a white collar and little piece of tie. It was eerie how they had organized themselves behind my back and decided on this as a group. I knew then that this was the ultimate; it was such a simple gesture. The guys had graduated; it was like Willy Wonka and the Chocolate Factory *at the end of the film. We now called it the* Willy Wonka *test, the unwritten things that you cannot dictate, you cannot write it in a manual.*

It is this kind of thing that sets us apart. I want to make The Geek Squad so that it is hard to copy I don't want it to be too systematized in that it can just be lifted.

This is what a Natural organization is all about. The customer and the Customer Experience are in the DNA: it's a living, self-perpetuating organism, where everyone just does things to improve the Customer Experience naturally. Would your organization pass the *Willy Wonka* test?

In the Enlightened organization, not only have emotions been understood and designed into the Customer Experience, it has also been realized that *depth* of emotion is important. The Natural organization has also realized that this is achieved by the extensive planning of stimulating the senses, as you can see from the previous examples.

Figure 9.1 and the following table show the report from a Natural organization.

Our algorithm places this airline in the Natural orientation, but in fact it has only just moved from the Enlightened orientation. One of the essential aspects of the Customer Experience it has learnt is the planned use of senses

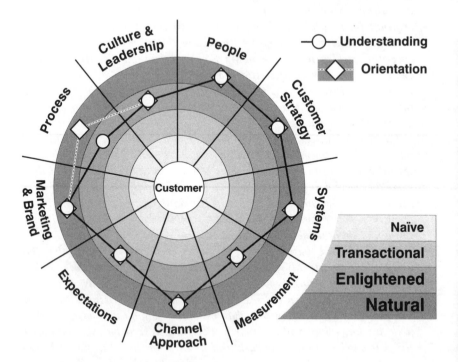

Figure 9.1 A Natural airline company

Orientation area	Orientation	Understanding
People	Natural	Natural
Strategy	Natural	Natural
Systems	Natural	Natural
Measurement	Enlightened	Enlightened
Channel approach	Natural	Natural
Expectations	Enlightened	Enlightened
Marketing and brand	Natural	Natural
Process	Enlightened	Natural
Culture and leadership	Enlightened	Enlightened

to stimulate and evoke emotions. However even the Natural organization has work to do to improve the Customer Experience. When we looked down into the indicator levels for this organization, we noted that:

- Customers' sensory expectations were not being captured.
- It understood that these needed to be included in the design of the processes.
- Once this has happened, these then need to be measured.

These are just a few of the items we noted that needed to be improved. There were others, so even when you have reached a Natural orientation don't think the work stops there!

These are the traits of a Natural organization. It has:

- a complete focus on the customer
- focused so much on the Customer Experience that it is in the organization's DNA
- a deliberate Customer Experience and a clearly defined Customer Experience statement
- built its system to improve the Customer Experience
- a culture that is designed, and aligned to the Customer Experience
- focused on depth of emotion
- consciously used sense to provide a captivating experience
- recruited people who are good at acting
- an integrated approach to the customer
- understood customer sensory expectations.

The Natural organization has customers in its DNA. It considers the customer throughout every part of the organization. You cannot have a meeting where customers are not mentioned. The Natural organization defines ways of even getting "deep staff" as we like to call them – employees who are the furthest from the customer – to engage customers. An example of this is Pret A Manger, which has "buddy stores." This means that everyone in the organization, without exception, spends time in one of its stores every quarter. The result is that everyone understands the customer and what customer-facing people have to deal with on a daily basis. One of the main differences is that the Natural organizations *deliberately* use the senses to Revolutionize Their Customer Experience™.

One example of the use of senses: when you pass building sites they now have "viewing holes" as they recognize that people are naturally curious to *see* what is going on inside. Another example in a similar vein is the growing number of restaurants that provide a window onto the kitchen. Not only can you *smell* and *taste* the food but also you can *see* it being cooked. The process is becoming part of the show, the story, the theater. Another extension of that is at Japanese restaurants where they cook your food on a table in front of you: now you can *hear* it being cooked as well. These examples, in their own small way, are bringing the organizations' processes, which were previously kept away from the customer, and putting them at the heart of the Customer Experience. They are making this part of the entertainment and a differentiated Customer Experience.

Consider a themed restaurant like the Rainforest Café where the animals periodically come to life and make sounds. You are plunged into darkness as the rain clouds form over the forest, and you see lightning and hear thunder. The Hard Rock Café has lots of loud music, great visual effects, and you can see all the rock memorabilia and take a nostalgic trip back in time.

Another great example is an office refurbishment organization that is looking to take the concept one stage further. This is a more technically advanced version of the viewing hole on the street. When it is renovating a building the organization plans to place a web cam on the floor it is renovating. Therefore the employees can view the camera over the Internet and see how their office is getting on. They can watch the progress being made and see what it looks like in terms of space. This also helps manage their physical and emotional expectations. Why do this? Well have you ever noticed that when you buy a house, over the months it takes to complete the sale, the rooms seem to get bigger in your mind? We have a tendency to exaggerate things in our minds if we don't see them for a while. With a web cam people can see the size of their offices, therefore helping to manage their expectations. This is the type of thought Natural organizations give to their Customer Experience.

Does it have implications for the organization? For instance, would the builders like being "on show" all the time? Of course it has implications, but the mindset of the Natural organization is different to the mindset of other orientations. It is wholly and totally focused around the customer. It would not even have this conversation as the builders, who would have been recruited for being very customer focused, would not even raise any issues – they would see the advantage for the customer and not even consider debating it. You see what we are debating here is an *internal* issue of what the builders would feel like. In the Natural organization the builders are proud to "show off" their work. This is another telltale sign of a Natural organization. If your organization would spend a lot of time debating the pros and cons of a decision like this, you are not a Natural organization.

The Natural organization understands how important the combination of senses are to its Customer Experience and has started to capitalize on this in the market.

Waynn Pearson, City Librarian, Cerritos Library, California:

> *We designed the library to appeal to all five senses, and we believe that we have succeeded. To reach people emotionally, we believe that you have to appeal to both sight and sound. By design, we provide a lot of "eye candy" for visual appeal, and we are not a typical quiet environment, but provide background music and other sounds, such as water and in the children's library the sounds of the rainforest. Many people visit us not because we are a library, but in spite of the fact that we are a library – and that is pretty cool – they see us as something other than just a library. We have this little byline that says, "All this and books too," which did not come from us or from some kind of marketing whiz but from a visitor. A few years ago, at the California Library Association's Millennium Conference, I gave a talk in which I used the phrase, "Convergence is the zeitgeist of the future." The Cerritos Library exemplifies that idea by merging the essential intellectual and learning qualities of the library with elements that have in the past been associated with theme parks or other entertainment venues. Our success is demonstrated by our foot traffic.*

Another example for using senses by Delia Bourne from Group Marketing at Hamleys:

> *Going back to the happy customers, when I have been to the Ideal Home Exhibition [Earls Court, London] and you get taken up with the salesman's patter and buy the whizzy pen or whatever it may be, you get it home and wonder, how does this work? They never seem to work as they demonstrate to you! All our demonstrations are very much hands-on with the customers. They don't just show the customer the product, they will give it to them, put it into their hand so they can touch and feel it and then have a go there and then before they buy it.*

"They put it in people's hands": this creates a connection, and the staff are using the sense of touch to create a bond. Another great example of use of the senses is a hotel we are aware of:

There is a hotel that has a very confused front area. The traffic is everywhere and the arrival and departure of guests is a very confusing experience as a consequence. Recognizing this, the hotel decided to do something about it. It could do little about the traffic but decided to have the concierge standing outside in a very visible uniform armed with a whistle. When the guests require a taxi, they are invited to ask the concierge. The concierge then stands in the street with his arm raised and, using the whistle he is provided with, whistles for a cab. This is not unusual, I hear you say. But in this case it is. The hotel knows the taxi drivers cannot hear the whistle, as there is too much noise going on, and they are cocooned in their air-conditioned cabs with the radio on! So why use a whistle? The purpose of the whistle is for the guests. It gives them a sense of reassurance that some order is coming from the chaos. It is part of the show!

Consider the impact on the psyche of the customer. Who are the types of people who have used whistles in your life? A number of them will be figures in authority: the schoolteacher in the school playground, the lifeguard at the swimming pool, a police officer, and a referee at a soccer game to name but a few. Planning this Customer Experience using a tool like Moment Mapping® is essential. With Moment Mapping® not only can you plan to evoke emotions, you can plan which sense to use to evoke that emotion. In this case the sense of sound created by the whistle is an Emotional Cookie™ evoking "confidence" that things are under control. The customers feel "assured" they are getting their cab. They "trust" the authority figure, the concierge, who will bring order from the chaos. All this from a whistle.

You see the easy thing would be to have missed this. I can imagine the conversation in one of the other orientations.

"There is too much confusion at the front of the hotel and it looks like chaos. What can we do to improve this?" "Why not dress the concierge in a bright uniform and get him to stand in the street with a whistle?" "I like the idea of the concierge, but there is no point in using the whistle as the taxi drivers can't hear them." "Yep, good point ... what color uniform should we give the concierge?"

The important point would have been lost in that split second the participants were discussing the whistle. They had already moved on. Why? Because they were focused on the transaction; they were focused on the task. They did not consider the effect on the customer. To the Natural organization every little detail is considered. Every little detail. Again this is a telltale sign.

We have a number of clients who, when we have shown them our Moment Mapping® tool, which plans such an interaction and includes what emotions and senses are integral to the process, have looked at us and said, "Do we really need to go down into that level of detail?" "Yes you do, if you are serious about Revolutionizing Your Customer Experience™." And in that split second, I look at their faces and see it is not a Natural organization. If they don't think it's necessary that's fine, they are the clients, but clients can be wrong!

Liam Lambert, Director and General Manager, Mandarin Oriental Hyde Park, London:

> *We started this at Mandarin Oriental in 1992. We had many focus groups within the hotel. We sat down and we wrote the Bible according to Mandarin Oriental. It was every standard you could possibly have and we actually called them Legendary Quality Standards. We counted them up and there was something like 1450. Far too many for one person to absorb. So we knew that these were the standards, we knew our guests' expectations, and we looked at these together from the guest perspective.*

Natural organizations are masters of detail.

So how do you evoke emotions, using sound, when the customer rings the call center? Well the Natural organization does not just accept the "standard" menu of sounds that are presented by the supplier, or leave it to someone in the organization to determine what music to play. It thinks outside the box. An insurance company we know has replaced its on-hold music with someone reciting poetry. It takes the customer by surprise and is a pleasant change to the "muzak" that is normally presented. Why can't your company tell jokes, if you are trying to create a "fun" Customer Experience? Why not list what is on TV that evening; why not have children singing badly as children do, if they are your target market? It doesn't have to be music.

But if you decide it is music you will play, as it will captivate your customer, the key question is, "What music?" How does it support your deliberate Customer Experience? The Natural organization has thought this through. But you also need to consider the other senses:

What smell represents your organization?

Have you thought about it? What smell exists in your Customer Experience today? In the shop, branch, rest room, reception of your HQ, and so on? There clearly must be one, so what is it? The Natural organizations have again thought this through.

According to our research 11 percent of organizations conduct market research to define which specific emotions and senses are required to meet their customers' expectations. However, only 4 percent of organizations talk specifically about how to meet and exceed customers' transactional, emotional, and sensory expectations, while 22 percent understand they should.

Let us give you an example. A number of you may have seen *It's a Bug's Life* in Disney World's Animal Kingdom, which provides a sensory Customer Experience. This is typical of this type of show, which is growing in popularity. In *It's a Bug's Life* you are given 3-D glasses, which make it look like the bugs are flying into the audience. As they do so, the flapping of their wings creates a wind, and again this simulates the feeling of touch. A dung beetle is also introduced, and the smell is not very pleasant, and then finally as the hornets fly around the room, one "stings" you, with a rod in the chair "poking" you in the ribs. All of this is done to great effect and great laughter. It is one of Disney's best attractions, and I would suggest this is the case because it is an assault on the senses. All the senses are used to heighten your experience. They have been planned. There would be little point in poking you in the ribs if hornets were not attacking you. It is the effect of seeing the hornets, hearing them, and feeling them via their wings flapping, and then being poked in the ribs that makes a great experience. Therefore you need to map all these moments of contact to produce the desired effect. Let us take this as an example. I imagine using Moment Mapping® for *It's a Bug's Life* would look something like this:

Table 9.1 Moment Mapping®: *It's A Bug's Life*

Moment	Action	Desired effect	Emotion	Sense being simulated
3-D glasses: bugs fly into audience	Give everyone glasses	Everyone tries to touch bugs	Anticipation	Sight, sound
Wind from bugs' wings starts to hit audience	Start wind machine and direct at audience	People feel wind on their faces	Surprise	Sight, sound, touch
More visual effects of bugs using 3-D	Create loud bang and visual explodes. Small amounts of water are sprayed over the audience	People are surprised at loud bang. People feel the berry juice hitting them	Excitement surprise, enjoyment	Sight, touch, sound
Dung beetle comes on rolling a dung ball	Start smell early to ensure it reaches audience	People smell the dung: released into audience	Disgust	Sight, sound, touch, smell
Hornets sting people	Ensure button is pressed at exact moment of sting	Hornets visually fly into audience. Fan starts to blow on audience. Small rod pokes people in the ribs as a "sting"	Surprise	Sight, sound, touch

You can use Moment Mapping® to plan the senses that you are going to implement to evoke specific emotions. Only 4 percent of organizations plot the Customer Experience at this level of detail at both strategic and tactical level, but 21 percent understand it should be done.

Another example of using the senses is when you visit Hamleys. At one time, on one of the floors you could hear the unmistakable sound of Darth Vader from Star Wars, breathing in the background. When you turned around there he was: a 6-foot Lego model with light saber in his hand and that haunting breathing! Natural organizations like Hamleys understand the significance of using the senses to evoke emotions. For instance Hamleys has an "open box policy". This is one of the signs for us of a Natural organization. You will recall that Naïve organizations typically have a "Do not touch" policy. Hamleys is the complete opposite to that: it has an "open box policy." This policy recognizes the fact that people like to see what they are buying and assess the quality by touching the toys. This is all built around the need for sensory interaction with the product.

Steven Hamilton, the Theatre Director, takes up the story:

> *Over the years with lobbying from the retailers the toy manufacturers have created boxes with windows in them so the customer can see exactly what they are buying. That is a step forward but we still get customers asking us to look inside. A lot of retailers would not like this, as when you open a product it is sometimes harder to sell after. Our answer is "Of course you can look inside." We take it out and show the customer what it does. The customers want to "connect" with the product; they want to see if it is value for money, what it involves, what the quality is like.*
>
> *The problem is that it is like a packet of crisps. When you buy a packet of crisps, you open the crisps and sometimes you may only have four crisps inside. I know I am exaggerating, but you get the point. You want to see what is in the box, you want to hold it, you want to look at it, you want to press the buttons, you want to shake it around, you want to put it on the floor and see if it does actually walk and flip over. And nine times out of ten you will buy the product as you know your child isn't going to be disappointed, it is safe if it does what it says on the box.*

What Hamleys has realized is that people have sensory expectations as well as physical and emotional expectations. Again, this is not normally recognized by the other orientations. A sensory expectation might be that you expect your food to come to you at a particular temperature. Now that may be somewhat basic, but it is very important in restaurants. What is the customer's sensory expectation? If you close your eyes now and think of a holiday to the seaside, what does it look like? Typically, people will tell us they can *hear* the sea, they can *feel* the wind on their face, they can *smell* the sea and the seaweed, they can *hear* the seagulls, they can *feel* the hot sand running between their toes. All these senses are built inside you, and as we have said before, these are your expectations. People expect to get boring music when they are put on hold during the telephone call to a call center.

The Natural organization and segmentation

Importantly the Natural organization has segmented its customers in a sophisticated way. It does not treat the customer as one amorphous mass. It has spent time thinking about their different needs. It has then spent time in aligning its Customer Experience to that segmentation. For example, Figure 9.2 shows the relative importance of different elements to different segments of a train company's customer base.

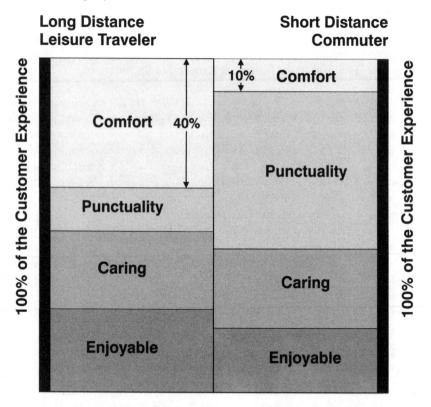

Figure 9.2 Customer Experience: transport

If you take the element of "comfort" in a train, this may be more important to the passenger who is traveling a long distance and who has paid for a first-class rail ticket than to the commuter who is simply traveling one stop up the line. The commuter may feel that punctuality is more important. In the work we have done with one train franchise the needs of the commuter, the leisure traveler, and the long distance traveler were all different. This did not mean that the franchise needed a new Customer Experience statement for each segment. However, it did need to recognize that the emphasis of each segment was different. The Natural organization understands this and not only amends its Customer Experience to meet that segment, but also realizes that each of these segments has different physical, emotional, and sensory expectations. In other words the experience recipe will be different for each customer segment but the basic ingredients remain the same.

The Natural organization is so customer-focused that it is just a state of mind. Let us give you another example from the airline industry. This is an example of lost bags. In many cases the airline knows shortly after you have arrived that your bags are not there. Most airlines wait for the customer to stand expectantly in line for their bags to come off the baggage carousel, evoking disappointment and anger when they do not appear. When this happens the customer locates the complaints desk to report the missing bag. He or she is asked to complete a long form before the airline swings into action. One airline has now put in place a process: when it is realized the bags are not on board, it contacts the destination airport and *pre-fills* a form ready for the customer to complete, as the airline has most of the basic information anyway. When the plane lands, the customer is immediately informed of the problem and asked to complete the final few questions for identification.

This is *proactive* and again another important trait of the Natural organization. This particular airline has also gone to some lengths to change the way it thinks about customers. For instance, internally it now classifies itself as being in the "leisure and entertainment" industry, not the travel industry. "So what?" I hear you say. Well, the leisure and entertainment industry has a different perceptive on life. This is an important part of changing people's mindset. To help this further it has implemented a program, with one of its partner hotels, where all airline staff now undertake the hotel's training courses. This is so that airline staff can learn how a hotel "serves" a leisure customer; from room service, to receptions, to making beds, all of which are equally important on an aircraft. A true piece of lateral thinking.

Natural organizations have realized that the employee experience needs to be the same as the Customer Experience, therefore they have aligned the two.

Robert Stephens, Founder and Chief Inspector (CEO), The Geek Squad:

If there is anything I could contribute uniquely to your book I would like to say that I think Customer Experience ultimately derives from employee experiences. What I originally thought was to differentiate ourselves to attract customers, but I had not known that the greatest impact on the Customer Experience was in that the uniform, these titles, these Geek mobiles, created a palette and some props to allow the employees to play a *character and that gave them an experience. These people **are** James Bond, they are Batman, only they are for real, they are the local celebrities and it's kind of the best of all worlds, they wake up everyday being themselves inside these costumes so we have given them this show to play themselves.*

Duane Francis, CEO, Mid-Columbia Medical Centre, Oregon

Ensuring we employ the right people and aligning our Customer Experience to our employee experience has seen us significantly reduce employee turnover. Currently it is about half what the industry average is. We have had a nursing shortage in the United States for the last two years, but we do not have any nursing positions open right now.

Mike Gooley, Chairman, at Trailfinders.

We insist our consultants are well traveled and they actually love and enjoy travel. They are personable, relate to people well, and have a good sense of humor. People who, generally speaking, get on with other people are the people that you tend to trust. The spirit in the company is very likeminded. I think we have just passed our 57th marriage where neither had set eyes on each other until they were both in full-time employment in Trailfinders. So they have a lot of things in common: same age, same social educational background, a great love of travel.

Therefore the people that the Natural organization recruits are totally aligned to the Customer Experience they are trying to give. The human resource, finance and IT parts of the business and any other internal function are measured on the delivery of the Natural organization Customer Experience to the rest of the company.

Organizationally the Natural organization may still have a VP of Customer Experience, but typically this person has been given more powers, or things may have evolved to a position where the Customer Experience is treated as natural and this role is no longer needed. If a person does have this role, then regular meetings are conducted with *all* parts of the organization to take a holistic view of the customer. This in turn helps the Natural organization adopt a seamless approach to the customer, which is facilitated by a "whole view" of the customer, irrelevant of business unit. Each part of the Natural organization has a measured focus on achieving the Customer Experience, and these include measurement of emotions and senses. Typically we have found that the balance of a Natural organization's key performance indicators is 30 percent physical, 40 percent emotional, and 30 percent sensory, with about 30 percent being internal and 70 percent being external customer measures.

The measurement of the Customer Experience is continued in the Natural organization. The best we have seen is in the entertainment sector. The BBC measures audience figures throughout the entirety of its programs. It knows exactly at what point the customer turns over to watch another channel or simply turns off the TV. This can be very enlightening. For instance in one program the BBC discovered that when the band came on, a number of people turned off. When the band was replaced with another group that was more acceptable, people kept viewing. Natural organizations know at which points the customers are *oblivious, distracted, engaged,* and *captivated.*

As the Customer Experience is so central to the Natural organization it will come as no surprise that classically the salary and bonus schemes in the Natural organization have a high degree of focus on achieving the Customer Experience, including emotional and sensory measures.

The high-level journey of a customer has been plotted into an experience map and the sublevels have also been defined. Here is an example from the banking industry in Figure 9.3.

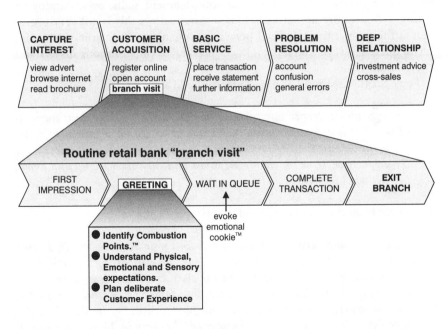

Figure 9.3 Moment Mapping®: retail banking

As you can see in the figure, the Natural organization has defined its very top-level process. It has then placed all of its subprocesses with each of the experience areas. Importantly this is independent of organizational structure, and from the customers' point of view. The Natural organization can then do a "deep dive" into the processes and into the detail and granularity of each of these. In the Natural organization this experience map and the underlying process are reviewed on a regular basis and maintained. This means that customer expectations are reviewed, and the processes are updated to ensure they are effective. Normally this is an area that other orientations fail to do. They have a "completed" mentality. In other words, they have now completed that task and do not have to worry about the process again for another 4–5 years. Nothing could be further from what happens in the Natural organization. They understand this and commit resources and people to maintain and update these regularly.

In the Natural organization the recruitment and culture of the organization is also different from the other orientations. The Natural organization realizes that one way to help engage the customer, help entertain the customer, and provide a show, is to look at its people and see if they can become part of the show. Over one in ten organizations is now employing people with the ability to act, role-play, and improvise. If an organization is using theater as a method for delivering a great Customer Experience, then it needs to train its people using acting and entertainment skills, even employing actors to "put more life into it." Our research shows this is not very prevalent at the moment, with only 2 percent of organizations focusing on acting techniques. However, interestingly, 39 percent of organizations understand they should be.

Peter Scott, Customer Service Director, T-Mobile:

> *We have used actors in our training to demonstrate what brings emotions alive, what it looks and sounds like, and how it feels for a customer. Actors are great because it creates an interactive learning experience, you can get the actors to increase the emotional input and turn the wick up and down, and see what happened.*

Let's hear from the retail entertainment people Hamleys.

> Delia: *It is more about your personality and your attitude, really, I think really the nature of the job, particularly the demonstrating side of the job, means that we look for larger than life characters. The demonstrators are all resting actors, dancers, magicians, lion tamers, flamethrowers, and so on. For example we have someone from* Blood Brothers *[a West End theater show] that works here and another who has been in TV commercials. It helps if they have had a background in the entertainment industry.*

This is great but only half the story. The Natural organization then needs to focus on how to get its people to perform, week in week out. The Natural organization has built a culture in its organization that recognizes this.

In Natural organizations they are focusing on the experience and not just the products. They have realized that the Customer Experience is not just about selling physical products. These offerings are also being segmented to different customers.

Some clever Natural organizations have realized this curiosity has reached such a peak that they can charge money for "behind the scene tours." People are so captivated by how it is done, the process behind the experience, or the product that they provide tours. I personally have attended tours showing you how beer is made, how whisky is made, what they do behind the scenes at NBC, the BBC, Disney, and Sea World. All these are creating an experience of their basic product. This is exactly the same as having a window on the building site; it is providing an experience of how these organizations operate. The Natural organization is proud of what it does and how it does it. Is there a demand to see it? Again this is a telltale sign. Do you have requests from people to see how your company operates? Would people pay for this experience?

The Natural organization also plays on the concept of "nostalgia." It sells products that can be collected and which create an affinity with the consumer. For example, Hard Rock Café sells pin badges and has created an industry of people buying and swapping these, as again Disney has. They think outside the square and consider what type of "experience" products they can sell. Let's hear from Steven at Hamleys about how it is now selling experiences as well as products: birthday parties and corporate parties.

> *We do not publicize the fact but we do birthday parties. But despite this fact we are booked up three months in advance and we only started doing them about two years ago as a bit of a side show. This is one of the areas that we are seeing people buy: experiences. Due to its success we have given up a fair part of the store for this. We have stepped it up and we have proved there is a considerable demand so we are now investing in a party area.*

These are great examples of how life is changing for the retailer. Space is now being given up to sell the experience. You can now buy experiences in a box in your local store. The Natural organization appreciates this and is capitalizing on it.

So in turning the page and completing the last self-assessment you will be able to complete the overall summary, which is also at the back of this chapter. This will give you an indication of the orientation you believe you are in. A larger test is available on our web site: www.beyondphilosophy.com. If you want to chat through your results then please don't hesitate to call or email our office.

But this is only the start … Now that you understand, what action are you going to take? What are the obstacles in your way? How are you going to embed the change in your organization? What are the barriers that will stop you? That is the subject we deal with in the next chapter.

> *I was taught very early that I would have to depend entirely upon myself; that my future lay in my own hands.*
>
> Darius Ogden Mills

Naïve to Natural™ self-assessment

Please answer the following questions and then transfer your scores to the summary sheet opposite.

17. Which of the following best describes the percentage of time senior managers spend with customers?
    a. A large amount of time.
    b. No time is spent with customers.
    c. A limited amount of time.
    d. A significant proportion of time.

Your answer [   ]

a = 3 points, b = 1 point, c = 2 points, d = 4 points   Score [   ]

18. Which of the following best describes your organization's complaints procedure?
    a. The organization has established a complaints department. Complaints are directed to it – there is little empowerment at the front line to deal with complaints.
    b. Complaints are treated with disdain.
    c. All our people are empowered to anticipate complaints and take proactive action to prevent and/or resolve them.
    d. Our customer-facing people are empowered to respond to and resolve complaints – they are authorized to spend significant amounts to achieve this.

Your answer [   ]

a = 2 points, b = 1 point, c = 4 points, d = 3 points   Score [   ]

Naïve to Natural™ self-assessment summary sheet

Now enter your scores from the end of each chapter and add the total of these scores together to find out which orientation your organization is in.

Chapter	Score
1	
2	
3	
4	
5	
6	
7	
8	
9	
Total	

To determine an indication of your Naïve to Natural™ orientation please take your score and see which category below you fall into. You can then go back and read the relevant chapter on your orientation. Please note this is only an indication, as in the book we have only used 18 of the 259 indicators that constitute the full Naïve to Natural Model™. A more complete version is on our web site: www.beyondphilosophy.com.

18–29 Naïve
30–47 Transactional
48–65 Enlightened
66–72 Natural

10 Understanding, action, and embedding

Others can stop you temporarily; only you can do it permanently.
Don Ward

A few years ago, during my time working in multinationals, I decided to attend a "behind the scenes" tour of Disney. I have always considered Disney as being great exponents of the Customer Experience and wanted to find out its secret. For a week, Disney staff presented their thoughts and showed us how they go about creating a great Customer Experience.

As I have always been a great believer in self-development, I have always been an avid reader of business books and have attended a number of business schools, including Harvard Business School. At the end of the week I sat quietly in my room at Disney, overlooking the Disney Institute with a blank sheet of paper in front of me. I wanted to capture a summary of what I had learnt.

*As I sat there I looked back over my notes and to my surprise I struggled to find anything of significance I had learnt. Yes, there were some nice bits, but nothing earth-shattering. I was shocked! This is Disney! Disney is renowned in the market for a great Customer Experience, it was far ahead of my own company's Customer Experience and yet I didn't learn anything? How could that be? Then it came to me like a blinding flash of the obvious. Disney had taught me things I knew already. But there was a critical difference between Disney and my organization. Disney had **implemented** the theory. We, I, my company, had not! In Disney it wasn't a theory, it was action, which had then been embedded. In my company it was just in other people's heads and mine.*

The biggest thing I learnt that week was the power of implementation. But this raised a bigger question in my mind, which was to stay with me from that day. If I knew what I should be doing, why wasn't I implementing it? As I sat there, I found myself making excuses...

- *They are different because ...*
- *It's easier for them because ...*
- *We don't have the money because ...*
- *Our market is different because ...*
- *We have started from a different position than they have and therefore it was easier for them ...*

As I like to put it, I was visiting the "land of excuses" and I had a great time justifying to myself my lack of action. I then realized these were just excuses. I realized the real answer as to why I hadn't implemented these things was:

I was not truly committed to the change, as perceived pain of change was greater than the pain of staying where we were.

In my experience this is true of many organizations today. This, in my view, is why the Customer Experience of most organizations is boring and bland. As you have seen from our research,[2] there are a lot of people who understand a great deal more about the Customer Experience than they have implemented. Like me, people enjoy the intellectual stimulation of the learning. They enjoy debating what they could do, and even what they should do. They enjoy reading the books, attending conferences and training events, and so on. But what has changed because of it? They may have changed their own personal "orientation" but the organization's orientation has not changed for the customers.

Therefore to Revolutionize Your Customer Experience™ it is key to go beyond the "understanding" and into the doing. You need to take "action" and then "embed" the change in your organization. *It is only when you embed something that this changes for your customers.*

Charles Handy[29] developed a great tool to explain this with his "S" curve. It can be used for many things. Handy says that as you go through your life, career or as an organization develops, initially everything goes well and you are on the way up: point X in Figure 10.1.

At some point this growth will plateau. You will stay at the top for a period of time but then you will start to decline. What Handy says is that as you start to come down the other side, you reach point Z and then you look around and realize things are going wrong, and you take action to change. This takes time to turn into positive growth again. However once this action takes effect you will start to move up the curve again.

Handy says that the time to change is when you have nearly reached your plateau, point Y, as this is the time you can then move on to the next stage of development and a new higher curve. This is the point when the organization has the most money and most resources. Most people don't do this though, as changing when everything around you seems great does not feel right. In my experience many industries miss the optimum time to change, and before they know it they are coming down the other side and chasing their tails. So where is your organization? Are you reading this book as things have started to go wrong? Or are you approaching the plateau and you have had the foresight to change? Whatever the case, "Understanding," "Action," and then "Embedding" are the key elements to Revolutionize Your Customer Experience™.

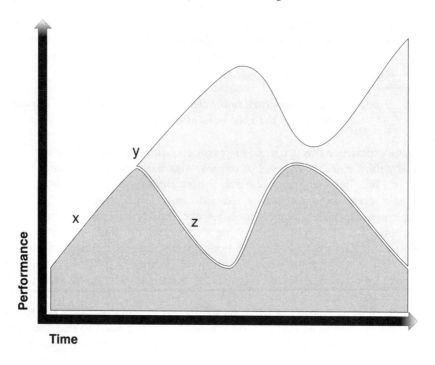

Figure 10.1 The Charles Handy "S" curve

Let's take this book as an example. You have invested a number of hours of your life reading it. I guess as you have been reading it you are now drawing some conclusions, and from the self-assessment you have an indication of which orientation you are in. Hopefully you also know some of the things you need to do to move into the next orientation. So what are you going to do? Nothing? Or something? The choice is yours. If it was just an intellectual exercise, I suggest you stop reading the book now and do something more constructive.

If you are going to do something, it will take work and there will be a number of obstacles in your way. We are going to explore what these are and how you can prepare yourself for them.

Over this chapter we are trying to give you our experience of working in multinationals and helping clients to do this stuff.

So let's start at the beginning. We have undertaken a great deal of research, and our Naïve to Natural Model™ typically demonstrates to our clients that they understand far more about the Customer Experience than they are actually doing and implementing. I challenge them, as I did myself that day at Disney, and say, "Why?"

Our research tells us that having achieved an orientation; there are three steps to changing and moving up an orientation.

1. *Understanding:* you need to understand more about the next orientation and what you are going to do.
2. *Action:* once you have understood what you didn't know, you then need to take action and do something.
3. *Embedding:* once you have taken individual actions/projects you must embed these in your organization to make a change permanent for your customers. This will then help change your orientation.

The Importance of understanding

The *Collins Concise English Dictionary* definition of understanding is:

1. *The act, state or feeling of a person who understands; comprehension, knowledge, sympathize awareness, etc.*
2. *The power to think, learn, judge, etc.*

Clearly, you need to understand something before you can take any action. The best model I have come across to explain this concept of understanding is the "conscious competence learning model."[30] This model shows that there are four levels of (increasing) competence:

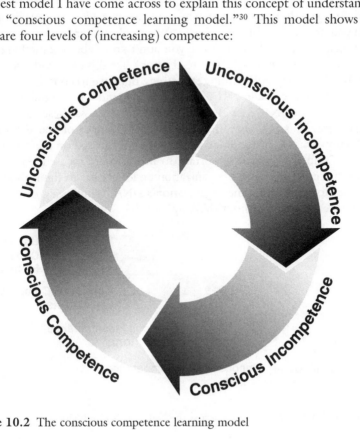

Figure 10.2 The conscious competence learning model

1. *Unconscious incompetence:* You don't know that you don't know.
2. *Conscious incompetence:* You do know what you don't know.
3. *Conscious competence:* You know and you do it.
4. *Unconscious competence:* You do it without having to think about it.

We all go through these stages when we learn anything and wish to become competent. To bring this to life when I was first explained this theory, I was given the example of learning to drive a car. If you have not ever seen or heard of a car before, you would not know that you couldn't drive it – *unconscious incompetence*. Once you discover a car for the first time, you would realize that you cannot drive it – *conscious incompetence*. Then when you learn to drive, you take all the correct actions but you need to consider them – *conscious competence*. Finally, you are doing it automatically; you do not have to think. Everything is automatic, and you drive home and cannot remember driving home as you have just done it automatically, naturally – *unconscious competence*.

The same steps happen as you discover more about the Customer Experience. At first, you don't know what you don't know. This is prior to "understanding." You don't even know why the Customer Experience is important. Then you discover why it is, maybe by having a Customer Experience yourself, which makes you think. You realize you don't know about something. Then you take some action. Maybe you read a book like this or attend a seminar or tour. You focus on implementing something but have to consider each action you take. Finally, you know what you are doing, and it is Natural.

We believe our Naïve to Natural Model™ fits across these four levels of competence. This is shown in Figure 10.3. A number of Naïve companies don't know what they don't know. They are not focused on the customer, as they don't know why it is important to be customer-focused. At the other end of the scale, the Natural organization no longer has to think about being customer-focused. It's in the organization's DNA. It builds a great Customer Experience naturally, without thinking.

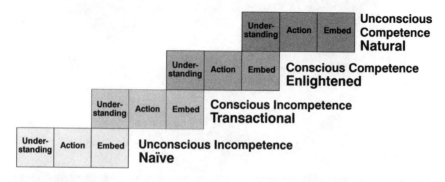

Figure 10.3 Competence levels across the Naïve to Natural Model™

The importance of "getting it"

The Customer Experience as a concept is a new area, and as such people are still only learning about it. We spend a great deal of time in converting people from unconscious incompetence to conscious competence. You will read some of the results of our training programs in the Yorkshire Water case study in the next chapter.

In our experience of the last seven years the most important thing that needs to happen is that people in the organization, in particular the board members, firstly need to understand what a Customer Experience is, how it manifests itself, and why it is important. In short people need to "get it." This is not an elegant phrase, but it is true. A few years ago we struggled to make ourselves understood to people who were not looking at the world as we were. We discovered we were not using the right language and not explaining it in an easy to understand manner. People were confused and they couldn't see what we saw, they couldn't picture what we had discovered. But over the years we have developed a very effective method of getting this over to people, one that we now use extensively. In essence we anchor the Customer Experience back into the reality of people's day-to-day lives. We talk about Customer Experiences they have had. There is no more satisfying part of the day, when the light comes on in a delegate's mind. It is satisfying because we are asking people to do something that is quite hard, to look at the world from a different paradigm, to look at the world through a different lens. We are asking people to examine the things that they have known to be true for years and put a different interpretation on them. This is all about "understanding," and ensuring people understand the Customer Experience is key for an organization to be able to Revolutionize Your Customer Experience™.

Interestingly enough, to date, we have not met anyone who has said, this is a load of rubbish and it is not happening. After some explanation of the new paradigm everyone buys in. Whether they then do something about it is entirely different! But one of the first steps is not to underestimate the importance of "getting it." It is vital that the senior team "get" this stuff. Again you will see how critical this was, *and is*, from the case study of Yorkshire Water in the next chapter.

Knowing me, knowing you

Understanding is not just about understanding the concept of the Customer Experience, it is also about being aware of what your Customer Experience is actually like. Who better to tell you this than the customer?

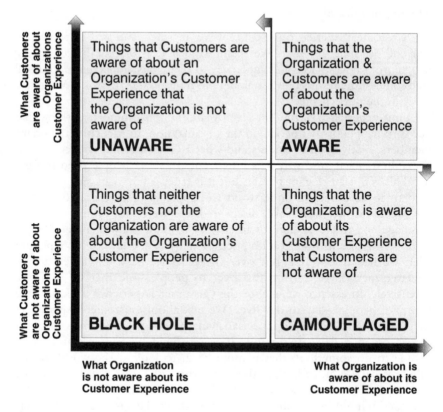

Figure 10.4 "Knowing me, knowing you" Customer Experience framework

Let us examine each of the zones in Figure 10.4.

Aware: this is where both the organization and the customer are aware of what the organization's Customer Experience is like. For example, the store is open between 10.00 am and 8.00 pm.

Camouflaged: this is where the organization is aware of its Customer Experience but the customer is not. For instance, all the calls are answered in India. Staff on the sales floor are paid on commission only. The reason it take four days for delivery is that the organization does not carry stock. The customer can become distrusting of the organization if these things are revealed at any point.

Unaware: this is where the customer is aware of the organization's Customer Experience but the organization is not. For example, delivery is so unreliable that customers always phone to check a delivery is on time. Or a particular member of staff is very rude when talking to customers. There is a cost of failure for organizations in this zone.

Black hole: this is where neither the organization or the customer is aware of the organiation's Customer Experience. For example, the store is just about to run out of stock of a product. Again, organizations have no control in this area and are prone to service and experience failures.

This is a useful model to assess your understanding of the Customer Experience. The idea is that you try to increase your understanding of your Customer Experience as much as possible, in order to minimize the effects of the Black Hole, Unaware and Camouflaged Zones. In your quest to Revolutionize Your Customer Experience™ it is important that you increase your company's understanding of what it is possibly not aware of. This can be achieved by talking with your customers more, and by looking critically at your Customer Experience and getting people to think through what the Customer Experience is about. In doing so, you will have the data that you will need to Revolutionize Your Customer Experience™. As we said before, all of this means nothing unless you are going to do something and take action.

The importance of action

Definition of action:
1. The doing of something.
2. An act or things done.
3. Bold and energetic activity.

You may not be responsible for your company's past but you are responsible for its future.

Anon

When we use the Naïve to Natural Model™ with clients, we look at what they are doing, what they know they should be doing, what action they have taken in the past, and what action they are taking today. "Action" is the one we have the most debate over. Clients will tell us about the committees they have set up. They show us wonderful plans written in MS Project. They tell us what they are "going" to do. They show us minutes of the meetings. But while all this is encouraging, in our view this does not come under the category of taking "action." Let us be very clear. Taking a pen out to write a project plan could be classed as taking action, but not by us. Calling a meeting of your team to discuss the matter could be classed as taking action, but not by us. We are not saying that you should not be doing these things, what we are saying is they are not what we would class as "action." When we talk about "action" we are talking about the act of changing something from what it was previously to something different. Our experience shows that until this happens it can be just talk.

In my career, I have personally managed projects which everyone internally agreed to and which everyone said were wonderful and that they fully backed them. But when we then asked them to do something, you start to see people change their tune. "Action" in our book is about changing something. Doing things is the only thing that will make a difference. Doing things! We believe this so much we have named our company Beyond Philosophy™. We believe that it is good to have a thought or a philosophy, but that you have to go beyond that and do something.

After action comes embedding.

The importance of embedding

Definition of embedding:
1. To set or fix firmly in a surrounding mass.
2. To fix in the mind, memory.

This is the toughest one, and the most important. We believe that you can only change the "orientation" of your organization in the eyes of the customer if you embed the actions. Embedding means it is no longer an isolated action. It is part of your being; you are doing this as a matter of course. It means, "This is the way things are done around here." It includes a process for organizational learning, to refresh and improve on what you have done. It is only when you reach here that you change your orientation. Undertaking action for action's sake is a waste of time.

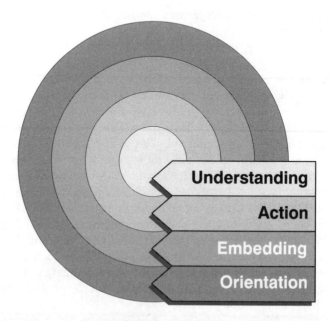

Figure 10.5 The steps to changing orientation

Actions can be placed under the category of "stuff" if they are not embedded. Why am I so disparaging? Because they never get anywhere! All that happens is there is a lot of action and resources ploughed into them and then they are not embedded into the lifeblood of that organization.

Let me give you an example:

*With one of our clients we had been working with them for some time. It was obvious to me nothing was really happening. Lip service was being paid to actually implementing any change. Why? They were not **really** committed. I decided to see their president and confront him. After a bit of a chat I asked my question, "Are you serious about this? Or just playing around, because if you are just playing around with this I suggest you stop, and save yourself the money. If you are serious then you need to be serious and do something!" He was a bit surprised by my candor but was appreciative of the challenge. Not many people challenged him. He agreed they were not really taking it seriously and that they did need to make a decision one way or the other.*

He called together a meeting for his main board within two weeks and asked me to attend and present my challenge. He told them he was disappointed with progress, especially as they had agreed it was the right thing to do. They all committed to take it more seriously. You see the president was able to inflict some pain on them. The pain of staying where they were was far less than the pain the president could inflict. They are now undertaking a great deal of work and reaping the rewards.

Therefore we repeat the question for you and your organization:

Are you serious?

If you are not, then don't bother. Save your time and money and opt for an easy life, as there is no "pixie dust." We can only reiterate the words of Winston Churchill at the beginning of the Second World War:

All I can offer you is blood, sweat and tears.

Having said this, do be aware! A total of 95 percent of senior business leaders believe this is the next competitive battleground, and if they are right, and you do not do anything, you have a problem, as you will be left behind.

Let us ask you another question. Is there something you could undertake that would improve your Customer Experience today? We are sure there is. So why are you not doing it? What is the reason? Like the story at the beginning of the chapter about my experience at Disney, I would suggest that consciously or subconsciously you have made a decision not to act on the knowledge you have. Let us look at the typical factors that stand in your way of taking action and embedding a new Customer Experience that would Revolutionize Your Customer Experience™.

Why people know what they should do, but don't do it

The simple answer is this:

> *They are not truly committed to the change, as perceived pain of change is greater than the pain of staying where they are.*

There are many barriers to Revolutionize Your Customer Experience™. As usual the reason stated is not normally the real reason the work is not moving forward, but instead a convenient excuse to hide behind. So let's look at these excuses. We have grouped them into the following five categories:

1. Not enough...

Typical objections:

- "Not enough time…"
- "Not enough money or resources…"
- "We are doing these other important projects."

2. Make it sound more difficult than it actually is

Typical objections:

- "I don't want to do this so I am going to make it sound more difficult than it is."
- "We have always done it this way."
- "How are we going to measure it?"
- "This does not align with our vision, mission and values."
- "I don't think we have the skills to undertake this."
- "I don't think we have the skills in the organization."
- "I know XXX does this but they are different, different markets, etc."

3. Deflecting the issue/blame

Typical objections:

- "I don't think the CEO wants to do this…" In other words: "I don't want to do this so I'm going to use the name of someone powerful in the organization to put the others off."

- "I don't think the executives are really bought in."
- "You want me to do that: then I will need to stop XXX [something important]."
- "How do we know this really works?"

4. The nay sayers

Typical actions. They will…

- attack you to show how clever they are
- put you down in public to gain political advantage
- wonder what's in it for them
- not like others taking the limelight or coming up with good ideas
- worry how this will challenge the status quo.

5. Say one thing, do another

Typical actions. They will:

- think that just because a decision has been taken they do not need to take any further action
- think planning means action – it makes them feels good
- present things that exaggerate the truth
- think that talking about things makes them sound important.

The final one is "We are so busy at the moment." The old adage remains true: "If you want something done, give it to a busy person."

> *If you always do what you have always done you will always get what you always got.*

As we outlined in Chapter 1, in our experience the danger is we can fill our days with "stuff." And boy, are we good at it. Stuff takes time, stuff makes us feel good, stuff fills our diary, stuff makes us look important, stuff is hard work, but stuff will not get you where you want to go. When people say they are busy or they haven't got the money or the resources, they are really saying, "This is not a priority." They *do* have the time, the money, and the resources; they are just choosing to use them elsewhere. Effectively they are saying that whatever they are doing is more important than improving the Customer Experience. This tells me something about their organization's orientation.

> *I always say to people, "Life is a choice … if you wanted to you could get up out of your seat now, catch a plane and fly off somewhere, and not let anyone*

know; you could never be seen again." Most of us choose not to for many reasons. But it is a choice. So when people say to you, "We cannot revolution-ize our Customer Experience because ..." it is rubbish. They can do what they want; it is just they have chosen not to.

Your job is to find out which is the case, and to structure your thoughts and actions accordingly.

The key issue is once you understand something to then take *action*. Most people don't. Therefore, there is competitive advantage to be found in implementation and engagement skills, and these should become key organizational competencies that should be built and nurtured and grown.

> **Competitive advantage comes from doing things others are not doing and cannot do.**

What excuses can really mean

- "I'm lazy. If we carry on doing what we have always done I don't have to think very much as I have precedents on which to make decisions and justify myself. That means I can do things without thinking about them."
- "I am scared. I have spent my life being good at the physical side of busi-ness and now you are asking me to be good at the emotional and sensing side and I am not sure if I am. Anyway why would I want to take the chance?"
- "I am not intelligent. I am not sure I understand this anyway so I will just ask some hard questions and hope it will go away."
- "I will be putting my bonus at risk. I am good at doing my job as it is and I am paid a lot of money as my bonus is paid on this."

Some of the real drivers that need to be addressed, as they are the internal reasons for failures

- Culture: the culture is not aligned to the change that is required. The culture restricts the ability of the organization to change.
- Poor leadership: people not being led in the right manner. Saying one thing, doing another.
- Apathy: is it really worth it?
- Initiative fatigue: this is just flavor of the month and if we keep our heads down it will go away.

In the middle of difficulty lies opportunity.
Albert Einstein

What you must do to make sure you are successful

- Adopt a principle of "Once we agree, then we do" – critical to the success of any project.
- Learn by doing – there is no substitute for experience, have a go, see what it's like.
- Adopt a process of ready, fire, aim – don't spend time perfecting things otherwise you will end in analysis paralysis. Instead start to implement and then adjust things as you go.
- Undertake a strategic and a tactical track – most organizations we work with have a desire, a need to prove this is working. Also the board wishes to see some quick wins. Therefore, we use an analogy. Imagine you are running a dog sledge and there are wolves chasing you. To keep the wolves busy, you sometimes need to "throw meat off the sledge" to occupy the wolves while you are busy making your escape. Therefore, undertake some tactical work to throw meat off the sledge. This should not be done to the exclusion of the strategic work but as well as it.
- Build a compelling story. Carry out a relevant communications exercise – a compelling story is vital to any change. Remember what we said earlier about storytelling. Time needs to be spent crafting this and then making it live in your organization.
- Construct a business case – "Show them the money." We have a number of business cases we have helped clients to write to prove the return that Revolutionize Your Customer Experience™ can have.
- Scope the project – make sure you know what you are tackling.
- Prioritize on those initiatives that deliver the maximum return – enough said.
- Run a pilot – prove it works and is not just a theory.
- Provide examples of how other companies should have done it – draw analogies with other organizations.
- Learn from other industries – the Naïve to Natural Model™ can provide you with an assessment against the many organizations we have now done this with.
- Increase understanding of the project with influential people – understand who the stakeholders are and make sure you put in place a plan to keep them abreast of any developments.

The most difficult barriers to overcome: the political barriers and how to deal with them

When I was in multinationals, people and friends outside work would ask me what I did for a living. I used to say, "I play chess." That was what it felt like. I equated company politics to chess, and to be successful we are all forced to play. Like chess, you need to think a number of moves in advance and predict what the other person is going to do and when. You then need to consider your moves well in advance, and plot different scenarios. I estimate in my final role, I spent 20 percent of my time on politics and a further 20 percent of my time attending meetings, which were a waste of time, but which I felt I needed to attend. In hindsight a sad thing to admit. But you cannot escape the fact that politics plays a big part in many organizations and can contribute to the reasons why organizations do not move through the cycle of understanding, action, and embedding. Politics can stop an organization from revolutionizing their Customer Experience.

Unfortunately to get things done you certainly need to understand how the politics work. You need to know who the "players" are. You need to understand who the people are who influence the players, and then plan your moves well in advance.

So in summary it is important that you follow the Understand, Action, and Embed™ cycle if you truly wish to Revolutionize Your Customer Experience™. In the next two chapters we case study two organizations that have Revolutionized Their Customer Experience™. One organization we have worked with: Yorkshire Water, while the other, Build-a-Bear Workshop, we have not. You will see and understand both of their approaches in how to Revolutionize Your Customer Experience™!

Success on any major scales requires you to accept responsibility – the one quality that all successful people have.

Michael Korda

11 Case study: from the most ridiculed to the most respected

The Kelda Group has turned itself from one of the most ridiculed water companies in the 1990s, into one of the most respected. It is now the second best performing company in terms of service levels and has developed a record for steady financial performance...

Financial Times, December 6, 2002

Yorkshire Water business customers have again placed the company top of all UK utilities in terms of customer satisfaction.

Energy Information Centre, December, 2003

WINNER – 2003 Gartner European CRM Excellence Award (Paris)
WINNER – 2003 Utility Industry Achievement Awards – Customer Care
WINNER – 2003 National Customer Service Awards
"Best use of technology in Customer Service"

Knowing Kevin Whiteman, the Managing Director of the Kelda Group, as well as I do, I am sure he will not mind me saying that it is not the most glamorous of companies. The group is made up of Yorkshire Water, Loop Customer Management, Aquarion (a water company based in Connecticut in the United States), and Keyland Developments (a property management company).

Yorkshire Water accounts for the majority of the Kelda group, and it provides a basic, but vital, service. The organization provides clean water to 5 million residential and business customers, as well taking away the wastewater and sewerage generated by these customers. Glamorous it is not!

But that is the very reason why we have chosen to feature it – to show you how it has gone about moving from the "most ridiculed to the most respected organization."

We want to share with you how it has Revolutionized Its Customer Experience™ and why it now enjoys the headlines listed at the beginning of this chapter. Importantly, you will also hear about the massive effect this has had on all its business and the financial returns it has brought. If you are in any doubt, below are the statistics to prove that a revolution has taken place in Yorkshire Water.

Here are some of its achievements:

- Opening times doubled from 37 hours to 85 hours per week.
- Customers are now offered narrower appointment time bands. A two-hour time band replaces morning or afternoon bands.
- A reduction in written complaints by 40 percent.
- A reduction by 20 percent of operational calls being received due to infrastructure improvements and implementation of systems and new procedures.
- A significant reduction in the number of repeat calls from customers.
- An increase in the number of calls closed on first contact.

This has resulted in:

Reduction of 50 percent unnecessary jobs.

Customer satisfaction up from 53 percent to 91 percent!

£8.5 million (approx $ 15.5 million) of financial savings made as a direct result of improving its Customer Experience!

We are certain that any organization would be proud of achieving these figures, and therefore surely this is enough reason for featuring Yorkshire Water. But there are two other very important reasons why we believe that it is a good case study:

1. It is not a new company. A great deal of business books look at how new companies manage to take their chosen market by storm. This approach is, of course, interesting but the advantage is that a new company has a blank sheet of paper. It is far more difficult when you have legacy people, legacy systems and processes, legacy customer perceptions, and legacy everything else!
2. Yorkshire Water operates as a regional monopoly within the privatized UK water industry:
   It does not have competitors. In addition it cannot generate additional revenues by encouraging people to use more water. In fact it is targeted to reduce people's consumption and therefore its revenue.

   An Act of Parliament prevents anyone else from selling water to the majority of the customers in the region. So forget improving the Customer Experience to gain loyal customers, it doesn't need to! Forget doing this to survive, it cannot go out of business! Forget doing this to increase sales, it cannot! What makes this case so interesting is that the activity it has undertaken has been done for many other reasons; reasons which are fascinating to explore. The question I have always posed to the company is, "Why bother?" You will soon understand why, as we reveal its journey of moving from the "*most ridiculed to the most respected.*"

This story starts back in 1995. The UK was going through one of its warmest summers in years. The water companies had been privatized under Margaret Thatcher, some six years earlier, in 1989. Years of under-investment, by both the government and formerly the local authorities, in the infrastructure of the water network had left the new water companies in a poor state.

For those readers not from the UK, Yorkshire Water is located in Yorkshire in the north of England. The organization employs around 5000 people, including its key service partners (utility contractors) who are employed to deliver the service to their customers. In 1995 it had not rained for 18 months in the western part of the region. The reservoirs feeding this area were very low and Yorkshire Water's under-invested network could not transfer water between east and west. In short the people in the west were facing the prospect of being without water. This threat was making national headline news, and the media took great delight in pillorying the organization for not being in a position to deal with the situation. Herculean efforts were undertaken by the company to solve the problem, and the threat of standpipes in the street to supply water did not materialize due to the hard work of a lot of Yorkshire Water employees. The crisis was averted, but still left a deep scar on the organization and the community it serves.

We started working with Kevin Whiteman, the Managing Director, and his team some time ago, and rather than me tell their story of how they have moved from the "most ridiculed to most respected," let's talk with Kevin and let him explain the journey for you. It's a story about how Revolutionizing Your Customer Experience™ can have a massive effect in many, many areas.

Colin: *Firstly congratulations on the wonderful results you have been getting recently. Can you tell us about the journey you have been on to Revolutionize Your Customer Experience™ since the drought?*

Kevin: *The organization came out of the drought in the mid-1990s having failed at nearly every level of business. Our basic service, which is a reliable, continual supply of clean water, had almost stopped. Customers were correctly upset. Emotionally we had really hurt them. It's interesting, although people tend to see us as a traditional organization, it is surprising the degree to which our business has a real emotional connection with customers and in fact everyone in the region. Water sustains life and they felt that we had well and truly let them down, both as customers and as a region.*

A group of us joined the company after that period as a new management team. It was clear that we needed to get the physical side of the Customer Experience right before we did anything else. Our customers *told us that this was fundamentally about **reliability** – the service had to be reliable and always there. We also needed to be **responsive** – so when customers contacted us we would respond and **resolve** their problem. It wasn't about saying, "Have a nice day," it meant that we had to solve their problems. We were still very oriented around resolving physical service issues.*

We put a lot of effort and energy into improving the physical Customer Experience just so people would say, "These guys are doing a decent job." It's funny to look back now, it doesn't sound a lot now, but at the time it was quite aspirational. Over the next three or four years we worked very hard to achieve that, we kept our heads down; there was very little effort at the emotional connection with customers. At that stage we just wanted to be a service that nobody knew was there.

Once we achieved that and we had reached the stage where the physical Customer Experience was good, we started to look to the future again. We decided to engage customers emotionally so we did some quirky things. We introduced "Tap Idols" where we had actors wandering about in ice cream vans in funny costumes, giving away jugs of water – just trying to make things fun. We hoped customers would think that dealing with us was enjoyable and interesting and not just see us as a water utility.

We started thinking about various management ideas and business philosophies. The "Customer Experience" was one that seemed to match our thinking as we tried to shift from just being an organization that lays pipes and delivers a clean quality product, into being a company that provides an emotional and enjoyable Customer Experience.

That's when we came across you guys. Using the Beyond Philosophy™ methodology we developed a "Customer Experience Hierarchy of Needs" which articulated for the first time the Customer Experience that we are trying to deliver, importantly both from a physical and an emotional point of view.

This drove us to think about how we should deal with customers and meet their needs at an emotional level. Importantly this wasn't constructed by a few of us sitting in a darkened room and determining what we thought, crucially it was in consultation with our customers.

*As you can see from the diagram [Figure 11.1] our customers told us that at a basic level they wanted **reliability**, **responsiveness**, and **resolution**. These were basic requirements that we focused on after the drought. However, from an emotional perspective our customers told us they wanted to **trust** us, they wanted to feel **assured** when they were dealing with us, they wanted to feel that we **cared**, and that we **valued** them. We also wanted to make it an **enjoyable interaction**.*

We are now investing our time and effort in driving the emotional aspects of the Customer Experience.

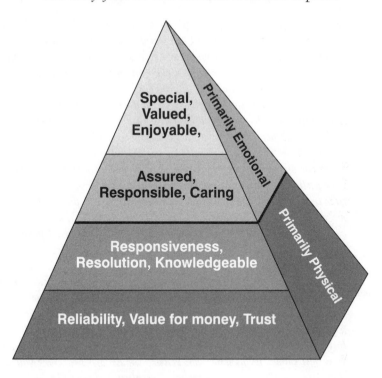

Figure 11.1 Yorkshire Water's Customer Experience triangle

*A number of people ask how we do this. Well we are looking at our processes and our measurement and a number of other areas. Let me give you a recent example where we were trying to combine an important business message and show that we are **enjoyable** to deal with. On April 1st this year we announced to the world that we had developed a drink that would help you lose weight! This was quickly picked up by the media and very soon the TV cameras arrived and the press. We provided interviews with customers who said that they had lost an amazing amount of weight by drinking this drink. This was in the media all day. We received some 10,000 calls into the organization with people wanting to find out more! ... but as I said, it was April 1st, April Fool's Day! It was an April Fool's Day joke with an important business message.*

*Our customers and everyone loved it, and it played on TV all day. This stunt was conceived and delivered to underline and reinforce the defined Customer Experience of **enjoyable**. At the same time however there is a very serious business message that underlies the message we were giving out. This business message was that we provide a high-quality low-cost product – drinking water. Drinking water is good for* *you and is not fattening! So if you drink water and not other drinks that contain calories, you will loss weight! Thus we managed to provide an **enjoyable** Customer Experience but also get over a serious message.*

Colin: *I saw the coverage as well and everyone was talking about it. Kevin, you know one thing that has always fascinated me about your organization is that you don't really need to do this. You are in a monopoly situation. So why bother doing all this work to revolutionize your Customer Experience?*

Kevin: *The main reason is initially in the mid-1990s Yorkshire Water was voted the worst company in Britain. This was a huge motivation for me personally, my new management team, and everyone else in the organization to turn the situation around. We asked ourselves, "What do we want to be?" Our answer was, "We want to be the best." To be the best you have to go further than anyone else. We wanted people to talk about us as being a fantastic water company. We believe that it is not just doing the physical things, there are a lot of companies that are good at that, if you are the best you have to go beyond that and provide an emotionally engaging Customer Experience as well.*

The really interesting aspect of this story is as we started to move from a physical experience into an emotional experience we actually created huge efficiencies as well! We discovered that when you start improving your Customer Experience you reduce the amount of work you have to do. Our complaints, for instance, are plummeting. This is because we not only provide a good quality experience, but are now also engaging customers at an emotional level. We have also gone from being bottom of the service leagues to top, and from being well down the efficiency league tables to top, so we've managed to do both.

Originally our intention wasn't to save money, and in fact a lot of people said that it would cost money. We have found that this is not the case. We have saved money and improved our Customer Experience.

There are other examples of where we've managed to improve the Customer Experience and save money. For instance, in the Loop Call centers, we discovered that approximately 25 percent of our calls were repeat calls. This was mainly because we hadn't done what we said we were going to do for the customer. Not only did we fail physically, but we failed to build trust or show them that we cared. We would continually send engineers to meet customers when we didn't need to. In addition, they would arrive at the wrong time and would miss appointments. This means that you would have to send the engineers again – often two or three times! This costs money and is annoying for the customer. So if you can deal with the customer at the first point of contact in the call center and solve their problem this improves your Customer Experience and costs £2–8 compared with £60–70 ($105–122) to send an engineer in their own van.

So if you can get it coordinated and correct, not only do you create a good Customer Experience, but it is actually a cheaper way of doing business. This means if the customer feels good about it then the financial savings impact on the longer term because you store up "good will" with the customer that is bound to stand you in good stead if things get a bit difficult in the future.

Colin: *So improving the Customer Experience saves money. What about the share price? Does improving the companies Customer Experience positively affect the share price?*

Kevin: *I'm absolutely convinced it does. The stock market is like anything else; it works on perception as well as reality. If every bit of news they get is about a transformed company, about our growing reputation of being an efficient company that delivers a good Customer Experience, about us being the best water company in the country, about us being an organization that has changed itself from one of the most vilified to one of the most respected, then it becomes self-fulfilling! The* Financial Times *quoted us last year and the market responds to that.*

Colin: *I know we have chatted many times about the positive effect on your people of improving the Customer Experience. Could you tell us a little more?*

Kevin: *People love to work for a company of which they can be proud; in my view it is the biggest motivator of all. If you have come from where we were then – where our people were insulted in the street – right through to the press saying "Yorkshire Water is doing a great job now," it becomes a source of pride. If you work for a company you are proud of and the company can maintain this position, it is the biggest motivator of all bar none.*

Colin: *So we sit here today and I know from working with you there has been a lot of work that has gone into improving your Customer Experience. Looking back over the journey, what would you say the main challenges have been?*

Kevin: *One of the key challenges is culture. When you are in an organization that is traditionally very engineering-focused, creating a culture and leadership style where people recognize that we live or die on our ability to be oriented around the customer is a challenge. The real issue is about alignment at the top. If the leadership and direction from the top is that the Customer Experience is everything, then people will respond and it will create the right culture.*

You see we had to decide if we were an asset management or a Customer Experience organization. Quite clearly we are a Customer Experience company. In this industry, we obviously need to be experts and excel at asset management to be able to deliver a good Customer Experience. It is about my team and I setting the agenda, then ensuring our people understand that managing our assets is actually only about the better managing of customers. We are responsible for changing our employees' focus. Today everyone who manages the pipe network knows it is also his or her job to make sure that the customer is happy. Not only are they focused on looking after the pipes but they need to look at how we can improve processes to ensure a positive impact on the customer.

The reality is that there is still a lot more to do – we now need to encourage them to not only look at the physical aspects of the Customer Experience but also how they impact on the customer emotionally.

Colin: *So when you started to talk to people about emotions in an engineering-based company what was the response?*

Kevin: *As a senior team we had to take time to understand if we wanted to do this – was it just all a bit ethereal or would it have a real impact? We had some fairly heavy discussions. For instance, if we went ahead with it what would it entail? If we are going to do it were we all signed up to it? Did we believe in it? The answer was that we did. The reality is that it entails quite a lot – a new way of thinking – but we reached the stage where we said and believed it was the right thing. We then put some weight behind it and we started to see some really interesting results.*

In the early days there was quite a bit of skepticism about what it all means. But there has now been a real change. The best thing for me is there is real excitement about it, people in the business like it, and we have quite a head of steam now. We want to be "known as the best" and if we really want to differentiate ourselves then we have to do something more than the other organizations are doing.

Colin: *Why are people excited by it?*

Kevin: *We've allowed our people to put a different pair of glasses on for the first time. People like to give a good Customer Experience. But histori-cally our Customer Experience was poor, not because people didn't want to do it well but because the systems weren't there, the processes didn't work, the support from the top was not there. The whole message was about keeping the customers at bay. A typical monopolistic attitude.*

We had traditionally always designed processes to suit the customer and the company. To suddenly say to our people; "Let's design processes purely to suit the customer and we need to generate these emotions," is quite empowering. To a certain extent ignoring the company perspec-tive has consequences of its own. You realize the consequences aren't nearly as great as you thought they would be. Some of the things that we've uncovered just look crazy. These things might not happen to the customer all of the time but some of our processes were causing such a bad Customer Experience and we didn't realize that. If we hadn't looked at it with our new pair of emotional Customer Experience glasses we would never have uncovered these customer emotions.

Colin: *Many organizations are worried that improving the Customer Experience will cost them lots of money. What advice would you give them?*

Kevin: *Firstly I would say there is something to be said in business about being brave and trying something different. Secondly, although you start with the mantra that this is going to cost you more, the reality is the opposite – the evidence is that it will save you money.*

Colin: *So you have a very impressive record and have achieved some great results. What advice would you have for those people embarking on this journey for the first time?*

Kevin: *Don't do it unless you believe in it, you are wasting your time. Secondly, make sure that everybody on your senior team is signed up for it – you only have to have one who is not and again you are wasting your time. It really has to be something that comes with real strength from the top.*

Thirdly, the first time there is an instance where something or some area is going to cost more, then spend it. Find it from somewhere else. If you don't there are those who will say, followed by the whole organization, that "the senior team don't really believe in this." So it's critical you provide this leadership early on.

Colin: *Thank you Kevin and congratulations again on your remarkable progress.*

At the beginning of the program to improve the emotional Customer Experience Kevin appointed Andrew Dunn to lead the change and "produce a step change in the 'feel of service.'" Andrew has been instrumental in implementing the Customer Experience in Yorkshire Water. So let's go down into the next level of detail and hear Andrew's story:

Colin: *Where did the step change in the feel of service come from?*

Andrew: *That came from Kevin Whiteman. He could see that we could do the physical elements but that there was another dimension we needed to aspire to – emotions and how it felt for customers. Some of us could understand what he meant but it was a bit strange for an organization like ours to be thinking like this. We weren't used to it. It was like getting a pickled onion out of a jar of treacle, you know it is in there but you can't quite put your finger on it!*

Colin: *So how did you go about understanding the Customer Experience?*

Andrew: *I started off by doing some research and increasing my understanding of the Customer Experience. I went on a Service Excellence Tour, which is where you go behind the scenes at some organizations that are widely respected for their Customer Experience. I met this absolute nutcase who kept asking every company we visited "What is the Customer Experience you and your organization is trying to deliver?"*

That guy was you, Colin! You made me realize that there was another dimension to the Customer Experience. What we recognize now and refer to as "feel" was in fact "emotional impact". The irony is that organizations are having an emotional impact on the customer all the time anyway, but they just don't realize it and they are not in control of it. As we were evoking emotions anyway I realized that perhaps we should find out what emotions our customers wanted us to evoke!

Colin: *I can remember the first thing we did for you was to conduct a "Mirror," walking your existing Customer Experience before developing your new Customer Experience. At that stage it was "inside out"...*

Andrew: *Yes it was, so with the help of you guys we asked customers what they wanted in a great Customer Experience and we discovered that emotions were what they truly wanted to feel from us.*

You guys led us through a process to discover the Customer Experience our customers wanted. We discovered twelve elements that you can now see on our Customer Experience statement (Figure 11.1). *Things like "trust," "caring," "valued." Each of these words has a massive impact throughout the business if we were to actually deliver them. So it was important everyone understood these implications and crucial that they agreed and got buy-in by the top team.*

Once we had agreed on the elements, we then asked our customers to prioritize them, and that's how we ended up with our "hierarchy of needs." What we have now further discovered is that all organizations have the same bottom two layers of the hierarchy of needs. The real differentiator comes in the top two layers, the emotional elements.

*Once you are delivering a **reliable** service where the pipes work, the water is clean, and someone answers the telephone efficiently, then this all starts to get taken for granted by the customer. If you can then start to engage with customers and show them that you **care** about them, that you **value** them, that you **reassure** them, and that you **know** what you are doing and that they feel **assured** of you, then ultimately you can create an experience they **enjoy**. It's that emotional feel for the company that will make them actually like us and give us the benefit of the doubt when things do go wrong. You don't get that when you are just delivering the basic physical service.*

Colin: *So you now have a deliberate Customer Experience. What are the benefits of this approach?*

Andrew: *Quite simply if you don't know where you're going you will never get there. You have seen the results we have achieved and this couldn't be achieved without a clear picture of where we were trying to get to. If you want to make the experience enjoyable for customers you have got to take out everything you do that is inherently not enjoyable. So if you think about the situation of roadworks: when we are doing repairs to pipes, then we now consider what enjoyable means. Not enjoyable is being delayed a long time, looking at scruffy workmen or tatty roadworks, and perhaps even being scared by the workmen's tattoos. So if you take away these elements, the experience has more chance of being enjoyable.*

A lot of our customers' experiences are unconscious ones. If they see our vehicles in the streets and they are dirty or they see scruffy looking road-works then they will consider us to be a tatty, rundown, scruffy sort of organization. So having a professional quality appearance in the street is important. Between 10 and 12 percent of our customers pass our road-works every year. We now use this as an opportunity to try and make customers feel **assured**. *We now make it very clear that they are our road-works, provide a helpline number for road users to contact us, and let them know what we are doing and how long we will be there. We also try and make it look clean, tidy, and professional to add that reassurance.*

The Customer Experience statement is about being sure that everyone knows where we are aiming for; if you don't do that you could end up anywhere. For instance when you used to ring our call center you would be answered and our agent would say, "Hello, this is Yorkshire Water, what is your billing reference and postcode, please?" Then they would do what they could to get you off of the phone as quickly as possible in order to deal with the next call. That's because they were driven by productiv-ity measures like average call handle time, percentage of calls answered in a given time, and similar efficiency measures. This was done so we could process our customers in the shortest possible time. This wasn't a deliberate policy but something that just ended up happening. Effectively this told customers we did not consider them to be a person as we were treating them like a transaction. That does not create a caring, valued, and enjoyable experience. Once we defined the Customer Experience we wanted to deliver, it was clear that we needed to change it.

When you ring up the call center we are now changing this to say, "Hello, my name is Kate, this is Yorkshire Water can I help you?" They will literally spend as long as is necessary on the telephone with that individual customer to solve their problem.

Colin: *So going back to the example of the way that the call was answered and the average call answering time, what element in your Customer Experience was that matching against? I believe it was caring?*

Andrew: *It was about caring but also about individual, about feeling special. We couldn't possibly create the feeling of being special and individual if we were referring to the customers billing reference number — so it was about showing that we cared for the customer and were able to deliver an individual special experience and make them feel more valued.*

When we checked back with customers after we'd made these changes, we were able to demonstrate much higher scores on caring, assured, and enjoyable.

Colin: *So how did you go about communicating this strategic change to people in the organization?*

Andrew: *It was very much about creating a pull, lighting fires rather than a sheep dip. As we were trying to work with emotions, it didn't feel appropriate internally to just go and force a communication package on people. We set out to create a buzz about the whole thing by running workshops to raise awareness. You'll recall that the Beyond Philosophy™ team customized and ran a structured program of workshops for us. We then asked people who had been on them to suggest and nominate colleagues who might also want to come. It's exciting because you're not quite sure where it's going to land but what was very clear after a couple of events was that there was a growing groundswell of people coming back and saying how thought leading it was. We were overwhelmed with the response from people. I think it was the weight of that evidence that gave us the confidence to move on. Roughly the agenda was:*

- *The Customer Experience Market Place – why this is important.*
- *The Seven Philosophies for Building a Great Customer Experience (from your last book) – what we need to do.*
- *The Yorkshire Water Customer Experience.*
- *How this can be applied in your day-to-day work.*

Here are some of the results:

- *Overall event score (1 = poor, 4 = excellent): the average score for 250 people was **3.65**!*
- *100 percent of delegates believed the Customer Experience is right for Yorkshire Water.*
- *100 percent of delegates believe that the Customer Experience program is fundamental to Yorkshire Water being "known as the best."*
- *100 percent of delegates believe the Customer Experience should be communicated more widely across Yorkshire Water and its partners.*

Here are some of the comments we captured from delegates:

"It made me think and review the way I deal with customers and how I could delight them"
"The Customer Experience is the next step change…"
" … the risk would be to ignore the Customer Experience!"
"Everyone needs to go on it. We should encourage them to come on the event"

These were excellent results and something we were proud of. This created a snowball effect, which galvanized further support.

Colin: *The Customer Experience is looking at the world from a different point of view. How important do you think it is that people understand the concept behind the Customer Experience?*

Andrew: *It is critical. You have got to "get it" and I think it needs enough people to "get it" in an organization to create a critical mass. Crucially it also needs enough people at the very top of the organization to "get it" because without the leadership it won't go anywhere.*

Colin: *A final question. What advice would you give to those people starting out on this journey?*

Andrew: *You have got to believe in yourself, and you have got to believe in the Customer Experience. As with any big change, if you want it enough you can create it.*

Loop Customer Management

Loop is an important part of the Kelda Group. It provides outsourced customer management functions such as a call center. It also has a number of diverse customers like the hardware store, B&Q, and the National Blood Transfusion Service. But importantly, it provides complete customer management services, including contact center, billing, and income collection for Yorkshire Water.

As it is dealing with Yorkshire Water's customers daily, it is vital that Loop is integrally involved with the Customer Experience Yorkshire Water is trying to deliver. To this end it has been involved in the journey to revolutionize Yorkshire Water's Customer Experience. But in addition, as Loop fundamentally believes the Customer Experience is a competitive weapon, and as it is in a competitive market – selling outsourced call centers – it is now focusing on the Customer Experience as one of the key ways of differentiating itself. Kevin Whiteman comments:

> *Loop Customer Management is in a competitive market. Routine call center work is a commodity and can be delivered by many and can be delivered very cheaply by many. Where Loop is now differentiating itself and its offering is on being a very high quality Customer Experience, based upon a great working environment, with a real commitment to delivering the emotional side of the Customer Experience for their clients.*

So to understand the next link in the chain let's hear from Mike Orlic, Loop's Sales and Marketing Director.

Colin: *Mike, can you talk about the work you are doing to help Yorkshire Water achieve its deliberate Customer Experience?*

Mike: *One of the key things that we've been doing is working in partnership with Yorkshire Water to understand the key behaviors our people need* to exhibit to support their Customer Experience and what sort of key measures, including emotional ones, they want us to achieve. Then we look at what improvements we can make in the call center. That needs some real rigor and thought put behind it from everybody involved in the process. We encourage our agents to come up with ideas and challenge our senior managers and directors with them. One example is the "right first time" initiative. This led to us removing the wallboards from our call centers, the ones that measure call durations and how long people had been on calls. We discovered our focus on this was creating the wrong behaviors. It forces the agents to focus on achieving that target or measure rather than the conversation they are having with the customer. Clearly this was not achieving Yorkshire Water's deliberate Customer Experience.

A team of us started to look at this more carefully. We asked what actually happens if we got things right first time and removed the regular call backs from customers who didn't get the answer to their calls first time. We saw with the productivity measures that customers were effectively encouraged off the phone so the agent could achieve their call targets. What did the customer do if they hadn't had their questions answered? They called back. We quickly realized that if you remove the pressure of measures that were driving inappropriate behaviors and gave people coaching and training on problem resolution and developing a more caring attitude – part of the Yorkshire Water Customer Experience – then this would have a great impact. We also discovered that this not only helped the Customer Experience but also the morale of our people.

You see our previous Customer Experience was not deliberate. It ended up being about speed and efficiency. If you are in a position to spend more time in resolving the customer's actual problem then there are immediate improvements for the customer as they are not forced to call back. It may cause a short-term headache for us as it means a longer call duration on the first call – but long term customers are not re-calling to get updates. The business benefit long term is in reduced calls, which clearly has a great effect on reducing costs.

Average call lengths as a measure have not disappeared. There are still planners using complicated formulas to plan ahead and make sure that we have got the staffing and scheduling right at all times of day. What we are not now doing though is passing that guilt trip of getting the resourcing wrong down to agent level through using average call lengths as a measure for them. It is not their fault that there are queues; it is our fault as the senior management team for not planning it right.

Colin: *So what effect did it have?*

Mike: *We wanted to make a statement about moving from a physical Customer Experience to a more emotional Customer Experience. We really had to make a song and a dance about it and make sure that actually symbolically people really understood what changes were being made and why. So we had a big launch day and made a big splash about the fact that we were removing the wallboards. We invited Yorkshire Water clients and had exploding balloons across the contact center with ticker tape flying everywhere. Then we served champagne and orange juice to everybody to celebrate. We were psychologically making a change, not just physically doing it.*

Colin: *What was the impact on the people?*

Mike: *The reaction has been very positive. We have seen an increase in morale. They really were being given the opportunity to improve the quality of service and they really sensed it, felt it, and were excited by it. The other way it manifested itself was indirectly through the regular staff feedback sessions every month. You can actually see people working with the client (that is, Yorkshire Water) and the feedback scores have increased in the right direction.*

We have also seen something like a 14 percent reduction in overall calls. This is very significant in terms of costs when you think about how much it actually costs to handle these calls. That is significant in itself but there are other benefits in terms of morale. This has had a positive impact on attrition. We do have a track record on improving our attrition rates in the area in the last few years and I think these ideas keep on helping us to go in the right direction.

Colin: *I know that a key part of your strategy for delivering a great Customer Experience is by providing a great employee experience.*

Mike: *Yes that is key. We were very pleased to move from 70th in the "Best Place to Work" study in 2002 to 33rd this year. Changing our culture and focusing on making it a great place to work allows us to deliver a better Customer Experience to Yorkshire Water and our other clients.*

Colin: *So is it about aligning the internal people experience with the external Customer Experience?*

Mike: *That has definitely been one of the key focuses that we had, as you are not going to get a great Customer Experience if your people are frustrated and not motivated. The ability to question and feel passionate about the Customer Experience is something we encourage. I think one of the key things outsiders comment on is that they can actually sit outside in reception and actually watch the buzz on people's faces. People actually smiling and asking each other questions; there is a healthy feel to it. Lots of people say that culture is a fluffy thing and you can't define it. Well you can definitely feel it here and it takes a lot of time and effort to create that atmosphere and once you have captured it the thing is not to lose it and to keep on improving it.*

Colin: *And you're aligning the type of people you require to the Customer Experience your clients are trying to deliver?*

Mike: *That's right. A good example of this is our client that sells power tool products. We provide a help and query line to give their customers some support once they have purchased the product. It is just good common sense that we recruit people who are very passionate about DIY and home improvements, who do this as a hobby or as an interest, or those who have had a prior role or job in DIY. So rather than having some 18-year-old who has never done any DIY for example you have got somebody who is actually quite passionate about it. That comes across on the phone. You are talking to someone who is actually interested in what your problem is and actually capable of resolving the problem. That is the real difference in terms of the customer feedback that we have had from our clients and the agent feels fantastic too, because they are actually interested in dealing with the query and are actually quite passionate about solving the problem.*

Colin: *Clearly you are in a competitive market. You have got a lot of competition out there and increasingly more organizations are moving and locating their call handling around the world. What are your key client messages at the moment?*

Mike: *Well the key thing for us is to actually understand what our clients' and our prospective customers' Customer Experiences are. A lot of them are still focused on initial cost savings and assume that by outsourcing to India this will impact their bottom line in a few years and will give them the savings that they need.*

From our perspective, we are challenging them and saying that if they want to attract the right customers that they need to focus on the Customer Experience they want to deliver. We show them how emotionally we can help them with that.

We're also talking to them about the role of call handling in creating loyal customers, how acquiring them in the right way is key and how they can improve the relationship through the Customer Experience.

Colin: *So what would your advice be to people looking to revolutionize their Customer Experience?*

Mike: *Perseverance: stick with it, believe in it, and follow your convictions. Follow your instincts, because the numbers will come and the performance will improve. Stick with your convictions and you will deliver the results.*

Some great words from Mike, Andrew, and Kevin. We are pleased and proud to play a part in helping them along the way. This certainly goes beyond the philosophy and into getting results.

Key learning:

- Align the top of the organization.
- Communicate to the people and get a groundswell of opinion.

- Ensure you ask the customer what they want in their Customer Experience.
- Develop a Customer Experience statement.
- Improving the Customer Experience can save you money.
- Improving the Customer Experience has many spin-off benefits especially with your people.
- There are things that you are doing that are costing you money, as you are not looking at them with customer eyes.
- Poor measurement can cause a poor Customer Experience.
- The right culture can improve your Customer Experience.
- Setting the right strategic goal is vital.

History has demonstrated that the most notable winners usually encountered heartbreaking obstacles before they triumphed.

B. C. Forbes

12 Case study: Build-A-Bear Workshop

Let me tell you about one of my favorite stores, Build-A-Bear Workshop, which we believe encapsulates a number of the aspects of the Customer Experience that are fundamental to all businesses.

While I was on holiday with my family we visited a shopping mall just outside Washington DC. In the mall we visited a Build-A-Bear Workshop store. I was astounded by what a great Customer Experience it was. From a technical point of view it is a wonderful combination of physical, emotional, and sensory experiences that all come together perfectly. For those of you who have not been, you are missing a treat! But as Build-A-Bear Workshop is already two years ahead of its business plan we are certain that it will shortly be in a shopping mall near you.

Let me explain what my family's experience on our first visit was. As we were walking through the mall we were attracted by activity that was going on in the Build-A-Bear Workshop store: a bear on a bike, I believe. As we entered the store a young person greeted us with a big smile and asked if we had been to Build-A-Bear Workshop before. We replied "No," so the person explained what we needed to do. We were looking for a present for my niece whose 21st birthday it was, and therefore personalizing a bear seemed the ideal gift, especially as Sarah is mad on pandas. We walked over to the right-hand side of the store and chose our bear "skin," a panda. The choice of animals is wide and varied, with rabbits and many other types of animal. With the "skin" we then moved to the next area. This is where you can install an animal sound or record your own message. We decided to record a message, a "Happy 21st Birthday" message for Sarah, which we all had fun singing! The next stage of the experience is stuffing the bear. The sign above the machine said, "Love is the stuff inside." The person operating this area was very pleasant and talked a lot to my daughter Abbie who had taken control of choosing the bear for Sarah. The bear maker asked Abbie to place her foot on the pedal so that she could insert the stuffing; Abbie thought this was great fun! Abbie decided that Sarah would have a soft bear although she could have put more stuffing in to make it harder, if she wished. Once this is complete you are invited to take a heart out of the box, kiss the heart and make a wish!

The next part of the experience is to move onto the fluffing up of the bear in the "spa for bears." It is a bear bath. Abbie combed and fluffed the bear

198

in the jets of air that were operated by a button she was pressing; these came from "shower heads" in the bath. The next experience was deciding what the bear should wear. You can't have your bear leave the store naked, can you? So on to the accessories. We chose a cheerleader outfit as a memento of our US holiday. There is a vast array of accessories: top hat and tails, superhero outfits, the choice is endless. Then, laden with accessories, Abbie sat on a computer and registered the bear and created a birth certificate. It is put into an exclusive cardboard condo, which is free, and your birth certificate or storybook is given to you at the same time, along with any special event information leaflets or promotions that are taking place (for example, a free gift with your purchase). This happens at the "Take Me Home" point.

Finally once this is printed you pay. Now how expensive do you think that would be? My first thought was this was going to be very expensive, but no, it was inexpensive. The animals range in price from $10–$25, with accessories being extra.

Finally, you pass the Bear Promise, which is hanging on the wall. It says:

The Bear Promise
My bear is special
I brought it to life
I choose it
I stuffed it
Now I am taking it home
Best Friends forever
So I promise right now
To make my bear #1 Pal!

I guess we were in there for about 30 minutes and had a great time, and really felt Sarah would love her new panda as we had taken the time to make it especially for her.

This is a great *deliberate* Customer Experience that is emotionally engaging and has designed-in the senses at different points to evoke emotions.

Now let us pull that Customer Experience apart and think of what happened. First, look at the whole process. A great deal of thought has been put into this Customer Experience. A great deal of attention to detail has been paid. The organization has thought how it is going to evoke its desired emotions.

Is this cost-efficient? That is not the issue! Build-A-Bear Workshop is more concerned with its Customer Experience than operational effectiveness. Is this organized in the quickest way to deal with the customer and move on? No. The organization has designed it with the Customer Experience in mind. It is built "outside in." From a physical aspect there are costs that have been designed into the Customer Experience that add no apparent value. However from an emotional perspective they are vital.

For example, when Abbie was asked to kiss the bear's heart and make a wish, I asked the person, "What function does that perform?" thinking the bear's heart might make a sound or light up or something. The person's reply was perfect: "Nothing," came the reply, "but you can't bring a bear to life if it doesn't have a heart, can you?" The sole purpose of the heart was to induce a deep emotional attachment, to bring the bear to life, and to make you feel responsible for it. If you have an emotional attachment then you will take care for the bear, you will love it, and I guess as a by-product you will buy it presents – more accessories!

The birth certificate again reinforces that you have brought this bear to life. It does not end here, there is an integrated web site and you can attend conventions where all the bears meet up and have a party. There are regular emails to keep you involved.

This is one of my best Customer Experiences because I believe it brings together a number of the essences of a great Customer Experience.

- It's about emotions: they are thought through and planned in.
- It's about senses: the organization has planned in a sensory experience.
  - Touch: the softness of the animal, skins, the stuffing, "Would you like your bear soft or hard?", the fluffing station where you fluff up your bear.
  - Sight: the store is very bright and appealing.
  - Sound: the sounds you can put into the bear.
- The experience integrates with the web and with the live events.
- The people seem to love their job!

I was so impressed with this Customer Experience that we decided to interview Maxine Clark, the Creator and Founder of Build-A-Bear Workshop. She has the great title of "Chief Executive Bear," and is based at World BearQuarters in St Louis, Missouri. Since early 1997, Maxine Clark has devoted her energies to creating Build-A-Bear Workshop, which calls itself a teddy bear-themed experience retail store. The first Build-A-Bear Workshop opened in Saint Louis Galleria in the fall of 1997 to a resounding success. Bear Builders[SM] of all ages are shopping at the innovative retail store that promotes creativity and encourages family entertainment in a fun and unique environment. There are over 150 stores operating throughout the United States and Canada. Build-A-Bear Workshop stores are also international.

The National Retail Federation (NRF) named Build-A-Bear Workshop as the "Retail Innovator of the Year" for 2001. Build-A-Bear Workshop was named "Best New Concept for 1998" by *Chain Store Age* magazine.

> Colin: *Can you just give us the story of how Build-A-Bear Workshop started and the concepts behind it?*

Maxine: *I think to understand the Build-A-Bear Workshop story then I need to say a bit about my past in the retail business. As a consumer I love to spend money. When I am out shopping I like things that are new and fun. You can have a good time shopping and that's one of the tricks. In my early retail career whatever I was doing, no matter what it was, I always felt that if you could add fun to it, if there was some kind of twist to it, then you could make it entertaining and you would be more successful.*

I was working in cosmetics and it fascinated me that it was so successful in the department store and never needed to have a sale. We did give away gifts with purchases but it was primarily about entertainment: making up the customers on the floor, having a grand event, even just having the cosmetics section at the front of the store. It was always so colorful, there were perfumes that smelt wonderful, and we were giving away samples. Everything was inviting.

Then the licensing phenomenon started happening in the United States with Strawberry Shortcake back in the late 1970s and Cabbage Patch Kids in the early 1980s; to me that was exactly what this was all about. I started utilizing the same kind of tools the cosmetic companies used in my department. We did great events with Strawberry Shortcake or Barbie coming to visit one of our stores. We made it fun. Quite simply we found when the customer is having fun they spent more money. We were very profitable because I always employed fun techniques and every day that I went to work there was a very important by-product; I was having fun too!

Then I became President of a Payless ShoeSource. Again I used similar techniques. We launched a Payless Kids program and we put in licensed footwear. We created special events around the premiers of Lion King, Pocahontas, *or* Beauty and the Beast. *The customer can come to our store and get something special that they couldn't get in any other store; they didn't come to us just because of the shoes.*

I just felt that I really couldn't do the things that I knew were possible working in a large company. I knew I had to reinvent retailing. So I decided to leave that company in 1996 and do something different.

I felt one of the flaws about retailing in the last 20 years or so is that markdowns have become so much a part of the business. It is sort of an oxymoron: you have to sort of devalue your merchandise so that the customer will value it and it doesn't really seem sensible to me.

When I was creating my business I wanted to create it so that newness drove the business and it was always about something fun and exciting. You were enhancing the value of the product and not devaluing it.

One of the things that were very popular at that time was Beanie Babies. My friend Katie and I – Katie was ten at the time – used to go hunting for Beanie Babies. We were in a store but they had sold out and Katie said to me, "We could make these," and I said, "You know, you are right." Katie meant go down into my basement and make like a craft project, but I thought something different. I immediately went home, went onto the Internet looking for a business that I could buy that might be a factory, toy, or a soft animal company. Everybody thought I was crazy. One day I went to a factory and I saw the factory in motion. Whilst I was there a group of kids were on a field trip in the factory, which gave me the idea of kids making their own bears.

Colin: *One thing that I have been impressed with is the way that you break the Customer Experience down and your attention to detail. Can you tell me a bit more about the philosophy?*

Maxine: *I have been a shopper and a retailer for a long time. I wanted to make the store experience the best of everything I have seen. I am a big fan of Disney. In fact I have had all of my major birthdays in Disney World. I have always been a student of Walt Disney and what he has tried to create. So I was thinking about how we could recreate that kind of feeling on a much smaller scale for the customer. I wanted it to be bright and cheery, you know all of the places when I walked into have always been bright, the people are friendly, you can help yourself if you want to, or you can be helped. The pricing is easy to understand. But in addition, as part of our Customer Experience, if customers need to use the telephone, because you want to call your husband and say that you will be late, we let you use the store phone. Or if you want to use the bathroom, we don't say, "Oh, we don't have a bathroom." You can use our bathroom. Or when you return something that you obviously bought there. I wanted all of the negatives to go away and all of the positive ones that I had experienced to be embellished upon. That to me was the basis for the store.*

Colin: *How did you involve customers in this design?*

Maxine: *We pulled together a group of kids to help me think all this through. A lot of these kids had been to Disney so they know what fun is and they know what imagination is. We really sat down and we organized the store so that people could understand it, without us having to tell them everything. We put little surprises around the store; things that we don't expect you to find the first time. We hope you will find them as you come and go.*

We make the merchandise to be flexibly displayed so that we could change as we went along. A lot of people are afraid to let customers do things, as they are afraid of legal suits. We made everything safe and everything at kid height so that they could do it. We tried to think of every detail. We also tried to make it larger than life, so for example; the bathtub is bigger than you would expect. The stuffing machine is bigger that you would expect. We take you on an adventure. When you enter our store, a friendly person greets you and makes you feel welcome, whether you are a kid of 3 or 103. Then once you are in the store and you pick your own animal, we don't try to sell you a higher priced animal or we don't try to sell you anything really, we let you personalize until your heart is content, you can have sounds, you can dress it in as many or as few things as you want, you don't even have to dress it at all. We give you a free hair bow or ribbon around the neck so that no bear would leave bare and you go through and you make the bear into whatever you want it to be.

Colin: *How do you use systems to improve your Customer Experience?*

Maxine: *A good example would be when I was ten years old I lost my teddy bear. I was very sad. I didn't want anybody else to feel that way so we created this system called the "Find-A-Bear ID system" and a unique barcode, which will belong to you, is inside every single stuffed animal and then when you go to the storybook computer you give us your name and address attached to that barcode and if that bear is ever lost or stolen we can return it, it can be returned to us, or it can be returned to you and we have done that for about 2000 animals so far in the last seven years.*

Colin: *What else have you designed into your Customer Experience?*

Maxine: *Well fundamentally we don't want to rush people through the store, we know it is a very personal experience especially with kids and a lot of people tell us that it is the one place that they can come with their kids and their kids aren't rushing to leave. They are also doing something together, as a family experience. That is a very special part of it and kids tell us that, "I love to come here because my grandma loves to bring me here," or "My mum loves to take me to Build-A-Bear Workshop," so I think it is a place that parents love as well. They are doing something that is fun and wholesome together. That is really a special part of it. For teenagers who are our customers that have come in to make a bear for their girlfriend or boyfriend that is another thing.*

One of the great things about Build-A-Bear Workshop is that we are all children at heart. All ages are comfortable in our store, it is not a kid store, it is not a baby store, it is a store for people who want to have a little bit of fun and who want to communicate something that is special; special feelings or emotion that you have.

We don't want it to be a one-time experience and a large percentage of our customers do repeat purchase, more than we had planned. They come back for more animals, they collect the animals, and they definitely come back for more clothes. Often, after, they go home and go onto our web site and play games, look at the calendar of events, and write us a letter and tell us what a great experience they had. Our web site is a very integral part to our Customer Experience and connection to our customers, especially those who don't live near our store: they can buy products on the Internet. We really use it to communicate with our customers about what is coming up at the store, there are e-cards that they can send, and whenever we launch a new product we create a special kind of activity.

We want to stay connected with them and we know that they might not be in the mall every week and we want them to know that we have new things. They give us their permission to communicate with them and we probably communicate several times a month with them.

Colin: *Since buying our bear we have been invited on a number of events. What are these?*

Maxine: *Well, throughout the year we create special events, usually about once a month. A new bunny or a new teddy bear that we are launching or a holiday like Valentine's Day or Easter or the Fourth of July, we will have a special event and we will tell our customers to come and usually there is some kind of promotion.*

It is our cosmetic strategy: adding value to the product, not taking value away as I said before. So if you are buying a monkey today you will get a free banana or if you buy the bunny you will get a free carrot. These are very successful and they usually create a lot of excitement. We have fashion shows in the malls where we will do a clothing fashion show and the kids are showing a bear dressed in something very similar and are always fun. Most of our events are within our store and they are developed around topical events. For example, we had a big weekend for leap day this year and we invited everybody within the United States of America whose birthday was on February 29 to come in and make a free bear. A lot of people did.

We have birthday parties in our store and what parents do is bring 8–10 children, along with the birthday child to make a bear and the party flavor is really the bear; we are giving a bear to everybody. These are phenomenally successful; we did about 100,000 parties last year in our stores – that's over a million kids and we get tremendous letters from our customers.

Colin: *So when people are buying a bear they are actually buying a whole experience?*

Maxine: *Well it is all in the package, not only package within a box. When a customer buys something in anybody's store, whether it is a cup of coffee in Starbucks or a watch in Selfridges in London, whatever it is you are buying, it is associated with the whole place: how the people treat you, what kind of box it goes in, what the bathrooms are like, especially for the female shopper.*

Colin: *One of the things we advocate is segmentation of your market. Are men or women more important in your environment?*

Maxine: *Women go to the mall or shopping environment and they already can tell you about their experience the minute they drive into the parking garage. If it is a hassle, that is what you are going to have to overcome as a retailer in that mall. You are going to have to say "OK that woman has had a real hassle and we are going to have to make this a good experience for her." Women watch the details and they want to be treated special and they want their kids to be welcome in the stores. They want to be able to use your telephone or return things easily, they just don't want the hassle, they want you to appreciate their business, I think men do also but since the majority of shopping is done by women – women are primarily responsible for organizing the family activities – then Build-A-Bear Workshop knew that we wanted to please the mums and we wanted to please the kids and we wanted to please ourselves.*

Colin: *How are you aligning your internal recruitment and culture to your Customer Experience?*

Maxine: *We are certainly looking for warm fuzzy people, people who are happy, who want to work with children, who like being on stage, being a little theatrical, and we look at anyone – from grandmas, adults, teenagers – we don't really have any restrictions. Customers can go anywhere to buy a bear. They have come into our store and they are buying a bear and it is an engaging experience. Our people have to be engaging and we put a lot of effort in that. We don't just hire off the street, we want people who want to work with kids and that isn't easy to find.*

It's quite simple really; we do it to make kids smile because that is really what we sell you… no, we don't care if you walk out of our store and you don't buy anything. But you walk out with a smile you will be back. If you walk out and you are not smiling we will never see you again.

Colin: *How would you describe your culture?*

Maxine: *Our culture is a fun-loving culture. I am very connected to our company. Our people have a profit share, our store managers have stock in the company and we have made them all owners because we could not be here without them and they are half of what we sell. I think we have a really mutual respect for each other, they know that I care for them as human beings and they know that I care about the personal issues that they face. You know we try to really be the entire thing that you want to work for, just trying to take care of everyone, and trying to create an environment where people can contribute to their potential.*

Colin: *How important do you think the storytelling element is in your communications?*

Maxine: *I think it is important for context. I think that people want to be connected to where they work, where they shop. I think that if you can make it realistic for people and they can understand the company values, they can therefore communicate the company values to the*

205

customer, they can live out their life like that. I have always understood the value of being able to tell your story, but then when I studied Walt Disney that was his whole thing; it is about telling great stories and creating great experiences because they won't tell the stories for you, and that is how the word of mouth and the excitement comes out of people because it is real for them.

Colin: *Given that you have created a great Customer Experience why do you think other organizations struggle?*

Maxine: *I think that most people are very tunnel vision and so they can see how we do it in our business but they can't see how to adapt it for their business. The other is it takes a lot of work and it is hard and expensive if your business model isn't set up for it.*

Colin: *I have just got one last question for you. There are a number of businesses just starting off on the journey of improving their Customer Experience. What advice would you give them?*

Maxine: *The first, I think would be talk to your customers and find out what they think could be better. Ask them, it doesn't always have to be on your shoulders to create great experiences. See if there is a way when you are engaging your customers in a brainstorming session, if you can get them to bring out the child inside them too and let them know that you want to do something really different and out of the box.*

I think that businesses also have to look at who are their customers, their primary customers, and who comes along with that customer. For a mum in a ladies clothing store, she is going to bring her kids into that store. So can she move the stroller through your store, is there a place for her to sit down, is there a place for the kids to be comfortable? Or if her husband is with her, is there a place for the husband to sit down if he doesn't want to be walking around?

So talk to your customers first, talk to your associates then think about yourself if you could be in the perfect place. What would you want it to look like? What would you want it to be? Where do you want to shop? If you were going to invent your business today from scratch what would it look like?

Colin: *That's great. Thank you very much, Maxine.*

As we have heard Build-A-Bear Workshop are now opening worldwide. We decided to chat with Steve Bedford, "Chair Bear" (Chairman) for Build-A-Bear Workshop in the UK, to add more detail and another take on the Customer Experience from the UK side of the pond.

Colin: *How did you get involved in Build-A-Bear Workshop?*

Steve: *Our company bid for the franchise rights for the UK and Ireland and we won it. I think we were successful because of our understanding of the brand and the experiential part of it, particularly the desire and need of customers to be entertained in a personal way. Every single animal we sell is created for that person, they put in the personality, they bring it to life, and we want to make that experience emotionally engaging, entertaining, and very individual.*

Colin: *Why emotionally engaging?*

Steve: *Fortunately many people don't **really** need many products nowadays. So when they consume they want an experience that makes them happy and entertained. Our prime aim is to make people smile in our stores, so they feel positive about their experience. This is important because in my view most interactions with businesses are poor. It is actually stressful buying things.*

Colin: *Why do you think that is the case?*

Steve: *In most businesses things are done for efficiency. This efficiency drives out time and reduces labor. Efficient retailers are always trying to reduce the amount of labor. It has a negative effect on the Customer Experience. I think that Customer Experience is a counterbalance for the drive for efficiency. Efficiency doesn't go direct to the soul, doesn't make you feel inspired. I think what Maxine Clark has created makes people smile, makes people dwell. If you look at the basis of competition in retailing, most people compete on the basis of price, quality, range of product, and choice. That's no longer good enough. Whilst all retailers look at the store environment the problem is the store environment only sells the visual sense. Most businesses do not consider the deep emotions: the sense of inclusion, touch, feel, conversation, interaction, and the emotional sense of something being done specifically for a guest.*

Colin: *I have been impressed by your attention to detail. Could you give me an example of that?*

Steve: *A good example is we don't sew up our animals; they are all pre-stitched via a patented system, so we seal the animals. Basically we draw a string together and it is tied. You could say we create a little mini umbilical cord! This idea came from a guest who asked if we were bringing her bear to life, then why were we hurting her animal with a needle? A good question! So we moved away from stitching and now seal the animals by drawing the string together.*

Colin: *How important are the people in delivering the Customer Experience?*

Steve: *It's absolutely critical that we have the right people doing the right things to deliver the right experience. We apply rigorous selection and training procedures, plus instore management processes, which ensure our people are motivated, ready, and prepared. We train our bear builders to think; "How can I make this the best thing that my guest will experience today?"*

The most important factor is the attitude and approach of our Master Bear Builders. They have to be willing to project, engage, and entertain. We look for people who have these abilities. For example we have recruited several Master Bear Builders at our Croydon store from the Brit School, which is a local performing arts college.

From the start I was impressed by how the desire to deliver a positive guest experience is followed through in all aspects of the company from recruitment to reward and measurement. The company has three priorities: number one is guest experience, number two is employee experience, and thirdly are smiles, which leads to sales and so we measure all of those things. For example every day we take calls from guests and we ask them to rate their experience. Their feedback is the most important measure of the store's performance.

Colin: *Thank you Steve, and good luck in the UK.*

13 Conclusion: dare to be different

Even if you're on the right track, you'll get run over if you just sit there.
Will Rogers

So we have reached the end of the book. Well done! You now have an advantage over those who haven't read it!

As we are fortunate enough to work across many industries we see what organizations are doing, and we know many organizations are now addressing the Customer Experience in a serious way. They are aware there is a path of higher profitability available to them. Other organizations we see are still running headlong to the commoditization precipice. We have heard about the way the baby boomer and subsequent generations are going to affect the economy. We have heard how in a more affluent society, such as ours, consumers will be demanding and seeking out experiences. We now understand why 95 percent of senior business leaders believe the Customer Experience is the next competitive battleground. We have heard from a number of leading organizations from both sides of the pond on what they are doing to Revolutionize Their Customer Experience™. We hope that you have undertaken your self-assessment and have an idea of where you are in the Naïve to Natural Model™. So, enough said.

We were considering how we should draw this book to its conclusion. Then it came to us: some time ago, when we set up our company we decided that we would name the company Beyond Philosophy™. Why? Because it articulates a key aspect of our beliefs. We believe it is OK having a philosophy or a good thought but this means nothing unless you go beyond the philosophy and do something with it. Hopefully we have increased your understanding, and you are now preparing yourself to take action and then embed this change to progress your orientation. So who better to tell you what you should do now than ten of the organizations that have already trodden the path before you? To enable this we asked these organizations the following question:

What advice would you give to organizations that are just about to start to Revolutionize Their Customer Experience™?

This is what they said:

209

Revolutionize your customer experience

Peter Scott, Customer Service Director, T-Mobile:

One of the challenges I am experiencing now is that people think the Customer Experience is about the physical stuff. The biggest issue is about trying to blend in the emotional engagement. The toughest aspect is in the first line and middle management, in terms of their ability to coach in an emotional sense as opposed to a physical sense. One of the lessons for people is to establish a management support structure, and that isn't just about putting them on a coaching course or putting them in a classroom for a day or two. If you really want to get this right then it is about taking on managers who have got the right emotional intelligence and who have got the right skills, capabilities, and experience and will be able to step it up a gear in their thinking. I think that is the thing where we are struggling most.

The first thing that I would suggest is that changing the Customer Experience is something people need to be patient with. It doesn't happen overnight. Secondly they need to get the total commitment across the organization. It isn't just one part of the business trying to do this; it is the whole organization that creates an experience. The third thing is I think people need to think hard about sitting outside the normal box, the normal framework. We for example have used actors to actually deliver the concept of the experience, that kind of training is not normal. So I think it's about really challenging the boundaries that one would normally operate in and daring to be different!

Waynn Pearson, City Librarian, Cerritos Library, California:

The sort of things that I would think about would be related to learning – you really need to take learning seriously. We talk a lot about "learning large." Learning large, for us, was the fact that we jettisoned everything that we had learned up to that point. When we started the project a friend of ours said, "Don't just get out of the box, throw the box away and start again." We did that. We had to go out and really do our homework and relearn. We changed our products from books and services to the user's learning experiences. Following our friend's advice gave us so many other things too. It gave us the learning destination concept – that was really crucial in terms of understanding what we are doing. It gave us the learning organization model – our organization is based on creative thinking, using your imagination for everything. And it is propelling us into the future thinking about a learning community. I think you have to look at every form of human interaction and activity so that you have a sense of how to provide experiences in different ways. We have a saying, "Beyond user satisfaction to user excitement." I think that is the key thing to think about.

Conclusion: dare to be different

Ellen L. Brothers, President, American Girl:

My first piece of advice would be to know your customers well. We know little girls better than anyone because we talk to them every day. What they tell us informs everything we do: from what products and experiences to develop to how we can make them more engaging. If you know your customer and respect them, great things can happen.

Duane Francis, CEO, Mid-Columbia Medical Center, Oregon:

I think the single most important decision we made was when we decided whether or not we were going to do this. You then really have to define who you are as an organization, you really have to set a course for what your mission and values are, and do so with your eyes wide open and with as much forethought as possible. Then you will become committed to it and make the right decisions, because it is the right thing to do. You need the confidence to stay on course because you will have peeks and valleys, ups and downs, that none can escape in any industry. To be committed, to be true to what you know is the right thing – that is the most important decision that you could make, because that sets the culture for everyone who works with you.

Kathryn M. Haley, Vice President, Client Experience, RBC Royal Bank of Canada:

Probably one of the barriers is time. Even though we have instituted pilots for accelerated testing of Client Experience elements, the critical part is capturing the hearts and minds of the entire organization. It takes time to embed this mindset into a cultural DNA.

I think the most important thing is to have the best interests of your clients at heart – to put yourself into their shoes – to really understand what they need and how it feels to interact with your organization. I believe that if we truly listen with understanding, empathy, and responsiveness, we will create memorable client experiences that have clients coming back again and again.

Rudy Tauscher, General Manager, Mandarin Oriental, New York:

Organizations need to stick to it over the long term. They need to make it an integral part of their company's structure and plan. It has to be part of the marketing plan, there needs to be one section on it that says Customer Experience. Customer Experience needs to run from the top to the bottom of the organization. It needs to filter through from the CEO to the line employee, and if that doesn't happen then the Customer Experience will not come together.

Elliott Ettenberg, Chief Executive Officer, Ettenberg & Company, Inc.:

There is so much to tell you, it depends on their business. The first thing I would do is redefine the marketing function and give it much more power. I am consulting with several corporations where we are adding greater responsibility. Every function has had an opportunity to lead businesses in the last 50 years. Engineering has done it, manufacturing has done it, accounting has done it, finance has done it, sales has done it. Marketing has never led business. I think adjusting to this new customer reality is primarily a marketing concern and a strategic marketing issue. Therefore marketers have to lead the business.

The first thing I would do is to make marketing a line function within the organization. That means, in retailing, instead of marketing being a staff position responsible for advertising and promotion, marketing would be responsible for merchandizing and for the store experience. Now if you tell that to somebody in retailing today, they would just start laughing at you. The second change I would make is the establishment of a customer council. The customer council should be an ongoing active board with funding that allows people to really set the marketing priorities and affect change. The third thing I would do is to take a close objective look at my product or service offerings and decide strategically whether I was in the needs or the wants business. From this decision would follow a tactical plan. If I wanted it to be a needs-driven I would also have to be the low-cost provider in the category. If I believed my future was in the wants segment, I would look to how I could deepen the relationship I have with my best customers.

Robert Stephens, Founder and Chief Inspector, The Geek Squad:

You will tend to find that what is important to the boss is important to me and that goes on all the way down the line. In my view it is not the people's fault. They are doing what they are paid and told to do. Leaders have to be the catalyst. It is not as though they are the dominant force – they are only the spark. Herb Kelleher is a great example at Southwest Airlines: he is not creating every Customer Experience but he set the standard. It takes time, that is where the patience comes in, but it will happen: little victories.

After you have started the process, a leader's job, I believe, is not to be the creator at that point; their job is to influence and inspire the organization. Continue that process and the organization will become self-sustaining, a chemical reaction, it will generate its own heat, its own innovations, and then the job of the leader at that point really is to keep telling the stories among the different departments and that is when the mythology surfaces.

Liam Lambert, Director and General Manager, Mandarin Oriental Hyde Park, London:

I really do think it has to start at the top of the organization. If I did not believe passionately in the Customer Experience and I was paying lip service to my team, they would pay lip service with their teams, and everyone would only go through the motions, but we would not do anything about it. I think I have to be the policeman, I have to be the inspirer, and I have to be the leader of that particular passion. When you look at the financial results driven from the Customer Experience it is as plain as anything, it is so obvious that this is the key to success; that you have to surround yourself with colleagues who are passionate, they will add value.

Mike Gooley, Chairman, Trailfinders:

If you are talking about an existing organization they have got a mountain to climb, and the bigger they are the more difficult it is going to be. If they are starting from scratch I don't believe you have any higher priority than setting standards and, if you like, walking in fear of the customer, because customers will decide your fate in the end.

Some great advice, good luck in Revolutionizing Your Customer Experience™, and if you have any questions then please do not hesitate to contact us in one of our offices in the UK or the United States or by mailing me direct at colin.shaw@beyondphilosophy.com with any comments, thoughts, or feedback!

We leave you with one final thought:

Opportunity rarely knocks on your door. Knock rather on opportunity's door if you wish to enter.

B. C. Forbes

Notes

1. "Customer Experience: Next Competitive Battleground" market research commissioned by Richmond Events for the Marketing Forum 2002. Reproduced in this book with kind permission of Richmond Events. Full report available free on the Beyond Philosophy™ web site: www.beyondphilosophy.com

2. Naïve to Natural™ orientation market research 2004. Available free on the Beyond Philosophy™ web site: www.beyondphilosophy.com

3. West Bromwich Building Society, April 27, 2004: www.westbrom.co.uk

4. Mid-Columbia Medical Center, Oregon, USA: www.mcmc.net

5. Cerritos Library, California, USA www.ci.cerritos.ca.us

6. Richer Sounds: www.richersounds.com serves ice creams to its customers during the summer.

7. Red Letter Days: www.redletterdays.co.uk

8. Alaska Glacier Refreshments (pure virgin water): www.alaskaglacier.com

9. www.icehotel-canada.com

10. Chapter 11 is a case study of Yorkshire Water (www.yorkshirewater.co.uk) and how it has improved its Customer Experience.

11. European Customer Management Conference 2003

12. Declan Coyle, Director, Andec Communications: www.andec.ie

13. Best Buy: www.bestbuy.com http://twincities.bizjournals.com/twincities/stories/2002/10/21/daily34.html

14. The Geek Squad: www.geeksquad.com

15. Elliot Ettenburg: www.ettenberg.com, mail@ettenberg.com

16. *Building Great Customer Experiences*. See www.beyondphilosophy.com for details.

17. http://newsmanager.commpartners.com/tappiaotc/issues/2004-04-07.html

18. The Advertising Association: www.adassoc.org.uk

19. Jan Carlzon's book *Moments of Truth* published 1989.

20. Michael Edwardson is the Principal Psychologist and Managing Director of Psychologica® www.psychologica.com

21. Details of the SOCAP Customer Emotions Study are available from SOCAP: www.socap.org.au
22. http://www.storytheater.net, 2504 Shalimar Drive, Colorado Springs, CO 80915, 001-719-573-6195.
23. Jean-Charles Chebat:
    http://www.hec.ca/profs/jean-charles.chebat.html
24. Dr. Alan Hirsch: www.smellandtaste.org
25. SkyTrax: www.airlinequality.com
26. http://www.airlinequality.com/news/news_extra/edit_low_ryan.htm
27a. www.blagger.com
27b. www.blagger.com: nayim1 at 22nd Jan 2004, 07:08PM
28. The "Mirror" is a Beyond Philosophy™ product that audits your (and, if requested, your competitors') Customer Experience. It evaluates what it feels like to do business with your organization, how it feels emotionally engaging with your people and how well you are meeting customers' expectations. We undertake reviews of your organization's Customer Experience across all the channels by which you choose to go to market. Alternatively, we can focus on putting a mirror to a single channel – perhaps your call center, your helpdesk, your sales force, or your web site. The key is that each mirror is tailored to your specific requirements and the industry or market in which you operate.
29. Charles Handy:
    http://www.pfdf.org/leaderbooks/l2l/spring2002/handy.html
30. Conscious competence learning model:
    http://www.businessballs.com/consciouscompetencelearningmodel.htm

Index

advertising, 28, 29, 43, 56, 85,
110, 116, 117, 118, 143, 211
affluence, 2, 6, 10, 12
airlines, 95–6, 121, 137–9, 159
Akers, A., 67, 76, 83–4
American Girl, 13, 54, 55–6, 67,
75, 142, 211
approach
fragmented/disjointed, 18, 19,
29, 39, 94, 103, 105, 110, 112,
115–16, 117, 118–19, 121
holistic, 19, 47, 143, 144
reactive, 94, 95, 107, 131, 141
proactive, 20, 82, 90, 106, 114,
120, 128, 131, 134, 140, 141,
159
see also understanding versus doing

BBC, 74, 160–1, 163
Bedford, S., 206–8
Beyond Philosophy™, xv, xix, 15,
62, 81, 136, 173–4, 184, 192,
209, 214n1, 214n2, 215n28
bonuses/incentives, 20, 36, 40–1,
80, 105, 118, 123, 131, 161, 178
Bourne, D., 76–78, 153
brands, xv, 9, 10–11, 28, 37, 43–4,
54, 82, 206
aligning with Customer
Experience, 21, 29, 109–10,
126, 142, 143
Brothers, E. L., 13, 54, 55–6, 67,
75, 142, 211
Build-A-Bear Workshop, 142, 180,
198–208

*Building Great Customer
Experiences*, xv, 16, 31, 36, 50,
133, 136, 144

call centers, 9, 19, 26, 27, 29, 56,
102–3, 119–20, 124, 155, 158,
172, 186, 193–4
scripts, 115, 191
calls, telephone, 19, 26–46 *passim*,
52, 53, 69, 84, 94, 99, 109–10
caller recognition, 144
Customer Experience of, 58,
116–20, 135, 191, 193–4
menus/routing, 28, 40, 69,
113, 114, 140
returning, 115
sales vs customer service, 105,
124
telephone skills, 131–2, 140
unsolicited, 106, 125
change, 31–3, 173
barriers to, 128–9, 167, 175–9
embedding, xvi, 20, 33, 98,
163, 167, 169, 174–5, 209,
212
S curve, 167
Clark, M., 200–6
Combustion Points™, 136, 137, 139
commoditization, xv, xvi, xviii, xx,
2–3, 6, 8, 9, 14, 30, 31, 33, 50,
68, 113, 209
complaints
customers' preparations for, 27
procedures, 94, 96, 97, 122–3,
145, 146, 164

conscious competence learning
  model, 169–70
Constantine, M., 87, 121, 124
culture, xvi, 20, 37, 44–5, 75, 94,
  100, 102, 103, 106, 110, 112,
  119–21 *passim*, 146, 149, 151,
  162, 178, 187, 195, 205, 211, 212
  blame, 44, 45, 94, 103, 112,
    117, 176
customer
  arrogance towards, 94–5, 96,
    99, 101–2, 115
  attention levels, 65–7
  blaming, 45
  expectations, 31, 42–3, 55–6, 129,
    131, 132–5, 138, 157, 184
  lack of focus on, 34–5
  loyalty, xv, xx, 7, 10, 11, 22, 31,
    53, 54, 182, 196
  management contact with, 98,
    112
  strategy, 39
  words to describe, 104
  see also Customer Experience
Customer Experience 41, 63
  average frequency of, 50
  as blend, 52
  and brands, 43–4
  building, 57–65
  channel approach, 42–3
  companies' awareness of, 5–6, 7,
    9, 12, 13, 15, 18, 19–21, 25–6,
    49, 72, 83, 92, 98, 100, 103,
    105, 112, 117, 118, 123–4,
    128, 131, 148–63, 167, 168,
    177, 189–90, 193, 202, 209
  customer response to, xvi, 26–30,
    65–8, 75, 83, 97, 99, 109–10,
    116–17, 118, 131, 134–5,
    135–46, 151, 167
  defined, 2, 50–6, 91, 96
  and employees, 29, 38–9, 44,
    99–101, 119, 120, 123,
    124–5, 145, 159, 195, 196,

205, 207
  evolution of, 30–3
  great, 8, 16, 39, 50, 76–9,
    81–2, 98, 127, 170, 198–200
  importance of, 11, 13–14, 25,
    93, 171, 182, 209, 212
  improving, 1, 6, 7, 34, 57–64,
    113, 130, 175, 182, 183–92,
    203
  measuring/targeting, 40–2, 56
  negative, 28–9, 30, 40, 58–60,
    61, 99, 106, 109, 120, 136,
    137, 138, 139, 207
  physical aspects, 9, 19, 30, 89,
    95, 105, 113, 114, 134,
    183–4, 188, 194, 210
  and public services, 14–15, 48,
    120, 148–9, 181–97
  purpose of, 56–7
  and stories, 73–4
  and strategy, 39, 49
  and systems, 40, 202–3
  Vice President of, 143–4
Customer Experience design:
  Moment Mapping® 112, 121,
    125, 130, 135–46, 154–5, 156–7
Customer Experience Hierarchy of
  Needs™, 63–4, 114, 132, 184, 190
Customer Experience Pyramid™,
  144
customer relationship management
  (CRM), 3, 21, 40, 119

differentiators, xv, xviii, 3, 8, 9, 32,
  96, 190, 207
Disney, 31, 75, 85, 145, 155, 156,
  163, 166, 168, 175, 202, 206
dreams, 12–13
Dunn, A., 189–92

economic cycle, 32, 33
Einstein, A., 16, 178
Elnaugh, R., 13, 27, 53–4
Emotional Barometer™, 136, 137

Emotional Cookie™, 136, 137, 139
emotions, xv, xx, 7, 20, 22, 31, 38,
    43, 48, 51–7 *passim*, 60, 64–5, 71,
    73, 75, 78, 96–9 *passim*, 105, 107,
    120, 123, 125, 127, 128, 129,
    136–40 *passim*, 142, 144–5, 146,
    148, 149, 159, 178, 183, 184,
    186, 188, 189, 190, 192–4 *passim*,
    198–200 *passim*, 203, 210
    emotional intelligence, 39, 125,
        130, 131, 145
    expectations, 16, 112, 131,
        132–5, 152
    measuring, 80, 160, 161
    negative, 28–9, 61, 98, 100,
        118, 120, 121, 183
    stimulating/evoking, xvi, 16, 19,
        47, 48, 53, 60, 62, 66, 68, 70,
        72, 74, 77, 91, 95, 110, 131,
        132, 147, 150–1, 153, 154,
        155, 157, 162, 199, 200, 207
    and stock market, 55
    see also customer; price
employees, 19, 29, 38–9, 146
    empowering, 127–8, 143
    personalizing codes, 124–5
    training, 145
    see also Customer Experience
Enlightened organizations/
    orientation, xvi, xix, xx, 3, 4, 16,
    18, 19–20, 27, 31, 33, 37, 38,
    42, 45, 53, 60, 70, 75, 94,
    127–46, 150, 165
    traits of, 131
Ettenberg, E., 10, 211

financial services, 6, 32, 37,
    110–11, 135, 136, 140, 161–2
Forbes, B. C., 197, 213
Francis, D., 7, 48, 81, 84, 87,
    127–8, 160, 211

Geek Squad, 7–8, 71, 97, 114–15,
    149–50, 159–60, 212–13

gender differences, 27, 135, 204–5
generations, 10–11, 12, 14, 209
Gooley, M., 104, 144, 160, 212
gorge, missing the, 4–5, 6, 9, 70,
    72, 129
growth, problems of, 99

habit, forming of, 97
Haley, K. M., xix, 6, 11, 54, 68, 83,
    89, 139–40, 212
Hamilton, S., 11, 25, 76, 157
Hamleys, 11–13, 25, 76–8, 153,
    157, 162, 163
Hard Rock Café, 72, 152, 163
"have a nice day," 84, 143, 184
hospitals, 1
    Mid-Columbia Medical Center,
        7, 48, 81, 84, 87, 127–34,
        160, 211
hotel services, 62, 141, 142–3, 154,
    155
    see also Mandarin Oriental

impulse buying, 25
inside-out focus, 18, 19, 44, 100–1,
    103, 114, 121, 190
    see also Naïve organizations;
    Transactional organizations
interaction, 29, 51–2, 56–7, 64, 91,
    115, 132, 138, 154, 162, 184, 207
Internet, xv, 9, 14, 56, 85, 87, 113,
    136, 141, 152, 202, 203–4
investment
    in Customer Experience, 25, 77,
        78, 163
    in R&D, 2

key performance indicators (KPIs),
    80, 94, 105, 113, 123–4

Lambert, L., 52, 141, 142, 155, 212
layout of sales areas, 25, 83, 148, 202
lead times, 35, 80, 124
leadership, 37, 44–5, 94, 98, 101–2,

106, 112, 120–1, 149, 175, 193
  effective, 16, 31, 97, 187, 189,
    212–13
  views of business leaders, xviii, 1,
    9, 13, 29, 31, 33, 38, 39, 43,
    134, 175, 209
  walking/not walking the talk,
    20, 98, 178
libraries, 1
  Cerritos Library, 14–15, 70, 72,
    75–6, 120, 148–9, 153, 210
Library Hotel, 62
Loop, 193–6
Lush, 87, 121, 124

Mandarin Oriental Hyde Park, 52,
  141, 142, 155, 212
Mandarin Oriental, New York, 75,
  98, 213
McDonald's, 114
measurement, 40–2, 144, 160
  of Customer Experience, 131
  of emotions, 80, 160, 161
mistrust *see* trust
Moment Mapping® *see* Customer
  Experience design
music, 8, 52, 53, 72, 75, 83, 84–6,
  153, 155, 158

Naïve organizations/orientation,
  16, 18, 22, 26, 27, 28, 30, 33,
  35, 37, 49, 52, 53, 60, 73, 75,
  87, 91–108, 110, 112, 113, 114,
  119, 121, 124, 125, 128, 135,
  141, 142, 145, 157, 170
  reasons for naïvety, 92, 128
  traits, 94
Naïve to Natural Model™, xv, xvii,
  xix, xx, 17, 21, 30, 31, 35, 36, 37,
  49, 55, 91, 94, 104, 118, 119,
  123, 129, 134, 137, 143, 145,
  165, 168, 170, 173, 179, 209
  decision to remain Naïve, 35
  key changes, Transactional to

  Enlightened, 131, 141
National Do Not Call website, 106
Natural History Museum, 88
Natural organizations/orientation,
  xv–xvi, xix, 16, 18, 20–2, 27, 31,
  33, 49, 51, 52, 53, 57, 60, 70,
  72, 73, 75, 81, 82, 83, 86, 87,
  128, 141, 148–65, 170
  segmentation, 158–63
  traits, 151, 160
  see also Naïve to Natural Model™

orientations, 16, 34–7
  see also Naïve, Transactional,
    Enlightened, Natural
    organizations
Orlic, M., 193–6

Pearson, W., ix, 14, 70, 75–6, 120,
  148, 153, 210
Peters, T., 22, 68, 135, 145
Philosophies, Seven, xviii, 16, 192
physical aspects
  basis for rewards, 40–1, 105, 123
  of Customer Experience, 9, 19,
    30, 89, 95, 105, 114, 134,
    183–4, 188, 194, 210
  Naïve focus on, 94, 104–5, 106
pressure, commercial/time, 3, 6, 7,
  12, 105, 124, 176, 191, 194
Pret A Manger, 111, 142, 152
price
  bargaining over, 29
  and customer satisfaction, 54, 128
  as differentiator, xv, 3, 9
  and emotion, 13, 54, 96, 97, 207
  falling, xviii, 2, 9, 31, 113
  and Naïve/Transactional
    organization, 52, 94, 113–14
process, business, 18, 56, 101–3,
  121, 130, 138–9, 159, 161–2,
  179, 182, 185, 188, 207
  end-to-end ownership of, 44
  see also complaints procedures

promises, broken, 29, 99, 102, 186

Red Letter Days, 13, 27, 53–4
Re-imagine, 22, 68
Revolutionize Your Customer
  Experience™, xvi, 22, 31, 32, 49,
  50, 52, 68, 72, 73, 76, 79, 82,
  106, 115, 154, 167, 171, 173,
  175–80 *passim*, 183, 213
rhetoric, false, 35, 36, 43, 100,
  109–10, 124, 177

S curve, 167
sales area
  layout, 25, 83
  smells/sounds, 85–6, 88
Scott, P., 6–7, 53, 98–9, 140, 162,
  210
scripts, 110, 115, 119, 143
Sea World, 86, 163
senses, 20, 52, 53, 81–3, 86, 153,
  157, 200
  general impressions, 191
  in sales areas, 85–6, 88
  sight, 83–4, 152
  smell, 88–9, 155–6
  sound, 84–6, 152, 155
  taste, 89–90
  touch, 86–88
  see also music
service, proper level of, 97
  poor *see* Customer Experience,
    negative
services, 6–7, 9, 11, 19, 27, 29, 42,
  53, 58, 95–8, 105, 112–14
  passim, 119, 120, 123, 124, 211
  and sales, 112
  see also call centers, financial
  services, Geek Squad, Yorkshire
  Water
Shaw, C., 34
  interviews, 58–59, 76–8,
    116–17, 183–96, 200–8
silos, 18, 19, 47, 90, 94, 105, 115,

  119, 121, 124, 147
"small print," 95
Southwest Airlines, 95, 213
Stephens, R. 7–8, 71, 97, 114–15,
  149–50, 159–60, 212–13
Stevenson, D., 72, 73–4
stories, 15, 70–9 *passim*, 127, 148,
  149, 179, 206
surveys, 12, 18–19, 35, 36, 99, 121

Tauscher, R., 75, 98, 213
theatrical techniques, xx, 8, 11–12,
  21, 71–5 *passim*, 77, 78, 79, 152,
  159–60, 162, 184, 205
  means not end, 49
titles, job, 103, 143, 159, 200
T-Mobile, 6, 15, 53, 98–9, 140,
  162, 210
Trailfinders, 104, 144, 160, 212
Transactional organizations/
  orientation, xvi, 16, 18, 19, 22,
  26, 27, 30, 33, 37, 49, 52, 53,
  60, 73, 75, 80, 94, 108, 109–27,
  128–9, 130, 131, 134, 135, 136,
  137, 141, 142, 143, 145, 165
  traits of, 112, 113
trust/mistrust, 26, 28, 29, 55, 63,
  71, 86, 99, 106, 109, 115, 119,
  121, 123, 124, 128, 137, 146,
  154, 160, 184, 186, 190

understanding versus doing,
  91, 110–11, 128, 130, 166,
  167, 168

Virgin Atlantic, 31, 111, 142

Whiteman, K., 181, 183–9, 193
Wolsey-Cooper, S., 131–2

Yorkshire Water, 181–97
yo-yos, 78

Zorb, the, 67, 76, 83–4